NOLS

A WORTHY EXPEDITION

THE HISTORY OF NOLS

KATE DERNOCOEUR

Edited by Ben Lester

An imprint of Globe Pequot
Falcon, FalconGuides, and Make Adventure Your Story are registered trademarks of Rowman & Littlefield.

Distributed by NATIONAL BOOK NETWORK

British Library Cataloguing-in-Publication Information available

Library of Congress Cataloging-in-Publication Data available
ISBN 978-1-4930-2607-4 (hardcover)
ISBN 978-1-4930-2608-1 (e-book)

♾™ The paper used in this publication meets the minimum requirements of American National Standard for Information Sciences—Permanence of Paper for Printed Library Materials, ANSI/NISO Z39.48-1992.

CONTENTS

On a broad level, this book is dedicated to all who know and understand
the transformative nature of NOLS and everything it stands for in terms of
community, the environment, and the preservation of wild places.

More personally, I dedicate this book to my first NOLS instructors,
who did, indeed, change my life: Willy Cunningham, Randy Cerf, and
Larry Marlowe (Winds Winter—1973).

The life that has unfolded, bolstered by the lessons from several
NOLS courses over a span of 40 years, has given me depth and value.
Among those I have come to know and love is one who
is most special—my daughter, Melody.
To you I dedicate all that I have received from NOLS, with love.

FOREWORD

The success of NOLS is a complicated story to tell. Effectively educating a quarter of a million students has required a series of timely and inspiring ideas, contributions from many individuals, and more than a bit of luck at important inflection points. Kate Dernocoeur captures so well many of these seminal moments in this book. As you pore through the story of NOLS, though, consider two broader themes without which the school could not have succeeded: the commitment and dedication of our staff, and the power and impact of our wilderness classroom.

For over 50 years the NOLS staff has made the difficult, daunting, and authentic happen on a daily basis. This dedicated community of talented individuals has worked across our planet, leading and educating students with purpose, passion, humor, and grace. They believe they can make a difference and on a daily basis they execute on that belief. They have developed positive, ethical leaders through life changing experiences. The story of NOLS is significantly their story and their labor of love.

The second key factor in making the magic of NOLS happen has been the power of our wilderness classrooms. The wilderness provides intense and transformational experiences, vast in scale and at the same time deeply personal to each who experiences them.

Our staff and wilderness have been tightly intertwined throughout the school's history. The link is personal, professional, passionate, and purposeful. Wilderness runs in our blood and nourishes our soul. We are proud of our many graduates who work as leaders in conservation, land management, and as policy leaders. We know firsthand the value of wild places, the importance of protecting them, and the urgent need to have them available for our children and grandchildren. We know it is important to develop future advocates and a constituency for these wild places, and that is core to our work.

As we look ahead to our next 50 years, our staff and our classrooms will remain at the core of the NOLS experience. However, the past half century has seen our school expand and diversify, bringing the NOLS mission to many new audiences and new locations. As you'll read in this book, integrating the new parts of NOLS with the old has sometimes been a challenge. To ensure that we can continue to support our core mission on into the future, the school undertook in 2015 the NOLS Branding Initiative, a process to refresh

Alaska mountaineering students approach the Matanuska Glacier. *Madhu Chikkaraju*

our brand and the way we present ourselves to the world. We emerged from the process with a newly focused message and "look." We also organized our brand into four pillars: NOLS Expeditions, NOLS Custom Education (formerly NOLS Professional Training), NOLS Wilderness Medicine, and NOLS Risk Services. Perhaps most significantly, we retired the words "National Outdoor Leadership School," largely because in the past 50 years, our school has grown well beyond the borders of the United States; the name that Paul endowed us with no longer reflects all we do. As we move into the future, the word NOLS will continue to stand, as it always has, for leadership, expertise, and the power of the wilderness.

This school has emboldened hundreds of thousands of graduates to step forward into their lives with confidence and skill. I hope and trust this story of our history will re-inspire you to carry forward as leaders in your workplace and communities and make our world an even better place. Carry on!

—John Gans **NOLS executive director**

PREFACE

During the year of writing this book, I often felt the reverberations of Paul Petzoldt's encouragement: *Go for it. You can do this.* That's what he told legions of young people in the 1960s and 1970s who came to Lander and wanted to do big things: scout out a branch location, start winter courses, climb big mountains, try any number of ideas. *Go for it. You can do this.*

Such trust he had in all of us, to do grand things. My opportunity to write the history of NOLS (grand in its own way) came about in such an unlikely manner: I overheard a conversation about it in a Dolomite *rifugio* breakfast nook. But, I thought, wouldn't that be something, to have that chance? And so I applied, got the interview, got the nod.

And then the immensity of it hit. How would I ever be able to write a linear account of a situation so multi-dimensional in time, place, circumstance? There were solitary months at my desk sifting and sorting, learning and organizing, interviewing and cross-checking, feeling overwhelmed by mountains of information. The goal was to make a 50-year accumulation of stories and events and big personalities make sense, to keep it honest and balanced, "warts and all." Luckily, I had phenomenal support from many people who understood the size and scope of the task. *Go for it. You can do this.*

So first of all, let me say that there is so much that is not here. This is a big story indeed. There are offerings from so many people that could add to the delicious texture of this history, yet were necessarily left behind. I was often sad, knowing I couldn't fit it all in. It was, in the course of writing, as if I had to let a great view pass out of sight as the turn in the trail carried me forward. To everyone who so graciously shared anecdotes and insights, I hope you know you do, indeed, have a place in this book, even if nuanced, even when your particular story isn't pronounced. I wasn't with you at your best or worst times; I met most of you just this past year. You are invariably people who I would like to know better. I hope and trust all of you who have a personal connection to NOLS will read this account and understand my limitations. As Howard Brodke said in his book, *Manipulations*, "I distrust summaries—any kind of gliding through time, any too great a claim that one is in control of what one recounts. I think that someone who claims to understand who is obviously calm, someone who claims to write with emotion recollected in tranquility, is a fool and a liar. To understand is to tremble. To recollect is to re-enter, and to be riven. I admire the authority of being on one's knees in front of the event."

At the same time, I feel as if my life's circumstances

Working together to cross a river in Patagonia.
Ben Fox

created the best possible scenario to be the writer of the NOLS history: I was a student, in 1973 (winter) and 1974 (summer)—in the trenches early enough to have a feel for the place, but not so much that I was part of the real blue center of the flame. Then I left, as we were told to do. I met Paul in Thermopolis in about 1976, when my 10th Mountain Division veteran stepdad introduced us. I remember that bear-paw handshake, his white brows, his keen look. In those few minutes, I felt his belief in me that I, too, could do big things with my life.

I became a writer—a journalist for 25 years and then an essayist with an MFA. I'm not a historian per se, but I understand the importance of seeking an objective, arms-length account when writing a work such as this. I remained far enough away from the school in those intervening decades that I never really considered how NOLS shaped me until during the writing of this book. So often, this past year, I sat back and realized, "NOLS gave me that." I have skills. Decent judgment. A sense of teamwork that can only be explained as expedition behavior. An eye for what is safe, and what is not. With that in mind, it is with a large degree of FONDE (NOLS acronym for Fear Of Not Doing Enough) that I offer up this book.

"Perhaps the healthiest tradition at NOLS is to take what we do with a grain of salt and a healthy skepticism, not glorify or exaggerate its importance and attribute profound meaning to every act... Nevertheless, if the school centered on providing mere thrills and adventure, it would just be another form of bungy jumping. What makes the school work ... is a shared sense of giving people an experience that will improve their lives," said Mark Harvey in the The Leader in 1995. This school matters. It does change lives, and it has done so for more than 50 years. Like it, this book matters. It serves to inform those who were not there of our roots, and it also serves to remind those who were there of what an amazing institution they have built.

Finally, I hope this book inspires readers to work on behalf of the wilderness. Everyone who loves wild places must help efforts to preserve them; you are needed. In coming years, education and advocacy for the outdoors will be critical. The work will be truly challenging. Conservation is part of the essence of NOLS. The past informs the future. As Paul would say, *Go for it. You can do this.*

—Kate Dernocoeur **April 2016**

Hiking in the Wyoming sun.
Liam Durkin

THE FIRST YEARS

All my life, people have asked the question, directly or indirectly, "Why the hell do you climb mountains?" I can't explain this to other people. I love the physical exertion. I love the wind, I love the storms. I love the fresh air. I love the companionship in the outdoors. I love the reality. I love the change. I love to feel the oneness with nature. I'm hungry. I get thirsty; I enjoy the clear water. I enjoy being warm at night when it's cold outside. All those simple things are extremely enjoyable because, gosh, you're feeling them, you're living them, your senses are really feeling. I can't explain it.

– Paul Petzoldt

On the morning of June 8, 1965, a group of 43 boys gathered six miles south of the sleepy ranching town of Lander, Wyoming. They had traveled from 20 US states to the mouth of Sinks Canyon, where they found themselves on the grassy lawn of a defunct hydroelectric power plant. Standing among them was an imposing man named Paul Petzoldt. He was an old guy, and big—a bear of a man. He stood six foot one, but seemed bigger due to his 240 pounds of heft, direct blue eyes, and imposing white bushy brows. A captivating storyteller, he used grand gestures and had a deep, booming voice and a hearty laugh.

Although not everyone thought the world of him, Petzoldt had the charisma and charm to make big things happen. That morning, he was preparing the group for a 30-day backpacking expedition into the nearby Wind River mountain range. Some of the boys around him had done similar things before, while others had never even slept outside.

From the dank interior of the pumphouse by the edge of the Popo Agie River spilled a mystifying array of items: wool pants and sweaters, Army surplus mortar carrier backpack frames, sleeping bags, canvas tents, rations, and various bags. As the boys fidgeted and fussed with the gear at their

feet, Petzoldt explained what to do with it. Put it in one of the three large zippered bags. Lash those bags to the backpack frame. Heft the load onto a knee, catch the unpadded, canvas arm loop on one side, swing the pack around onto the back. He told them not to mind the itchy wool pants and shirts. With rain or snow almost guaranteed in the next 30 days in the wilderness, the wool would keep them warm when wet.

In his own way, Petzoldt was contributing a small piece to the sea of change occurring around the nation. In 1965, Gemini 4 astronaut Ed White performed the first US spacewalk. The Houston Astrodome opened. The first skateboard championships were held in Anaheim. President Lyndon Johnson declared war on poverty and established Medicare and Medicaid. Bob Dylan shocked folk purists at the Newport Folk Festival by going electric. And the monthly number of draft notices doubled as the war in Vietnam started to escalate.

That summer, Petzoldt was 57—an age when many people were eyeing the ends of their careers. For more than 40 years, he had built a resume of mountaineering, guiding people in the mountains, and teaching them ways to live there safely and comfortably. With this group of boys, though, he was trying something different. Petzoldt's goal was to train outdoor leaders, people who could go on to stand where he was and teach what he was teaching. He was starting a school from scratch, and calling his experiment the National Outdoor Leadership School. This was its inaugural course.

The territory Petzoldt planned to use for his classrooms was vast and wild, filled with peaks and glaciers and rivers difficult to cross—but in traversing it the students would emerge as capable leaders with the judgment and skills to lead others back in someday. Along the way, the students discovered NOLS to be something far different from camp or military school or a guided tour. Through the direct experience of falling while roped, using a map and compass to navigate off-trail, summiting a peak, creating meals from a variety of ingredients, and leading their peers in situations where they themselves were learning too, they discovered their own limitations and also how to help each other. They rode back to Lander dirty and happy and flushed with a sense of success.

Not that it was always easy or fun. When "issue day" at Sinks Canyon was done, the students hauled themselves and their gear into the school's cattle trucks for the 55-mile ride to Hidden Valley Ranch, where they discovered during a downpour the first night out that the army-surplus tents leaked badly. Petzoldt then led them uphill, to the pass at the top of Dry Creek. For the next two weeks, they hiked and climbed and fished near the North Fork of Bull Lake Creek before returning to the roadhead, warming (and rinsing) themselves in the hot springs at Fort Washakie, and returning

Emma, Paul, and Ranger the dog in Twin Falls, Idaho.
NOLS Archives

to Sinks Canyon. After re-rationing, they hiked back into the mountains for the remaining two weeks.

The second NOLS course, in July, left for the high country from Dickinson Park, and the third, in August, from Moccasin Lake headed northward toward Gannett Peak. By the end of the summer of 1965, about 100 young men had followed Petzoldt and his assistants into the mountains. Those first courses led to hundreds more. Between expeditions and, much later, classroom-based courses, more than 250,000 others would graduate from NOLS in the next 50 years.

—————

Born to a farming family in Creston, Iowa, in January 1908, Paul Kiesow Petzoldt was the youngest of nine. His father died of diphtheria before Paul was four years old, and that same year his family enrolled him in school. Petzoldt became an avid reader, a passion ignited by his schoolteacher sister, Lily. He spent hours, often alone, exploring the woods and fields near his home, his vivid imagination and sense of adventure bolstered by stories of big landscapes and exotic places as described by the likes of Zane Grey and Jack London.

By the age of six, Paul was responsible for whichever farm chores his older brothers didn't want to do and thought he could handle. He brought in the cows, slopped the pigs, tackled and butchered chickens for his mother Emma's cookpot. He was also entrusted with the traplines along the nearby Grand River, which yielded muskrat, mink, possum, coon, and civet cats. Skunk pelts might bring a dollar or two each, according to his biography, *On Belay*.

During World War I, the Petzoldts lost their farm. The large family had begun to scatter as the older children left home, and it became impossible to keep up with the loan payments. When Paul's brother Louie came home from the war, he found Emma and the remaining children in a rented house, struggling to raise enough food on a small plot. But the potato fields of south-central Idaho showed promise, and the family decided to move to a small farm near Twin Falls.

Looking north from their new home, Paul could just barely glimpse his first real mountains: the snowy, 11,000-foot peaks of the Sawtooth Range. Closer by were the tall cliffs of the Snake River Gorge. Soon, the boy—not yet 10— began scrambling up and down the high cliffs until they seemed like his own back yard.

When Petzoldt was about 12, he plotted a trip to the Sawtooths. He showed his plan to Emma and convinced her to let him take the family horse, Shorty, to pull the buggy. Accompanied by his friend, Chico Martinez, and his sheepdog, Ranger, and provisioned with food, including jars of Emma's home-canned peaches, he headed out. For three weeks, they made their way 80 miles north, traveling past Shoshone, where Paul reassured the inquiring sheriff that they had his mother's permission. When they arrived in the mountains, they were disappointed that the area was nothing like the picture books of the Alps; the tall spruces and pines shuttered the views of the valley below, and there were no grandly steepled peaks. After fishing and exploring for a few days, the boys headed home.

On the way, Shorty, who was mostly a saddle horse, was overwhelmed by a steep grade. The buggy picked up speed. With wheels spinning faster and faster, the buggy careened into a ditch and the brace connecting the axles snapped in two. Dazed but unhurt, the boys found a way to pile their gear onto the remaining front axle. They had to walk beside Shorty much of the rest of the way home, but Petzoldt's first expedition was in the bag.

After that brief taste of the mountains, Petzoldt—possibly contrite for wrecking the family buggy—tried to settle down, but it really wasn't in his nature. He was constantly interested in finding answers to his dreams, and his newest one became getting a bicycle. The walk to school was just too long. But the family's battles with money never waned. Without the cash for such a luxury, Emma offered her son an acre of ground to raise a crop of onions. Surely, this would bring in enough money for a bike.

Petzoldt tilled and planted his crop, watering and nurturing it all spring and summer. It was a good crop, and as harvest time approached, he snapped the green tops off to encourage the onions to ripen. But the market in 1922 was disastrous for farmers. It would cost more to harvest the onions than Paul would make selling them. No onions, no bike.

Worse, the rest of the family's crop had to be abandoned in the ground as well. It didn't matter how industrious they were, or thrifty; the Petzoldt family, like hundreds of thousands of others, lost their farm and disbanded. Several of Paul's siblings went to California, two for careers in horse racing. His older but much smaller-statured brother Curly (Eldon) became a successful jockey. Others returned to Iowa. Just after New Year's 1923, Emma broke the news to her youngest son that she would be moving to New York to care for an elderly cousin in exchange for room and board. Petzoldt, who was about to turn 15, stayed with his brother, Willy, in Twin Falls to finish eighth grade.

After graduating, Petzoldt headed west to live with his brother Louie, who had moved to Long Beach, California. He attended Polytechnic High School there in the fall, but generally avoided the crowded household where he felt he was in the way. Instead, he spent hours at the public library, reading insatiably, including books by the likes of Plato and Mussolini. He also liked to listen to the wide array of soapbox rabble-rousers at the city park, who were proclaiming radical ideas ranging from communism to socialism and beyond—concepts that Petzoldt found fascinating but confusing, yet were instrumental in the continuing self-education that helped form the independent young man's worldview.

After one school year in California, Petzoldt returned to the familiarity of Twin Falls. He did not want to stay with Willy, whose crowded home was several miles out of town. Instead, he supported himself with a series of jobs, finally landing one as a waiter at the Prine Hotel that included accommodations. Around then, he also learned to hop trains, an exhilarating means of transportation that yielded a way to indulge his wanderlust—and the opportunity to visit his mother in New York.

When school let out for the summer in 1924, Paul was 16. He and a buddy from Twin Falls, Ralph Herron, 17, decided to head for Jackson's Hole (as it was then known), which had grown from a fur-trading center in the early 1800s to a well-known cattle ranching area by the 1920s. Herron had relatives living in the area and, knowing how Petzoldt loved mountains, he thought Paul should see the Teton Range. They had hitchhiked 185 miles to Rexburg, Idaho, when Petzoldt got his first view of the mountains.

The Tetons are young, their ancestral rock pushed up in the Cretaceous period some 80 million years ago when part

From the west, the Tetons rise
without warning from the foothills.
Heidi Hatcher

of the floor of the Pacific Ocean pushed its way beneath the North American plate like a gopher under a lawn. For more than 50 million years, earthquakes, erosion, and volcanic activity shaped the uplift into the mountain ranges that cover much of the western United States. But about 13 million years ago, a 40-mile-long fault near the border between modern Idaho and Wyoming was thrown into a series of seismic convulsions. The eastern side of the fault fell thousands of feet, and the western side was pushed still farther into the sky. Today, Jackson Hole sits just on the edge of that depressed eastern block. Rearing 7,000 feet above it is the western block, shaped into the spires of the Grand Teton and the rest of the Cathedral Group by glaciers and earthquakes, and still too newly exposed to have eroded into foothills and gentle slopes.

From the west, the view is perhaps even more improbable, as the Grand Teton and its companions erupt without transition from behind rolling hills like fangs of rock, stretching into the sky from nowhere. "Our lives changed when we rounded a bend near Rexburg and saw the Tetons," wrote Petzoldt in his book, *Teton Tales*. "Suddenly we had another goal. We were going to climb the Grand Teton."

When they reached Jackson's Hole and asked the locals about climbing the mountain, people mostly laughed. The concept of mountain climbing was regarded in those days with suspicion and sometimes disapproval. People openly wondered about the value of it, not to mention the safety.

Luckily for the boys, there was one man visiting in Jackson's Hole that July who understood their zeal: William O. "Billy" Owen. In 1898, he had been in the first party to definitely summit the Grand Teton (the truth of two other claims in 1872 and 1893 have never been verified). He warned them that it would be very difficult, but gave them some advice and drew a rough map of a route near the East Ridge.

Bolstered by Owen's confidence in them, off they went, full of innocence and enthusiasm, knowing that a crowd of skeptics back in Jackson expected them to fail. They stowed their scant gear in quilts donated by sympathetic townsfolk, and tied the bundles into horseshoe-shaped packs. Owen arranged a ride for them out to a closer starting point at the Lucas ranch, where they then bushwhacked along the lower reaches of the mountain, past a lake to a small flat field. There, in a warm, sunny meadow, they stashed their coats, blankets, cans of pork and beans, sardines, and candy bars and headed off to tackle the steepening terrain. They were wearing cotton shirts, bib overalls, and cowboy boots. They carried just an old hay rope, an old box camera, and a pocketknife.

Despite Owen's map and advice, the boys veered off to

the East Ridge itself, "and suddenly found ourselves in a different realm of mountaineering," recollected Petzoldt. They encountered steep, dangerous, and terribly exposed conditions slick with ice and snow in places. When evening was upon them and it started getting cold, they realized it was too late to climb down, so they retreated into a crack on the south side of the ridge for what little protection it could offer.

Then a storm blew in. Gale-force wind was followed by hard rain, as if someone was pouring a bucket over them. After a short reprieve, the darkness was punctuated by hard-driven snow. They wished for their coats. In the summer of 1994 at the 70th anniversary of that ascent, Petzoldt told reporters, "It was awful. We did everything wrong . . . If we had known what hypothermia meant, we would have frozen to death!" Realizing that this failure of judgment was not a dream or storybook adventure, the boys endured a night that felt like eternity.

By sheer luck and determination, the boys made it without harm back to the meadow the next morning and collapsed onto their quilts in the sun after gorging on their provisions. They didn't wake up until late the next morning. Refreshed, they debated what to do. They had quite enjoyed the notoriety that their plan to climb the Grand had sparked on the streets of Jackson and didn't want the inevitable

Paul Petzoldt on the summit of the Grand Teton during his guiding days. *NOLS Archives*

ridicule of failure. So, humbled, but with a remaining stock of youthful pride, they rested and cut pine trees for hiking staffs, then started out again the next day.

They traversed snowfields and found the route that Owen had described. By 2 p.m., July 25, they stood at 13,775 feet, on top of the Grand Teton. Theirs was likely the fourth ascent of the iconic mountain. Petzoldt, in his cowboy boots, was the youngest ever to accomplish it.

When they finally reached a road and hitchhiked into town, their boots were wrapped in strips of blanket, the soles nearly worn away. People in Jackson doubted their story, but Billy Owen asked them to describe the summit, and he verified the claim. They were vindicated, and became instant local celebrities.

He told that story hundreds of times in later years, not for acclaim or accolades, or to caution people against risk-taking. Rather, he used that tale and many others for instructional purposes: "Here is what I experienced; you would be wise to learn from hearing this."

———

Petzoldt wanted to stay in the area. He found work in the Lucas ranch hayfields and also guided three more parties up the Grand that summer—including his boss, Geraldine Lucas,

age 59, and, on another climb, a re-ascent by Billy Owen.

Inescapably drawn to the Tetons, Petzoldt returned to Jackson's Hole for many summers. On his first year back, one hot, sweaty day in 1925, he was pitching hay at the Lucas ranch in the shadow of the Grand Teton when two men showed up to ask if he would show them the route up the Grand. When they agreed to pay $100, the wheels of enterprise began to turn in his mind. Their offer was "a whole season's wages for two days of 'work'!" he said later.

It was his first truly professional guiding gig. He knew from reading and speaking with people who had climbed in Europe that, in those days, professional guides there literally hauled their clients up and down mountains. That approach seemed both dangerous and unappealing to Petzoldt. He saw a better way, a "more responsible" way, he said.

His thinking was influenced by two sobering experiences in 1925 that left an indelible mark. First, his friend Ralph Herron fell off a pinnacle far up on the Grand Teton known as the Molar Tooth. His belay saved his life, but he sustained serious injuries that required an arduous evacuation by piggyback.

Then, a man named Theodore Teepe was climbing with another group when he lost his footing and slipped down a snowfield, crushing his head on a rock. The sheriff sent for Petzoldt and asked the budding mountaineer to lead the effort to bring him down. After engineering a descent using ropes, the rescuers slid the tarp-wrapped body down a snow chute to the packhorses. Later dubbed Teepe's Glacier, the area stood as a lifelong reminder to Petzoldt of the darker aspects of the alpine world.

"I thought of an analogy between mountain climbing and playing golf. If a golfer sliced a drive into a lake, it cost him a ball and a couple of strokes. But if a climber sliced on a mountain, that's the last chance he got," he wrote in *Teton Tales*. From the start, Petzoldt insisted on teaching his clients how to be in the mountains safely and comfortably.

Petzoldt climbed prolifically in the Tetons in those years. In the 1920s and 1930s, his name appears every 10 signatures or so in the Grand Teton's summit register, usually while guiding climbing parties. In his spare time, he did many first ascent climbs on various routes up the Grand Teton and on the surrounding mountains.

When he wasn't in the Tetons, Petzoldt wandered. He rode the rails or hitchhiked, doing odd jobs—haying, picking fruit, washing dishes, or waiting tables—making enough to get by while mostly avoiding the authorities (except for one horrific beating from the railroad cops in Grand Island, Nebraska). He often visited the public library in whatever town he happened to visit. At first, he was mostly just trying to get warm, but then he realized no one would bother

Paul on the golf links in Europe in 1928. *NOLS Archives*

him if he sat down to read, which he did avidly. He also finished high school in Toledo, Ohio, after winning $2,000 in a card game.

In 1929, Petzoldt was awarded the first mountain-guiding concession in the newly created Grand Teton National Park. He named his enterprise the American School of Mountaineering (later the Petzoldt-Exum School of American Mountaineering, in partnership with another legendary mountaineer and climber, Glenn Exum).

By 1933, Jackson Hole had become the western summer playground of many wealthy and influential people. Among them that summer was Sir Albert Baillie, Dean of Windsor and private chaplain to the king and queen of England. Baillie, a thoughtful man of about 60, saw something appealing in Petzoldt's thirst for knowledge. He extended an invitation for Petzoldt to spend a year at Windsor Castle as his guest. Not having the funds for a ticket, Petzoldt hopped a freight train to New York that October, then walked into a shipping office looking for help. The charismatic Petzoldt talked the vice president into reduced-rate ocean passage on the *American Farmer*. The man was Kermit Roosevelt, son of the US president at the time.

In England, Petzoldt suddenly found himself in high society, far from the cowboy world of the American West. He enjoyed long conversations on various topics with Baillie and other highly educated people, and read voraciously in the extensive castle library. He learned to play golf with the king's knights. It was a far different sort of education than his several attempts over the years to attend college in America when his pocketbook permitted.

After nine months, despite a deep friendship with Baillie, Petzoldt's urge to wander rose again. He left England, curious to see Germany, where Hitler was already chancellor, and the Alps, which he had always longed to visit. On a shoestring budget, he made his way by bicycle southeast across several countries and over steep passes to Zermatt, where the 14,780-foot Matterhorn pierced the sky.

Of course, he had to climb it. There, he witnessed trekkers being guided in ways that horrified him. As he reported years later in *The Leader*, "My approach was totally different from the European approach. In Europe, you hired a guide who top-hauled you up and hauled you down. They would not even tell you the time of day. It was all a secret. They didn't want to wise up a sucker. They didn't want anyone learning enough to climb on their own. They were in business." One day, he encountered three exhausted older people who had been left behind by their trekking group, and bivouacked with them overnight before seeing them safely down.

Then he met a New Zealander, Dan Bryant, who was

The 1938 K2 expedition team. *NOLS Archives*

looking for a climbing companion. Together, the young men accomplished the first double traverse of the Matterhorn in one day—a major feat—and other challenging climbs before Petzoldt returned to the United States on a freighter, flat broke, in late 1934.

Petzoldt's burgeoning reputation as a guide and moun-

taineer didn't escape the attention of the exclusive eastern US climbing community. In 1938, he was invited to join the first American K2 expedition to climb the second-highest mountain in the world (28,251 feet). Sponsored by the American Alpine Club, the official mission of the expedition was to reconnoiter the mountain for another attempt planned for 1939. The expedition leader was Charles Houston. Halfway through medical school at the time, Houston went on to an illustrious career as a mountaineer and high-altitude physiology researcher.

Petzoldt was a late addition to the team roster, and despite a promising start, he remained an outsider to the others, who were all from elite East Coast social backgrounds and already close friends. His rough-hewn Western style, plus various differences in opinion that arose during the expedition, led to disagreements, especially between Houston and Petzoldt, which were never resolved.

Some of the issues arose from disputes over money. Petzoldt mistook his agreement with an original member of the expedition who had to cancel and then recommended Petzoldt, offering to cover his costs. The confusion left Petzoldt with no spending money. Another strike against him was his temerity to teach rope and piton use to the Sherpa porters.

In addition, some questioned Petzoldt's suitability for the climb; in those times, there was a perception that large men couldn't handle altitude, according to his biography, *On Top of the World*. It didn't help that he suffered a debilitating illness—possibly dengue fever—on the trek in.

After weeks on the journey, Petzoldt and Houston happened to be in the best position on the final day for climbing. The summit bid had to be abandoned, but in the course of that attempt, Petzoldt climbed past 26,000 feet without supplemental oxygen—a world record at the time. (Petzoldt would attribute this feat to the techniques he developed called "rhythmic breathing" and the "rest step," which he later taught at NOLS).

Different versions of the K2 tale leave a murky understanding of what actually happened, but by all reports, group dynamics on the 1938 expedition were far from ideal. Multiple references hint at disdain, intolerance, and disagreements among a group of men with strong personalities, including Petzoldt. And in later years, Petzoldt in particular would express frustration with the circumstances that prevented a successful bid. But based on the lessons he integrated at NOLS in later years, there is little doubt that the experience helped fuel the concept he eventually dubbed "expedition behavior."

During World War II, Petzoldt worked in several capacities. At the start of the war, he worked in the Department of Agriculture, buying food to send to Russia under the Lend-Lease program. Then he applied to the newly created 10th

Mountain Division, the first unit specifically created to do battle in the harsh European mountains. His initial application was rejected (possibly because he was already 34 years old), but then he received orders to report to the training grounds at Camp Hale, Colorado. After an inauspicious start scrubbing the bathroom floors, PFC Petzoldt was recognized and immediately promoted to staff sergeant. He was given the job of preparing hundreds of 10th Mountain Division soldiers for battle. He also got an assistant, a man named Ernest "Tap" Tapley. Petzoldt quickly realized the young man was one of the most accomplished all-around outdoorsmen he had ever met.

Together the two men used their experience and knowledge to develop systems for the evacuation of sick and injured soldiers, which happened frequently on the rigorous training grounds surrounding Camp Hale. They also developed rapid, large-scale cliff evacuation procedures that involved belaying soldiers descending on zip-lines. And Petzoldt, ever a proponent of the warming capacity of wool, taught vivid lessons on how to dress properly. As he wrote many years later in the *NOLS Alumnus* (the precursor to *The Leader*), "When I was in the ski troops they had some pretty good cold weather equipment, but they had officers in charge who were not outdoorsmen.... They would put on all their wool clothes and then put a cotton sweatshirt under-

10th Mountain Division soldiers. Paul Petzoldt second from left. *Frank Chuck*

neath, because the wool was scratchy, they thought they were allergic to wool, or some other reason. Consequently, because of using cotton next to the skin, we had a lot of frostbite, amputations, pneumonia, etc. Our hospital was completely filled with victims of cold weather. I was given the job of lecturing . . . 11,000 troops to tell them how to dress and actually wear the good clothes that they did have." Petzoldt did not fight with the 10th in Italy, but instead went to officer's candidate school (graduating as a second lieutenant) and served the duration of the war instructing soldiers.

———

After the war ended, Petzoldt worked in Europe for the army for a while and then returned to the Teton mountain-guiding concession, which his partner, Glenn Exum, had maintained during the war. They decided to alternate years running it. After losing a guide, Fred Ford, on the Grand his first summer back, Petzoldt decided to hand things over to Exum for good. The company was renamed Exum Mountain Guides, and Petzoldt faded from prominence in the mountaineering community.

He had heard about a homestead raffle to be held in Riverton, Wyoming—his wife's hometown. Petzoldt and Bernice Patricia McGarrity, married in October 1935, had shared many adventures that are richly told in her book, *On Top of the World.* By the post-war 1940s, it seemed appealing to get some free land and stability. Perhaps his status as a war veteran gave him an advantage; his was the third name drawn. Years after the onion crop had failed in Idaho, Petzoldt found himself back in the business of farming.

Their homestead was 20 miles north of town, and with a great deal of effort, he and Bernice developed 160 acres of cropland and raised high-quality alfalfa seed. Then came trouble. In about 1957, Petzoldt stored a harvest of several hundred thousand dollars' worth of seed at a warehouse in Sterling, Colorado. Ever the deal-maker, he had used the receipts for the seed as security for a loan from the bank. But word came that the warehouse was bankrupt. Farmers were at the warehouse, getting their seed out. It was a melee.

Petzoldt wasted no time driving south. This was his livelihood at stake. "Witnesses described how this man came down from Wyoming with a large, double-headed axe in each hand, and was waving those axes around," recounted a source who knew Petzoldt well in those days. "He was grabbing the seed that was his. He managed to save a substantial amount of seed. Eventually, the sheriff came and got some order to it, and Paul had his seed in a pile and was patrolling it with those two axes."

Bankruptcy proceedings went on for more than two years, finally reaching the Federal District Court in Denver. Petzoldt took a financial whipping for his efforts, and he and Bernice ended up losing the farm.

The couple moved to another homestead, this time in Arizona, but the acreage was not tillable, and they eventually traded it for a bar back in Dubois, Wyoming. Around that time, Bernice experienced amplifying mental health issues, and the marriage fell apart. She moved back in with her family in Riverton. With debts piling up, Petzoldt turned his remarkable deal-making skills to selling real estate and, more lucratively, cars in California, Arizona, and Texas. Along the way, he broke both shoulders in a bad wreck, according to a friend. Eventually, he was able to pay off more than $70,000 of debt with his self-described used car "racket," but overall, the 1950s were a dark time for Petzoldt.

In 1961, he relocated to Lander. After several years of estrangement, his marriage with Bernice ended in divorce in 1962, and on December 29 that same year, he married a Lander woman, Dorothy "Dottie" Dewhurst Reed.

The two had met when he was operating his Rams Horn Saloon in Dubois, where she and her friends used to go for the dancing. Originally from Pennsylvania, she was station manager and co-owner of the Lander radio station with her sister's husband, E.J. Breece. Breece, who later became a state legislator, also owned the local newspaper. They were well connected in the small community of about 3,000.

Noatak river valley in northwest Alaska.
Stéphane Terrier

Petzoldt Returns to the Mountains

IN THE EARLY 1960S, Petzoldt increasingly returned to the mountains. After moving to Lander, he noticed youngsters climbing the cliffs along Sinks Canyon south of town without any instruction or attention to safety. Concerned that someone might get hurt, he approached the town council and proposed that they let him teach rock climbing to community youngsters through the Lander Parks and Recreation Department. They agreed, and for the next several years, his American School of Mountaineering, as he named it, bolstered interest in the wilderness out the back doors of Lander townspeople.

In the winter of 1962-63, Petzoldt organized a climb up the Grand Teton with his Lander friends. There were about eight people on the expedition, according to his friend and lawyer, Jack Nicholas, who participated.

"During that climb was when I developed respect for what kind of guy he was," he recalled. The snow was shoulder deep and upward progress exhausting. The party got strung out, and the teenaged son of a Lander man was struggling. His boots were ill-fitting, and he was very cold and frightened. Paul talked to him, calmed him down, rubbed his feet, and somehow found him some bigger boots.

"That kid would have died if Paul didn't handle it the way he did," said Nicholas. "He handled that so nicely. It made me realize that the guy had something to teach."

Throughout his difficult post-war years, Petzoldt kept alive the idea of someday starting a school based on his love for the mountains. Then, in 1962, Petzoldt read in *Reader's Digest* that an American version of the famous British school Outward Bound had been founded in Colorado. He also discovered that his old Camp Hale assistant, Tap Tapley, was an instructor there. Petzoldt contacted Tapley, who told the

Rob Hellyer and Paul Petzoldt. *NOLS Archives*

founders of Colorado Outward Bound School (COBS) about Petzoldt. In 1963, Petzoldt became their chief mountaineering instructor.

The innovative Outward Bound program was launched in Wales in 1941. The mission of Outward Bound hinges on helping students find untapped personal strength through dealing with extreme adversity. The concept was originally developed in response to puzzlingly high death rates among British merchant sailors as they awaited rescue after their vessels were torpedoed in World War II. Whereas older men tended to survive, many younger men died despite relatively short waits for help, resulting in the theory that survival was as much a mental thing as physical. Outward Bound purposefully put its students in challenging situations to help them learn how to cope. The concept worked, and Outward Bound grew into a worldwide organization.

A young man named Rob Hellyer also heard that Outward Bound was coming to Colorado, and immediately knew he had to be part of it. The son of a public affairs officer in the Foreign Service, Hellyer was with his father in England in 1962 and had been on three Outward Bound courses in the UK. In the spring of 1963, in an era before Internet or cell phones, he simply made his way, unannounced, to the headquarters in Marble, Colorado.

"Really, the stars were aligned," he said, "because I got up there in the afternoon, and there were only three people there: Tap and his wife [Lee], and Paul. So I said I'd been to Outward Bound, and they said that's great and said I could sleep in the office. Paul wanted to learn the country around there—he'd only been there a day or so—and Tap said, 'why don't you take that kid with you?'"

The next morning, Petzoldt, age 55, and Hellyer, age 20, went out to explore the nearby Rocky Mountains for a few days. "He took me under his wing. It was the opportunity of a lifetime. I fell into it," reminisced Hellyer.

They worked for Outward Bound that summer, leading students on courses and managing logistics. But Petzoldt recognized that many of the instructors, while capable educators, floundered trying to plan and execute trips into the wilderness. Many of the Outward Bound staff were unable to read maps or cook in a sanitary fashion. He also witnessed good rock climbers who were not skilled at showing kids how to camp. Worse, some were motivated more by their own chances on the rock than helping youngsters learn. In other words, trained leaders who could demonstrate safe and practical camping and mountaineering techniques were sorely needed.

Petzoldt pitched an idea to the founders of Colorado Outward Bound: let him start an Outward Bound branch in the Wind River Range of Wyoming, where he could prepare leaders adept in all areas of outdoorsmanship. The specialized branch of the school that he envisioned would generate competent instructors for Outward Bound so they could safely and effectively lead their students into the backcountry.

His enthusiasm generated talk—serious talk, including presentations to the Lander town fathers—of starting a branch of Outward Bound in the small town, then home mostly to ranchers and miners. He asked Jack Nicholas to look into the legal feasibility of the concept. It could be a boon to a place where Main Street had only been paved since 1959, and where most of the side streets were still dirt and gravel.

WILDERNESS WITH NO CONTRIVANCE: THE WIND RIVER RANGE

By Molly Herber, instructor

For many a NOLS graduate, the Wind River Range is iconic. Its granite peaks form the backdrop of uncounted photos framing grimy, smiling adventurers. It's where the school began and where its headquarters have remained for 50 years. In a school whose denizens are perpetually hungry for new vistas, what has kept the center of the school in the same place?

In some ways, Paul Petzoldt began his outdoor school in the Winds for pragmatic reasons. He was already familiar with the range from years of working as a mountain guide in the nearby Tetons, and from farming in Riverton. He had scouted the mountains by airplane as a place to train Outward Bound (OB) instructors. And after he split with OB, it still made sense to start his own school in the Winds: OB was already well established in Colorado; the ranges in the Pacific Northwest had unreliable weather and too many roads; and Alaska's vast wildernesses were simply too far away.

But the Winds offered more than convenience. They contain dozens of granite cirques for training mountaineers, clear lakes for fishing, and miles of trail-less terrain that demand technical skill to traverse. It's an area roughly the size of Delaware, almost entirely roadless. Courses could be true wilderness expeditions, without endlessly looping back through the same terrain to avoid roads and overcrowded trails. Early instructors Rob and Martha Hellyer aptly summed it up: "It was the only place that had everything."

The Wind River Range was the home of my own first introduction to an extended stay in the wilderness, and I believe that many of the reasons Petzoldt chose the Winds remain true decades later. Today, we have the added benefit of seeing the impact that a decision made in 1965 has had on the school and its students over time.

As I look through my journal from my 2008 mountaineering course, I find that I often used the same words to describe both the Winds and my feelings: "wet," "cold," "long," "sore," "tough," and "beautiful." Those words appear in various forms in nearly every entry. Maybe the repetition came from fatigue, but maybe, in their simplicity, those words best fit the landscape as I saw it.

The Winds have remained a big wilderness. Horsepacker re-rations allow students to stay deep in the mountains for the duration of their course. This means more time to hone outdoor skills and develop a sense of place without interruption. When the only reminders of the outside world are airplane contrails in the sky, the experience becomes fully immersive.

Such immersion also demands commitment. You can see almost nothing of the Winds from campsites at the roadhead. You have to hike for miles and get dirty and sweaty and tired to earn the sight of the sweeping spires of the Cirque of the Towers, Gannett Peak's summit ridge, or the crystalline blue of a nameless alpine lake. Traveling through the Winds, students learn to respect and value that commitment, and to work through the physical and mental challenges that the

environment presents. They learn to value the slow trudge.

The Winds are not defined by a single, iconic site. Instead, day after day and mile after mile, you'll find another valley dotted with scarlet wildflowers, another granite spire bathed in alpenglow, and be just as stunned by what you see and smell as you were on the first day. In the Winds, each place is equally powerful.

When NOLS was founded, mountains were its heart and soul. But as the school has grown, so has our understanding of that heart and soul and what it can teach us. In addition to mountains, wilderness is also embodied in gravel coastlines reached only by a few hardy paddlers, or winding desert canyons, or sweltering jungles. Leadership doesn't only mean attaining a summit in good style; it also means forging relationships across cultures and acting decisively in an emergency.

What our origin in the Wind River Range gives to students and the school is the shape and style of the leaders we seek to create: leaders who are humble, who value hard work over recognition, and who seek the wilderness for the joy of it. The rugged, quiet strength of the Winds has room only for thoughtful, deliberate striving. That striving, formed in the mountains that have been the school's backbone for decades, will keep NOLS moving forward as we develop new leaders and improve our own practice of leadership, pursuing only the objectives that demand the very best we can give.

The founders of Colorado Outward Bound, Josh Miner and Joe Nold, even traveled to Lander to look over the area. Notes from one meeting, held December 11, 1963, at the home of a Mrs. McCloy, refer to the "Wind River Outward Bound School." Other correspondence between Miner and Petzoldt refer to it as the "Outward Bound Leadership School."

It was not to be, however, for what are reported to be a variety of reasons. Other Outward Bound locations were being developed in Maine and Minnesota at the time. And egos on both sides of the Wyoming branch idea were large, according to some sources. Petzoldt was never one to hold back when differences of opinion arose on matters he cared about, and the founders of COBS weren't shy, either. They overruled Petzoldt's insistence that students wear wool, not cotton. And then they stipulated that Petzoldt raise $300,000 seed money and build a mess hall before commencing operations in Wyoming. In August 1964, the Outward Bound board decided not to support Petzoldt's train-the-trainer concept and rejected his idea of a branch in Wyoming. Petzoldt left COBS and went home to Lander, where he pondered ways to teach people to go into the backcountry safely and responsibly, without hurting either it or themselves.

Petzoldt was already aware of the importance of conserving the backcountry as it began to beckon to more and more people. A couple of years earlier, in September 1962, Rachel Carson's seminal book, *Silent Spring,* had been published, calling attention to the impact of rampant human development on the natural world. Summer camps and scouting trips were beginning to supplant the appeal of dude ranches. Outward Bound had come to North America. People were discovering the fun of camping and being in remote places, and were increasingly eager to explore ways to use the "great American outdoors," as President Lyndon Johnson called it when he signed the Wilderness Act into law on September 3, 1964.

The Wilderness Act was an important moment for outdoor enthusiasts, defining, as it did, the nature of "wilderness." It was a long time coming, requiring eight years, 66 revisions, and 18 hearings before it was finally passed. It was nurtured through its long legislative gauntlet mostly by Wilderness Society executive director Howard Zahniser, who died just four months before Johnson signed it into law. Petzoldt was a passionate supporter of the concept and testified about it before Congress. Initially, the Wilderness Act preserved 9 million acres of wilderness in 13 states. By 2015, those numbers grew to 110 million acres in 758 places in 44 states.

Paul's response to the winds of social change took flight in the bar at the Noble Hotel. Sitting on the northeast corner at

3rd and Main in Lander, the three-story brick hotel with 61 rooms was built in 1917 as an upscale way station for tourists on the road to Yellowstone. Builder H.O. Barber named the hotel after his investor Fred F. Noble, who owned the land where the hotel was built. When Barber died in 1930, the hotel was purchased by Harold D. Delmonte, who refurbished it and redid 10 rooms in historical themes and 9 others with "Indian" themes. The lobby, with its tiled floors and big stone fireplace, was grand. High ceilings opened to a mezzanine on the second floor where, years later, the NOLS administrative offices could be found.

One day in January 1965, Paul and Dottie were having a drink at the Noble with their friends and neighbors, Jack and Alice Nicholas. Living just two doors apart on 3rd Street, the couples spent a lot of time together in those days. Nicholas was a lawyer in town and the city attorney, and Alice was busy raising their five children. Jack first met Paul in divorce court when Bernice retained him as her lawyer, but the two shared backgrounds and later became friends. Nicholas had run away from home and traveled the West as a boy of 13. His father came after him, but he ran away again at 14. He taught himself the classics by age 19, finished high school through a correspondence course, and made his way through law school.

"He was always talking about wanting to start a school," recalled Nicholas. That night, "Paul got to talking about how he didn't know how to go about it, and I said, 'Well heck, let's just do it.' So Dottie and Alice came to our house and we went into the office. We sat there and I said we had to name it, so we picked out the name. We got a board of directors—a good board that could draw people." It included Petzoldt and Nicholas, as well as Tapley, Glenn Exum, some local people, and a legislator. They built the board phone call by phone call until after ten o'clock that night. "In the morning I drew up the Articles of Incorporation and took them around and started getting them signed," said Nicholas.

It took more than a month in the slower days when typing with carbon copies and sending items via the postal system were the norm, but the NOLS Articles of Incorporation were finally signed and certified by the state on March 4, 1965. While waiting on the paperwork, Nicholas and his secretary scoured the *Encyclopedia Britannica* for the names of every school, college, and university in the United States. They filled 25 pages with 20 addresses per page of high school and private school addresses, and built an equally sizable stack for colleges and universities. Then they sent off letters announcing the start-up of the newly formed "National Outdoor Leadership School."

Handwritten letters also went off to everyone Petzoldt knew, including former guiding clients and those Outward

NOLS YUKON

The evolution of NOLS Yukon began with Patagonia, according to Molly Doran. If a place as remote as Patagonia could become a viable NOLS location, what else was possible? A scan of the atlas brought western Canada to the forefront. The vast tracts of British Columbia showed abundant untracked open space dotted sparsely by a few cities and towns. The vast mountain ranges looked promising, and outside of the population centers near the US border the whole province was hardly settled at all. Perfect.

Mount Edziza Provincial Park, 650 miles north of Vancouver as the crow flies, looked remote enough for the first NOLS Western Canada Mountaineering course in that area in 1994. That first course was run out of the school's branch in Washington, and then Willy Warner, as director, moved the base operations in 1995 south 320 miles along Highway 37 to Smithers (population 5,000 in 2015). They rented shipping containers for the gear hauled up from Washington, and a house for an office. For the next several years, the branch ran five or six courses each summer. Then increasingly the rivers of the north—those free-flowing arteries through the dense, untrammeled forests—begged the question: Why not add canoeing to the mix? The first combo course was added around 1996, and for a classroom they chose to go north to Yukon—which seemed fine until it took three days to drive the 600 miles from Smithers to the McMillan and Hess Rivers.

Even with that introduction to Yukon, Warner and his crew could sense the vast possibilities of the territory lying just north of British Columbia. Its capital city of Whitehorse was bigger than Smithers, and the airport decent. In 1999, Warner, a Canadian from Winnipeg, and his wife, Abby, also an instructor, rented a warehouse in Whitehorse, notable mostly for its pink floor. The base was renamed NOLS Yukon.

It was a hit. By 2001, a year after Rich Brame arrived to take the director position, 160 students departed on a dozen or more courses. The core offerings at the branch were hiking, mountaineering, and canoeing, but there were also combo expeditions lasting up to 45 days. There was also a semester, with NOLS Alaska hosting a sea kayaking section. In 2003, a Yukon outdoor educator backpacking and river course began.

After Brame left in 2004, Jim Chisholm became director until 2007, when Jaret Slipp took over until 2014 (Slipp also organized and led the Baffin Island expeditions from 2006 until 2009). He was succeeded by Briana Mackay. NOLS Yukon was started as an independent branch, but when Jim Chisholm became program manager, it was brought under the NOLS Alaska umbrella. When Don and Donna Ford retired in 2012, supervision switched to Teton Valley, where Abby Warner, with her deep knowledge of Yukon operations, had become director in 2002. Over the years, however, the PNW had gradually extended its operations farther into Canada, and by 2015 it made sense to shift Yukon to the PNW family.

In 2013 the branch dumped its pink-floored airport warehouse located in a commercial area—never high on the charming scale—in favor of a 10-year lease at nearby Takhini Hot Springs, a retreat center 25 minutes out of town with much improved ambience.

Canoeing in the Yukon. *Roo Riley*

Bound students who had given him their addresses. "I started writing 40 letters a day, six days a week, until I got 100 students for the first year," he said later. Andy Carson, who first met Petzoldt at Outward Bound, got a letter and signed up for the first NOLS course. Bill Scott, who had been on the very first COBS course, said, "I could not go because of college. But as soon as I graduated I went, in 1967. I didn't know Paul, but the letter was very personal. It said, 'We really want you to come,'" he remembered.

With no start-up funds or other revenue sources, only the course deposits from students provided money. The school had "nothing, nothing, no sources at all," Petzoldt told an early NOLS historian, Del Bachert, in 1987. Early expenses, largely postage, were paid by Nicholas. The letter-writing campaign was already yielding results—much to everybody's surprise—by the end of February when, Nicholas remembered, "Paul came to the office and said, 'Do you realize we have $30,000 in the bank?'" Course deposits had begun to arrive in the mail. The school was real. The summer ahead loomed.

Petzoldt had to get a handle on a daunting list of details. He needed to procure supplies and equipment, find faculty assistants, and arrange for rations and transportation. But in the 40 years since his first climb up the Grand Teton, Petzoldt had honed his organizational and logistical skills, as

Paul Petzoldt and Tap Tapley. *NOLS Archives*

well as a friendly, convincing manner that motivated others to pitch in. He also had help from two capable, trusted colleagues: Tap Tapley and Rob Hellyer.

Tapley hailed from Amesbury, Massachusetts. He was a soft-spoken man who taught mostly by demonstration. Tapley was unusually humble and calm, according to those who knew him—a good foil for Petzoldt's more flamboyant style. Bill Scott met Tapley in 1962 at COBS. "Tap would be standing out in the middle of this water watching all of us go through on the morning run, just standing there in the freezing cold river. That's when I developed a great admiration and respect for Tap. He was like the wilderness god there."

On early NOLS courses, Petzoldt and Tapley could often be seen consulting with each other, figuring out the best way for a course to unfold. Andy Carson recalled watching the pair on numerous courses, first as a student in 1965 and later as an instructor: "It was a fluid day-by-day process of deciding what to do, where to go, what to teach. They were working out what a NOLS course would ultimately come to entail, in terms of skills. You watched Paul and Tap talk it through out loud." There were many topics to address; the art of it was to recognize the fluid nature of the outdoor classroom and the teachable moments it offered. When a good lake came along, it was time for the fishing class. When someone was hurt, it was time for first-aid lessons. When it rained, it was time to discuss ways to keep raingear handy.

Rob Hellyer was also a crucial member of the early NOLS team. Although he was serving in the US Army in 1965, he was able to get a look at what was happening that summer when he came back to Lander on leave. He returned full-time in 1966 after he left the service.

"Rob was so versatile and energetic, he quickly became Paul's man Friday," said Andy Carson. "Rob would take care of every problem. By 1967 . . . Rob would be in with a course maybe for five days, but then he'd have to slip away to go organize the re-ration. Very quickly, whether he liked it or not, he'd do anything to make things work well, so he was out of the mountains more than he was in. Paul could count on him absolutely."

Much of the clerical work of NOLS occurred at first in the basement of the Nicholas family's large brick home, later moving to the basement of his Main Street office at the Nicholas Building next to the Noble Hotel. But the school needed more space for supplies, logistics, and personnel. By April 1965, use of two properties had been arranged. The first was north of the State Training School on the road to Riverton, an unused property given to the Lander Alcoholic Rehabilitation Foundation known as the "AA Building." NOLS purchased it that spring to use as a staging and issuing area, and later for storage. The second was Alfred Ellerby's Hidden Valley Ranch on Dry Creek, 55 miles up Highway 26 near Burris in the heart of the Wind River Indian Reservation.

Nicholas soon helped arrange a much better location for NOLS operations. Just six miles southwest of town on the Popo Agie River, the old hydroelectric power station in Sinks Canyon had made Lander the first electrified town in

Rob Hellyer. *NOLS Archives*

Wyoming in 1890. By the 1960s the site was in disrepair. Pacific Power donated it to the city of Lander and pulled out. Nicholas, who was city attorney at the time, secured a lease for NOLS to use the property in exchange for caretaking it. Rent was just right for the NOLS budget: a dollar a month.

Clipping to protection on a climb
in the Rocky Mountains.
Pascal Beauvais

Launching the
First Courses

IT WAS A SCRAMBLE IN THE SPRING OF 1965 to acquire the needed equipment, supplies, food rations, and everything else to launch 43 boys and their instructors into the backcountry. But Petzoldt was a master scrounger. He took the student deposit money and went shopping. Petzoldt headed for a surplus center in Sydney, Nebraska, where the school, as a qualified educational institution, had access to loads of post-war material. His first purchase: a two-and-a-half-ton stock truck. Then he filled it to the brim.

Another source for gear was in Denver, in the person of an accommodating military surplus rag merchant named Leonard Joseph. Petzoldt met Joseph during his COBS years. Joseph understood Petzoldt's "rob Peter to pay Paul" methods for getting things done, often agreeing to let him pay when the money came in. Best of all, the surplus stores had no shortage of woolen pants. Now that he had his own school, Petzoldt could set the rules, which meant that NOLS

garments would be wool. (He allowed synthetics in later years, but never cotton.)

There was no way NOLS could have pulled together the clothing and equipment they needed, course after course,

Stock trucks transported students and gear in the early years. *NOLS Archives*

without Thelma Young, whom Petzoldt hired in April 1965. Although she claimed she wasn't even looking for a job when he approached her, she had been sewing since age five and quickly earned her place as an essential member of the team. In coming years, she would listen to various ideas for back-country equipment and clothing, and create whatever was needed: tents, windshirts, Dacron booties, etc. One of her early innovations was to cut off the bottom half of one wool sweater

and sew it to another, creating a garment that extended to the knees. Thelma was still working for the school as its longest tenured employee when she died at age 69 in November 1999.

Petzoldt's shopping and Young's alterations resulted in what would become the iconic NOLS uniform: a floppy felt or woolen ski hat, wool pants with a heart-shaped patch of dense wool from scrap overcoats sewn onto the butt, Thelma's customized double wool sweater, and later, a gray or red woven-

Thelma Young, NOLS equipment guru, at her sewing machine. *NOLS Archives*

The NOLS uniform in the early years—wool from head to toe. *Ken Jones*

Early NOLS packs were surplus frames originally designed to haul mortars. Duffels were lashed to them, creating the (in)famous "three-bag system." *Ken Jones*

Before the advent of backpacking stoves, cookfires were the norm. Students were taught to dig down to make the fire, and later replace the topsoil. *NOLS Archives*

wool, Nehru-collared shirt with a striped NOLS patch.

Backpacks for the initial courses were also vintage. Petzoldt purchased loads of army-issue stuff bags and British Army pack frames with canvas arm straps and no hip belts, originally designed as mortar carriers. Then he showed students how to strap three of the bags onto the frames, thus launching the (in)famous NOLS "three-bag system." As with many NOLS systems, it wasn't fancy or expensive, but it worked. The bag containing two pounds per person per day of food was a hodgepodge of smaller plastic bags containing about 70 ingredients ranging from "Cream of Punishment"

(oatmeal) to rock salt, grains, flour, blocks of electric-orange cheese, macaroni, and more.

In the mid-1960s, it was customary to build bonfires in the backcountry. Early NOLS movies show impressively large fires, but before long, those were replaced by smaller cookfires. Students were taught to dig out the sod and burn their wood on the inorganic layer. Coals were drowned and stirred into a slurry and the site returned to its natural state before moving on. Conservation and care of the environment were non-negotiable (if still evolving, in actual practice) core tenets of a NOLS course from the outset.

Course structure was loosely based on the military model familiar to both Tapley and Petzoldt. Instructor teams consisted of a course leader (CL) for the overall group, a patrol leader (PL) for each of the smaller groups, consisting of 10 to 12 students per patrol, plus one assistant instructor for each patrol.

In the first summer, the CLs were Petzoldt and Tapley. The first four patrol leaders were Bruce Barrus of Cleveland, who was working on his PhD in geology, Bart Redmayne, a Harvard student, and Jack Hyland, of Denver, all recruited from Outward Bound, plus a missionary from Fort Washakie named Jerry Taylor. From Lander in the first class were Dan Hammerstrom and Chuck Erickson, who was son of the school's physician, Bill Erickson, working as an unpaid assistant. Tom Warren came from Riverton as one of the school's first scholarship students.

Course curriculum included climbing, hiking, shelter building, map making and map reading, fishing, packing, and "all the arts necessary to enjoying the outdoors in safety and comfort," according to the *Wyoming State Journal*.

True to his original proposal to Outward Bound, part of the mission was to develop people who could capably lead others in remote areas, even in trying circumstances. After weeks of skill-building, Petzoldt's "final exam" was called "small group survival." Students burned whatever food rations remained in their bags, and spent the last five or so days finding their way back to the roadhead in small groups without instructor support. A passage, a conclusion, a commencement of sorts, it was a way to prove (at least to oneself) that the essential teachings of NOLS had been grasped. Through time, the precise implementation of independent student travel has been scrutinized, altered, and renamed, but the basic premise of survival has been an integral, quintessential part of the NOLS field experience from the very start.

When the first course ended on July 8, 1965, the hungry students and their instructors were served a spaghetti dinner at the Episcopal Church parish hall prepared by Jean Erickson, Alice Nicholas, and Dottie Petzoldt (who discovered, upon finding no strainer for the noodles, that the screens off the church hall windows worked just fine).

The next day, Friday, July 9, the instructor team turned right around and began again. This time, they left from Dickinson Park, and Lonesome Lake, Wind River Peak, and Grave Lake were on the itinerary. In the mix on the second course were four boys from the state hospital at Evanston, sponsored by the State Vocational Rehabilitation Division. Perhaps because of his own personal story, Petzoldt believed that NOLS could help troubled boys. Although they weren't the easiest students (they had been placed in the state hospital for a reason), according to Hellyer, the NOLS experience had a positive impact on many of them. Sometimes, he said, "It was tough. They were tough. They had to go absolutely cold-turkey from the drugs they were on, but it was the best thing ever" for them. According to John Johnson of the Mental Health Center in Lander, NOLS was "an extremely profitable experience for them and they did wonderful." From a business point of view, too, it was also helpful that the state paid an extra $100 tuition per boy. The eight boys from the state hospital who were students in 1965 pioneered the way for many more before the affiliation was eventually discontinued.

Petzoldt also felt deeply that NOLS should be within reach of everyone, not just the wealthy with the pocketbooks for such an adventure. "He'd take anyone who asked," said Hellyer. "He never said no. He took everyone in, gave 'em a scholarship." In his travels to promote the school, according to Nicholas, Petzoldt often returned with a scholarship student. He also invented the "Pay Back When Able" (PBWA) scholarship system: come to NOLS, and pay off the tuition when you can. This scholarship program made NOLS possible for many students, who often stayed as instructors or staff, sometimes for years. (By 1970, 71 percent of the 1965 PBWA scholarship outlay had been paid back.)

"Paul Petzoldt totally 'got' what youth was going through in the 1960s and '70s," recalled longtime instructor Q Belk. "He would give the opening speech in the Lumberyard or on South Pass to my courses, and you could just see the students experience their individual epiphanies: 'Here is an adult I can trust. My parents are stupid but this is a Great Man I can follow.'"

After the third and final course finished that summer, Petzoldt, Tapley, Hellyer, and the rest of the still-nascent NOLS community could look back on the season with pride.

"We are extremely satisfied not only with what we accomplished but also with the enthusiasm of the people who went through the course . . . that is, in our small way, spreading better leadership to all groups interested in using the outdoors," said Petzoldt to the *Wyoming State Journal*.

Later that fall, Petzoldt delivered a six-page "Review and Report to Trustees, 1965" to his board. It included a positive recap of the first summer, as well as 20 recommendations for the future. These included field logistics, increased emphasis on "actual mountain climbing and snow and glacier techniques," better organization of supplies and equipment, improved office organization, future contact with graduates, a course for women, public relations, and more. He also recommended three men be added to the board of directors.

HOW I SPENT MY SUMMER . . . 1967

By Gene Bates, Adventure Course, 1967

It was June 1967; I had turned 13 years old, and I was about to embark on one of the greatest adventures of my life. I had been chosen to attend NOLS's very first course for juniors, later renamed the Adventure Course.

I was a rebellious young boy in a time when there were few options for dealing with juvenile problems. Because of behavior issues, rather than criminal activity, I had been expelled from school, and my parents, who were ending their marriage, admitted me to the juvenile program at the Wyoming State Hospital. During this time, the hospital and NOLS had an agreement to allow select youths to attend courses in Lander.

The trip from Evanston, Wyoming, to Lander was an adventure of its own, as we were all on our own and traveled by Greyhound bus. We were welcomed to the school headquarters by the biggest man I had ever seen: Paul Petzoldt was huge, both in stature and personality. He was friendly and kind, physically imposing in his sweater and knicker-style trousers with socks and boots and a wool watch cap. Standing in the early morning sunlight on the steps of the front porch, arms akimbo, speaking in a strong but gentle voice, he epitomized the outdoorsman that he truly was.

Petzoldt took the time to inform me and one other boy selected from the hospital that we would not be singled out or treated differently than any other young man in the group. I am quite sure that it was never mentioned that we were "patients" of the hospital.

The group started out on foot a short way and encountered the river. It was swift and deep, a pole-and-rope bridge the only way across. As a kid who was afraid of heights, had zero self-confidence, and was skinny with little upper body strength, little did I know this was the first of many tests and the first step on a life-changing journey. The roar of the river was deafening, and taking that first step out onto that pole carrying a pack that was half my body weight made my heart race and my stomach churn. The noise, the movement of the water beneath me, and the swaying of the bridge made me want so very badly to turn around and get back on that truck! I looked back at the parking area and realized the truck was gone! I now had no choice but to put one foot in front of the other and get across that bridge.

We camped that first night on the far side of the river. We had been separated into two-man teams who were tent mates, climbing buddies, and cooking partners. The team concept applied to pretty much everything we learned or did. Each of us was responsible for and to each other. If your partner was lazy, you had to work harder or work with him to step it up. We learned early on that if one person was strong in a certain area or skill, he could benefit the group by helping those who were lacking.

The next few days were a series of tests, lessons, hardships, excitement, and rewards. We got our first blisters and learned how to take care of them and what to do to prevent more. For a collection of city kids and even us few Westerners, the daily hike to the next stop was hard work. We started with short distances and worked our way up. Every direction we turned seemed to be uphill. We learned to balance those awkward pack frames and to cross streams deftly. Nearly everything we did was a new experience, and there were many opportunities to receive instruction. As the days stretched into weeks, we became stronger, more confident, self-reliant, and disciplined.

During one climbing class, Petzoldt "encouraged" me to be lead climber on a short but difficult rock face. As we prepared to rope up for the climb, he handed me a sling of pitons and hammer and said he wanted to watch me lead. Although I never really overcame my fear of heights, I learned to put my fear aside and do the work necessary to reach a goal. I found that I could push beyond my comfort zone with confidence. Petzoldt was, I believe, a good judge of character and encouraged all of us to do our best and try again if we failed. What a gifted teacher he was.

My experience during that summer shaped me in ways that I was completely unaware of at the time. Some of those subtle lessons didn't come to light until many years later. Physical and mental endurance, logical thinking, calm and deliberate problem solving, and so much more have steered me in my adult life and through a career in the military and law enforcement. At the time, I saw the hardships of life on the trail

as drudgery and couldn't wait to make camp and rest. Climbing filled me with fear and apprehension. I was a good navigator, but initially lacked the self-confidence to step up and lead. I endured the daily hikes, the discomfort of the unpadded canvas pack straps cutting my skinny shoulders, sleeping on the ground, not realizing that I was growing, maturing, and learning life lessons that hardly anyone in the world would ever have the opportunity to enjoy.

This is not to say that I missed the awesome beauty of the world around me: the cold crisp air in the mornings and the flower-covered alpine slopes, ice-cold pure water flowing from snowfields or glaciers over granite on its way to the Green River and beyond to the valleys and desert of southern Wyoming. From standing on the summit of Lizard Head in the Cirque of the Towers and viewing the world from a place that even eagles rarely venture, to stepping across the Green River at its source, I knew that this was something special.

I reflect back on that summer often. With age and maturity I appreciate the experience more and sometimes regret that I never returned or kept in touch with Petzoldt. I would have liked to tell him what a life-altering experience I was privileged to have gotten and what an impact he personally made on me. We never really ever know what footprints we leave on another person's soul, but Mr. Petzoldt surely left them on mine.

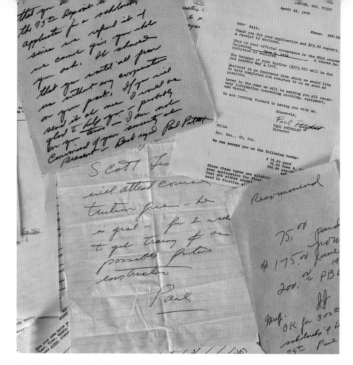

Paul believed in the power of handwritten correspondence and in the benefits of letting students come to NOLS first and pay later. *NOLS Archives*

His report also included a financial recap of the year. The document shows "Cost" (revenues) of $40,000 against "Actual Cost" (expenses) of $35,600, leaving a balance for 1966 of $4,400. He also noted how effective the "PBWA" scholarship program had proven.

Another recommendation that is perhaps the seed of an ongoing theme of NOLS finances across the years was that "the school should be self-supporting from an operational standpoint . . . To give donations for operational expenses might lead to financial sloppiness and waste in programming, purchasing, and management. This, we feel, was the case at the Colorado Outward Bound School . . . " In future years, both the insistence on operations paying for operations as well as the inevitable comparisons (good and bad) with Outward Bound would rise again and again.

In the report as well are comments written by 10 "instructors" (which is what he called his first 100 graduates). One was written by a boy from the state hospital at Evanston: "I want to thank you for making me see a lot clearer how to get along in this world."

In the fall of 1965, Petzoldt appeared at the Outing Club of Colorado State University in Ft. Collins. After his presentation explaining the NOLS program, a petite 19-year-old woman approached him and asked why there were no girls in the slides he had shown. Did he allow girls on the NOLS courses, she wanted to know.

"No," she recalls him saying, "but I don't know why not. You want to come?" Petzoldt wrote down her contact information and later wrote a letter inviting her to NOLS. The "PBWA" scholarship he offered sealed the deal. She informed her parents of her summer plan. The woman was Martha Newbury, and the summer ahead would change her life.

In late December 1965, Petzoldt led 15 climbers on a New Year's attempt to climb the Grand Teton. The effort failed, but it garnered widespread national publicity for the school, with numerous TV and radio interviews, plus articles disseminated by the UPI and AP wire services. Ever charismatic and quotable, Petzoldt was good copy, and the story of his exploits on the Grand meshed well with his enthusiasm and dedication for this new school. Much of his time that winter was spent on road trips to promote NOLS. He was invited to speak in March at the American Camping Association's annual convention in Chicago, and also at the Midwest district conference for the National Recreation and Parks Association in Kansas City.

"Really, the salesmanship was incredible," said Hellyer. "He had incredible discipline." His earnest belief in the power of a handwritten letter with a real signature persisted. Over time, he pressed others into service, including Hellyer and Skip Shoutis and other early office assistants. (Later, when letter-writing ramped up dramatically, Shoutis often sat across from George Newbury—Martha's cousin who arrived in 1970—at an old army double-desk, writing letter after letter in reply to the bins of queries about the school that were flooding in.)

Promotional efforts paid off. The three courses in 1966 were larger, with about 50 boys each, including the "carefully screened" boys from the state hospital in Evanston. Petzoldt also gave scholarships to students from the Lander area. A special bus from the Kansas City Park and Recreation Board arrived with 36 boys for the July session.

On June 8, 1966, the first course for girls headed into the backcountry. Martha Newbury was one of seven led by NOLS's first co-ed instructor team of Tap and Lee Tapley. Also attending was 16-year-old Patty Nicholas, daughter of Jack and Alice Nicholas. The July course had seven females, and more came in August. The girls carried less weight and used a packhorse that summer, but that practice was soon discontinued.

By 1966, Sinks Canyon was the center of NOLS operations. There were four buildings on the property: the big concrete power plant building that had housed the two turbines (which some called the pumphouse), a nice log house that housed the office, a garage used as a small shop and for storage, and a small white dorm-like house with a kitchen and bunks. Much of the property was dilapidated, requiring work to be habitable even by NOLS standards. The roof in a corner of the pumphouse had been knocked out to remove the two turbines, according to Hellyer, so he and a crew of helpers patched it and re-tarred the roof.

The office building, according to Nancy Wise Carson, who worked there after her student course in 1967, had a little porch room facing the river with a kitchen where she cooked many a turkey and 50-gallon batch of potato salad. Other cooking was done on an outdoor grill by the pumphouse, next to the fish pond. For a fledgling organization short on cash but populated by enthusiastic and willing young people, it was a great location.

With the Popo Agie River running through the back yard, NOLS students suffered a tradition borrowed from Outward Bound: Everyone was required to jump in the water in the morning. Once a college professor from Berkeley refused to jump in, but Petzoldt told him it was mandatory, so they threw him in, recounted Nicholas. "He said he was going to sue the school, that it was his constitutional right not to take a bath, but we just laughed at him."

Although some clerical work was still done in town by Nicholas and his secretary, the NOLS office at "the Sinks" was a tightly run ship captained by one of the earliest full-time employees of NOLS: Mrs. Jean Johnson, with an assistant, Mrs. Helen Rawalt, at her side.

"Jean was in charge of everything," Nicholas remem-

NOLS's first headquarters, in Sinks Canyon.
NOLS Archives

bered. "She was a very nice lady. She didn't have an outgoing personality; you asked a question and she'd answer and not add to it. She wouldn't sit down and have a conversation with you. She cut people pretty short, and that caused some consternation to some people. But she did everything that was needed to be done."

"She probably thought we were dirty, irreverent, young people. We were!" said Andy Carson. "But she worked hard and was dedicated to the school. You didn't want to upset her."

Many documents in the school archives show the sort of orderliness Mrs. Johnson insisted upon. Course records until at least 1974 are neatly handwritten, and it's a fair guess that many of them are in her hand. Precise handwritten lists also were kept of items held by the office for safekeeping while students were on their courses: wallets, money, paper airline tickets, and more.

———————————————

As much as Petzoldt touted that NOLS was a school for leaders, it was also a place for adventure—and with it came risk and the inevitability of loss. The school's first evacuation occurred on the second course in 1965, when a young man from Albuquerque got sick and was evacuated by packhorse. The boy wasn't seriously ill, and was offered a chance to return to NOLS later.

But on Wednesday, July 20, 1966, student Arthur Saltus, 18, of Morristown, New Jersey, was leading up a short section of rock in a couloir on Kagevah Peak. He was roped and on belay, but hadn't placed any protection as he climbed. In rock climbing, "protection" refers to devices driven or wedged into the rock and then clipped to the rope with a carabiner. With well-placed protection, a climber who slips from the rock won't fall all the way to the ground. According to his patrol leader, Andy Carson, "He peeled off, and ended up at the base of the short wall, unconscious but not outwardly broken up or bloody or horribly disfigured." They made a litter out of small trees and lowered him down some 450 feet of scree to a meadow where a helicopter could land. He never regained consciousness and died in the afternoon. An autopsy showed a fractured rib and pelvis, multiple internal injuries, and a subdural hematoma. Saltus's ashes were scattered at Sonnicant Lake the following week, his godparents in attendance.

The NOLS "classroom" had taken its first victim, and the tragedy dampened the spirits of the people at the school, just as Teepe's death in the Tetons had been a grisly wake-up call for Petzoldt in 1925. Saltus was the first of 12 deaths on NOLS courses in the first 50 years—half of those occurring in the school's first 10 years.

In discussion in camp afterwards, said Carson, it was hard to know what he or the other instructors might have done differently. Learning more about the boy, who had shown himself to be a risk-taker, "was a lesson in itself, and also to learn that some people will take greater risks than one might oneself, in the same situation, was another lesson for some of us younger instructors, with fewer life lessons under our belt. The swift violence of his death—everything's great until suddenly it isn't—was hard to shake, but with Paul's leadership and experience of other fatalities, we absorbed it as best we could and continued through the next several weeks."

In 1967, after another failed attempt at what had become an annual New Year's effort to climb the Grand Teton, Petzoldt went on a whirlwind of more than 30 speaking engagements throughout the country to promote the school.

NOLS was growing. That summer, there were once again three regular expedition courses. An addition to the course lineup was the NOLS "Adventure Course" for 13- to 15-year-old boys. According to the *Wyoming State Journal*, one impetus for developing courses for younger students was that Petzoldt had, the prior year, turned away one of Senator Bobby Kennedy's sons for being too young.

During those early years, Petzoldt was experimenting with variations on the main theme of NOLS, such as course size and length; the first Adventure Course ran from July 10 to August 19—nearly six weeks. Courses in 1967 also mushroomed in size to 50 students or more to accommodate as many people as possible, and they would become even larger in coming years, sometimes with more than 100 students. Courses were co-ed, with 22 girls attending in 1967. Although they initially camped in separate patrols, everyone participated jointly in lessons and activities. Course length ranged from 30 to 35 days. Innovations such as these led to inevitable questions about the impact on the backcountry, a situation that would eventually lead to course-design changes.

Another innovation was a special 10-day trip for 25 Boy Scouts from Elizabethtown, Kentucky. And there was a customized NOLS experience for diabetic boys, a program that lasted several years, led by Jim Halfpenny and John W. Walker, a track coach and member of the physical education department faculty at the University of Wyoming. The concept of specialized, customized NOLS experiences existed, as shown by these examples, well ahead of the creation of NOLS Professional Training in 1999.

The school got an important boost in legitimacy with the advent of college credit. Starting in 1966, Kansas State Teachers College offered college credits in ecology and biology. In addition, the University of Wyoming began offering two semester hours of recreation credit to students, largely through the school's relationship with Walker, who also became a long-term member of the NOLS Board.

Rob and Martha Hellyer. *NOLS Archives*

Paul teaching route finding. *NOLS Archives*

In all, 150 students graduated from the regular expedition courses in 1967. Each course enjoyed a final banquet, and diplomas were awarded. The atmosphere at the school was buoyant. Even Mrs. Johnson was light-hearted; she was quoted in the paper as saying, "We had a lot of humorous incidents which we don't talk about."

On the same day that the second course of the season issued its gear, Monday, July 10, Petzoldt was uncharacteristically absent. He took a few hours off to host a special occasion at his home in Lander: the wedding of his righthand man and assistant director, Rob Hellyer, to the young woman from the CSU Outing Club, Martha Newbury. After her student course, she had become an instructor for the school. In December, Martha would join Petzoldt and her husband as the first woman on the team for the third annual New Year's attempt to climb the Grand Teton.

What NOLS Students Were Learning

FROM THE FIRST, Paul, Rob, and Tap had a clear idea of the principles they were trying to pass on: Judgment. Leadership. Outdoor skills. Care of the environment.

The bedrock NOLS concept was judgment. Ever since his cold, dark night on the Grand Teton at the age of 16, Petzoldt knew the importance of judgment, especially in the unforgiving world of the wilderness. "Judgment in my estimation is the greatest safety factor you can have," he believed. With it, the risky nature of the outdoors is better managed—that is, safer, as safe as a place with cliffs, rivers to ford, avalanches, steep terrain, and harsh weather can be. Paul's way to disclose risk and set safety expectations at the beginning of the course, according to Skip Shoutis, was to say something on issue day like, "Turn to your right, turn to your left. The person you are looking at may be responsible for your safety. You are responsible for their safety." In that way, he emphasized the responsibility each had for the others.

He also liked to say, "rules are for fools," or, to quote a less pithy version from 1965, "excessive rules are for beginners." What he meant by this misunderstood maxim is that it is impossible to write a particular rule for every eventuality, but beginners need rules because they haven't developed their judgment yet. Perhaps he came to regret using that word, "fool," but he wanted it to be clear that, with experience and judgment, a leader can relate knowledge and technical skills developed from one specific situation to other similar situations; if you're lost, you'll never be lost in the same place again, but the principles for dealing with it are the same. "He was ahead of his time," said NOLS risk management director Drew Leemon, in 2015. "Way back then, he was talking about expertise and heuristics."

Predictably, the specifics of curriculum shifted over time. Axmanship, for example, was once on the skill list, as was how to fight forest fires (Tapley actually once needed his

Petzoldt's experiences in the mountains had taught him the importance of judgment. *NOLS Archives*

fireman's axe to put out a small forest fire). Use of firearms was taught, and how to kill and butcher animals. Although Petzoldt described using cows in the earliest years, instructors later purchased sheep from high-country herders. On one course in 1966, a moose was shot and butchered. "At that time, people were allowed to do survival-type training," according to one source. "It was at least gray-area legal, so we butchered the whole thing. It was more than we wanted to carry and more than we could eat right there, so we were actually smoking it so we could take some with us." Apparently, when the folks from the Wyoming Game and Fish Department heard what was going on, they "kinda got upset about this and said 'no, it should really be survival training. You can't use a rifle, and you have to take an animal by natural snares.'" Porcupines and other small animals remained "fair game" for some years after that.

Petzoldt's teaching methods were designed to leave an unforgettable impression. "Paul was not beyond taking what might be considered radical steps to get a point across," said Bill Scott. "They included things like having people stand up and take off their clothes and throw them in the fire if they were wearing cotton, in front of everybody."

Likewise, he wasn't above having slow, sleepy students thrown in a lake, sleeping bag and all. Or tossing items he felt to be out of place or unnecessary in the wilderness far out

Mary Jo Newbury. Fishing was part of the NOLS experience from the very beginning. *NOLS Archives*

into a nearby lake. Or reminding those who forgot their rope signals, not by lecturing, but by aiming a well-placed rock missile in their direction.

Many times, a class would evolve from whatever situation was at hand. If someone was lost, Petzoldt made a class out of the search; if hurt, then he'd teach about first aid and evacuation on the spot. His style relied heavily on the importance of using not just common sense but also the wisdom that comes from direct experience: the stuff we learn from doing things repeatedly.

"He was captivating. When you think back, he had good presence," recalled Haven Holsapple, a student in 1967 and still working for the school in 2015. "He had kind of a booming, good voice that carried well, and an easy laugh, but at the same time you knew he was serious about what he was teaching. That's what carried through."

Tapley and Hellyer were perfect foils for Petzoldt's blustery style. Both men were uniformly praised for their abilities at the head of the "classroom." Tap was notoriously sparse with words, teaching mostly by example. And Hellyer was likewise a notably capable and dedicated teacher, very good logistically, very caring.

Petzoldt did not invent the idea of taking people into the backcountry for an extended period of time. Others, such as Outward Bound, were already doing that. His primary innovation was recognizing the need for outdoor leadership, and he helped train leaders by putting students in leadership situations, at first under the watchful eyes of NOLS instructors, then increasingly in student groups traveling independently, and at last during the final days of "survival." The point was to teach students so that, in a stressful situation, they could successfully lead others safely through the mountains.

As the school grew, Paul, Tap, and Rob were stretched more thinly. Rob took on innumerable logistical tasks, including the packhorses and re-rationing. Although Paul and Tap still went out on most courses or at least made a point of visiting with every course at some point, they had to begin depending on others to do some of the teaching. They drew from the growing ranks of patrol leaders, who had repeatedly observed the three powerhouses of NOLS instructing. The instructor corps began to build.

After that first crop of PLs, recruited mostly from COBS, new instructors were recruited from the top tier of NOLS students. Course leaders—initially Paul, Tap, or Rob—watched their students carefully. Paul, especially, would put people in situations to see what they would do. For example, said Skip Shoutis, "when he was teaching rappelling, he'd give you perfect examples, and how you can't let people mingle around the edge of the cliff. He'd say, 'Here we are, and oh, look at that eagle' and show how easy it would be to hit a buddy with the pointing arm and knock 'em off the cliff. . . . You don't forget that sort of thing," said Shoutis.

Students who performed well were asked to come back as instructors. Instructor ranks grew as the 1960s drew to a close, and became vital glue for the school. "We were pioneers. It was the best thing in the world for a bunch of young people to have an old man (so he seemed to us) listening to our ideas and letting us do things, and putting all those young people out in the hills for 30 days with even younger people," recalled Shoutis. "It was a huge responsibility. We were empowered. Those were the happiest days of my life."

In 1967, the school purchased five horses and borrowed a couple more, and from then on used packhorses for re-rationing courses that were too far in the mountains to reach by truck. At two pounds of food ingredients per person per day, students could carry about 10 days of food at a time. Rob and Martha Hellyer could often be seen wending their way into the high country to rendezvous with a course and deliver both fresh rations and news of the world.

When Bill Scott did his first pack trip in August 1969, he said, "Rob needed help to take supplies to the North Fork of Bull Lake Creek from Elkhart Park, 30 miles over Indian Pass. I'd done a little riding, but I'd never packed horses. Martha was pregnant. I mean *real* pregnant. She helped us pack up the horses, then drove back to Lander.

THE YOUNGEST NOLS "GRAD"

Possibly the youngest "graduate" of a NOLS course is Jim Hellyer—not for his 1988 Alaska mountaineering course at age 18, but for his participation as a toddler in 1970. His instructor-mother, Martha, saw no reason why not to depart for the backcountry as usual that busy summer. With a Kelty pack specially modified with mosquito netting and a rain fly sewn by Thelma Young and Martha, Jim rode in style on her back, protected from the sun by a surrey-like awning over his head. "The ball fringe was added just for fun," said Martha. To help carry the cloth diapers and entertain the 10-month-old toddler while she taught, Hellyer brought along her "baby Sherpa," Patty Nicholas, age 18, a veteran from the first all-girls course in 1966.

Jim Hellyer in his carrier.
Martha Hellyer

"Rob and I went over Indian Pass for my first time leading a pack string. It was a great experience. When we got over there, there was a student having intestinal pain. Paul was with them and thought he had appendicitis and wanted a helicopter, so they sent me out on a horse with another student who wanted to go out. We rode all night to get back to Elkhart Park, drove back to Lander, got there about dawn to meet the helicopter.

"Meanwhile, it turned out Martha had had her baby. I got the basics: boy, weight, all that. I got in the helicopter to show the pilot where to go. Rob was camped three or four miles away, so I wrote a note, stuck it in a little nylon sack

NOLS EAST AFRICA

The history of NOLS in Africa belongs to dozens of committed people. It started when Paul Petzoldt went to Mozambique with the Lander One-Shot Antelope Hunters club on safari in 1973 (where, incidentally, he also met Joan Brodbeck, who would soon be his third wife). He scouted the region from February to April 1974, with instructor Mike Williams and his wife, Jill. "We circled two-thirds of the country, up to Mount Kenya, through Maasai country, down to Lake Victoria and back, mostly on our own in 110-degree heat in a tiny Peugeot sedan," Williams said.

Visiting Africa on safari was one thing; starting a NOLS branch was another. "Paul was a fish out of water there," remembered Mike, as they worked through multiple stumbling

Getting close to lions. *NOLS Archives*

blocks, many of them cultural. Many times, the logistics of transportation, equipment, schedules—all the things Petzoldt relied on Rob Hellyer to handle at home—raised Petzoldt's ire. "He was not adept at bumping into things," said Williams. Finally, they befriended Phil Snyder, at that time the warden at Mount Kenya Park, who traded the permits the school needed for equipment from PPWE (Paul Petzoldt Wilderness Equipment).

Paul returned to Wyoming, leaving the Williamses headquartered in a house in Otiende Estates, a subdivision outside Nairobi. They had been joined by NOLS grad Vince Fayad and his wife, Chris. They went to Africa as newlyweds to work as graduate assistants for a University of Michigan program, but then heard NOLS was starting the Kenya program. The four did further scouting and continued to prepare for the first course, which ran from June 17 through August 24, 1974.

It was a 10-week program, a harbinger of the fully fledged semester course programming that was soon to come. The first three weeks were on the flanks of Mount Kenya for basic camping and mountaineering classes, and climbing Point Lenana (16,354 feet) on Mount Kenya. The course then moved to the Great Rift Valley for cultural components and geology lessons about the valley and its soda lakes. From there, they went to the Maasai Mara to visit a baboon research center and learn about wildlife biology—including hunting and harvesting gazelle. A move to the southeast took them to Tsavo National Park, from which the students traveled independently in small groups to a coastal base camp at Ras Ngomeni, near the town of Malindi. There followed more cultural opportunities,

Students and wildlife in East Africa. *James Kagambi*

snorkeling, and fishing—sometimes overnight—with the local fishermen. The final banquet was in Nairobi.

When the course was over, Mike was already late for law school in Spokane, so he and Jill boarded the plane with the students—neglecting to mention to the Fayads that they were leaving.

Left holding the bag, the Fayads almost single-handedly kept NOLS in Africa in business for the next two years. During that time, "we fumbled and stumbled," recalled Vince in 2015. Mike Blumenthal, a student on the first course, stayed on to provide invaluable help. They contended with an unscrupulous investor who soaked the school for funds and once ordered his sidekicks to brandish steel pipes in a showdown in Malindi when Fayad refused to pay. In April 1975, they moved the headquarters north to Granny Kenealy's Wanky Wonky Farm, a hostel in Naro Moru at the foot of Mount Kenya. Lacking privacy there, they moved again in September to a place rented from an expat named Minto, who eventually sold the eight-acre spread to NOLS in 1997. The Fayads stayed on through eight courses in all, with help from various instructors from the States; Tap Tapley came for the second course and Jim Halfpenny for the third.

More than anyone, the Fayads deserve credit for the very existence of NOLS in Kenya. In 1976, they handed the directorship over to Horace Bone, who was followed from 1977 to 1979 by George and Mary Jo Newbury. Many directors and assistant directors from NOLS followed, usually for two-year stints and usually as married couples. The best continuity for the school—with so many North Americans coming and going—was provided by East Africans. Shikuku Ooko, who worked from 1988 until 1997, was described by instructor Nene Wolfe as "one of those rare people in this world. NOLS launched him into a career of environmental education in Kenya, which evolved into an Africa-wide program involving environmental education." James Kagambi (KG) arrived in 1987 and was instrumental in launching courses for East Africans known as the NOLS Outdoor Educator Program (NOEP). A Tanzanian expat named Lolly Didham guided scores of 1980s students through the marine reserve she helped create off the coast of Malindi. (For lack of such a resource, John Gans taught the snorkeling section for his own semester course in 1979.) Didham's helper, Omari Haji Baruku (known as "Omari-Bob") taught about Swahili Muslim culture and the history of the coast. Later, the coastal sections were farther north, in Lamu, where students helped their skippers sail dhows up the coast to the Somali border.

Recruiting and training East African faculty was somewhat different from North America, where outdoor education and recreation were more common. In one case, instructor Stephen Kabiru was literally the "boy next door." More often, instructors came from secondary or university teaching backgrounds, and many went on to instruct NOLS courses in other parts of the world. KG had taught grade school and coached soccer before coming to NOLS. During his tenure at NOLS, KG completed three

of the Seven Summits, was the first black African to climb Denali (1989), and represented Africa in the UN Peace Climb for the World on the Eiger (1991).

Stories enough to fill a book of its own accrue to the school's experience in Kenya. For "survival," students were tasked with traveling in small groups on local transportation with a minimal budget. Wildlife encounters caused harm, but no fatalities—including one when a lion tripped on a tent guy line and got tangled in the tent while students were sleeping inside. One student was seriously injured high on the flanks of Mount Kenya by a Cape buffalo, and another was bitten in the face by a hyena that got into her tent. A course in 1994 was robbed at gunpoint by 10 bandits.

Renamed NOLS East Africa when the courses also began operating in nearby Tanzania in 1999, the branch was closed in 2003 for various reasons, much to the regret of many. The property was sold to Fred Roberts, who was branch director from 1986 to 1991, and his wife, Elizabeth Goodwin; they continued to run it with other NOLS veteran instructors as Batian's View, an experiential education center.

In 2011, through the efforts of KG and Kenyan instructor Muthoni Muriithi, a 13-year NOLS veteran and recipient of the NOLS Annual Field Staff Award, Africa rejoined the school's list of locations with a new version of NOLS East Africa, this time in Tanzania. Muthoni was at the helm. As KG said, "I believe that Africa has great classrooms for the outdoors, and the cultural base is a great teacher. This base in Tanzania prides itself in cultural exposure, the ability to meet different tribes and learn from them. Where else can you visit and hunt with the bushmen, hike with the Maasai alongside giraffes and other wild animals, [and] hop from one volcano to the other?"

and dropped it to him, letting him know he had a boy."

As the 1960s drew to a close, American society was beginning to reel with change. Women picketed the 1968 Miss America contest as a chauvinistic enterprise. The 1969 draft lottery spurred resentment of the Vietnam War. Burgeoning resistance to authority by long-haired, unkempt people calling themselves "hippies" signaled the rise of the drug culture and rejection of "The Establishment."

That made someone like Petzoldt good press over what the "grand old man of the mountains" was doing with and for young people in Wyoming. His annual efforts to climb the Grand Teton in winter failed the first four years, but the drama and danger lent a healthy dose of cachet to him and the school. Media attention began to build. In March 1968, the popular outdoor magazine *Field and Stream* published "Outdoor Finishing School," written by Raye Price (later, Raye Ringholz, author of the Petzoldt biography, *On Belay)*, who had spent time with the first all-girls course in 1966, along with her daughter.

The December 1969 issue of *Life* magazine—a household treasure in those days—featured NOLS in a full spread by Jane Howard with the alluring title of "Last Mountain Man? Not If He Can Help It." It was reportedly going to be the cover story, until Charles Manson and his grisly California cult murders supplanted it. To this day, Manson's face is

Bringing the groceries in Patagonia. *Ignacio Grez*

startling as his wild eyes stare eerily off copies of the magazine stowed in the NOLS archives. But the article introduced important Petzoldt educational philosophies, including his concern for the environment. After describing Petzoldt as an intrepid adventurer, Howard wrote, "Besides his gusto for skirmishes with the elements, he has a militant reverence for the natural world, as those whom he ushers into the wilderness soon learn. Once he made two boys walk back 12 miles to pick up a couple of pieces of tin foil."

On January 1, 1970, the New Year's climb of the Grand Teton was at last successful. The press covered it eagerly. "I was pushed and pulled the last 300 feet up to the top," said

From left: Michael Wadleigh, Rob Hellyer, and Paul Petzoldt during the filming of *Thirty Days to Survival*. *NOLS Archives*

Petzoldt, by then age 61. As if summiting successfully wasn't enough, the group that year was unusually newsworthy. Two of the climbers, Mr. and Mrs. Joe Nixon, were newlyweds who had tied the knot on December 14. Both the bride (the former Nikki Peck) and the groom were NOLS graduates, he

in 1966 and she in 1968. As a press bonus, Nikki had been the reigning Miss Indiana during her NOLS course.

The nation was well primed by both the *Life* magazine article and the New Year's climb, for the main event. In a day when there were just three broadcast channels, one of the most popular TV programs was the *Alcoa Hour*, and on Tuesday, January 20, 1970, it broadcast *Thirty Days to Survival*. A Life Films project that was picked up by Alcoa for distribution, the movie was made by Michael Wadleigh, Charles Grosbeck, and Fred Underhill. The men followed a course for a month in the backcountry during the summer of 1969 as the students learned to camp in early-summer snow, cook, fish, climb, and rappel. (Wadleigh and Underhill went on to film another momentous American event after completing their work in the Wyoming backcountry: the three-day music festival at Max Yasgur's farm in Woodstock, New York.)

Getting the job of filming done placed an extra logistical layer on top of the process of sending a course into the field. The course ran as usual, with an independent unit operating on the side for the film crew. Diane Shoutis and Susan Delissa cooked and supported the filmmakers and their team, plus the eight young men who were hired (at $1 a day, according to Haven Holsapple, who was on his first paid job with NOLS) to run the heavy reels of film and early-generation cadmium battery packs back and forth to town. The support crew was nicknamed "barwai" and "barwini"—an attempt at humor, referring to a city in India known for its mountain porters.

A particularly poignant part of the film occurs near the end. During the five days of survival, the film crew follows a patrol that discovers a cache of forgotten food at the bottom of someone's pack. This leads to great debate over what to do. Only the youngest boy, Danny, age 13, chooses to eat. When the patrol checks in at the roadhead, the expression of regret and chagrin on Danny's face when he reunites with Petzoldt captures without words the desire students to this day place on themselves to measure up to the high standards of the school.

The week before the show aired, a review appeared in the *New York Daily News*. It reads, in part, "They triumphed over bitter cold, gnawing hunger, and exhaustion—a thrilling ending to a fascinating documentary . . . During this time of hippies, junkies, and other social dropouts, here was a feature that gave one hope for and renewed one's faith in the youth of this country. This special should be shown in every school of the land."

As a result of *Thirty Days,* the school rocketed into the 1970s with a velocity few could have predicted. NOLS had arrived on the national radar.

NOLS Archives

Beautiful climbing in Patagonia.
Rainbow Weinstock

1970-1975

THE BOOM YEARS

Through a series of events in early July 1973, I found myself sitting on a bridge over Dry Creek on Highway 287 in Burris, Wyoming . . . Soon an older model car with a large white-haired gentleman with bushy eyebrows pulled over and offered me a ride, and he introduced himself as Paul Petzoldt. [He] proceeded to tell me about this outdoor education leadership school he was the head of, and by the time we arrived in Lander an offer had been made to allow me to take a course and work for the school to make the money to pay for it. . . . My life has been spent here in Lander and Fremont County . . . I couldn't have asked for a greater life experience.

– Bruce Cartwright, instructor

The *Alcoa Hour* presentation of *Thirty Days to Survival* catapulted the school into overdrive. From graduating about 300 students per year in the late 1960s, student volume more than tripled to 989 in 1970. Courses, which were sometimes as long as 35 days, left for the field each week, rather than each month, as in prior summers.

In the documentary, Petzoldt and his assistants are shown teaching students how to climb, to fish, to hike all day and arrive in camp with enough reserve energy to pitch their tents or flies and cook in the snow. One clip shows everyone laden with immense backpacks hiking over a 13,000-foot pass. "We want to build self-reliance, and an appreciation of wild places," he says. The film is compelling, and is filled with such classic Petzoldt comments as, "Leadership can only be learned by leading," and "Knowledge without judgment is pretty useless."

Through the 1960s, Petzoldt was the face of a relatively small organization. But the 1970 whirlwind of growth in Wyoming also coincided with geographic and seasonal

Stills from *Thirty Days to Survival.* *NOLS Archives*

expansion. That summer, Bill Garrison led the first NOLS East course, and in March of the next year, Tap Tapley inaugurated the first courses in Baja, Mexico. Winter mountaineering made its debut first in the Wind Rivers in 1970, and then the Tetons in 1972. Instructors scouted new locations and routes in Alaska and elsewhere. In 1971, there were 24 Wind River courses and 15 "expansion" courses elsewhere.

"Paul couldn't say no to anybody," recalled Bill Scott, who had been part of the scene since 1967. "So when it became a matter of, instead of 300 students, that we were going to have 900, Paul and Rob never said 'can we do this?' They just said 'we *gotta* do this.'"

The flood of student applications that arrived in the mail during the late winter and spring of 1970 created an "all hands on deck" atmosphere in Lander. Geoff Heath, a student from 1966 who had worked for NOLS through 1968, dropped out of Utah State in February to help Petzoldt comb student files in search of people who might come to Lander and help prepare for the upcoming busy summer and work courses. Realizing the need for more space, Petzoldt and Hellyer borrowed $22,000 from First National Bank in February and purchased the Foster Lumber Company, a four-building complex at 502 Lincoln Street. Vacant and in disrepair, the property was nonetheless just what the school needed. Until then, NOLS staff numbers had necessarily dwindled in the off-season from September to May; there was not enough to do to support a big staff year-round.

Suddenly, a small army and an explosion of effort were

needed to stay ahead of the mushrooming interest in NOLS. Hired for a pittance and fueled by belief in the school, instructors filtered back into town early, and former students came looking for meaning and purpose (and adventure). Everyone helped pull off the summer season. "That was just the attitude that people had. It was infectious," said Scott. "You made it happen, whatever it took, you made it happen."

"I dropped out of college and drove my '66 Mercury to Lander in mid-April 1970, right after they bought the Lumberyard," recalled Steve Gipe, who had been a NOLS student in 1967. "There was a whole tribe of us. We were living in wall tents up in Sinks Canyon, right across from the HQ. . . . [In] the white house where Rob and Martha lived . . . there was a kind of a kitchen, so we'd do meals there. And then we'd go down and work on the Lumberyard. We redid it, painted it, reroofed it, hand-sanded all these army-surplus trucks and painted them, all this in a couple of months." Hellyer had asked a retired British military officer, T. K. Creighton, to oversee the work. "He would go around and yell, 'Keep working!'" recalled Gipe. "He could make you work hard while at the same time you would like him."

By June, when the first students arrived, one of the buildings on the corner of Lincoln and 5th Street had a front room for seamstress Thelma Young and her crew and an

Lumberyard crew in the early 1970s. *NOLS Archives*

office. In others were a huge storage area, the rations department (then and now called the Gourmet Gulch), and an outfitting area with room to store equipment and supplies and to outfit students on issue days. The property also housed the school's vehicle fleet and a two-story barn-like structure with dorm and toilet facilities used by many instructors between courses.

What is a NOLS Course?

In the beginning, the content of a NOLS course was passed along in classic oral tradition. Not much was written down or codified. Most instructors were those who had been identified in their student courses as having potential, so course content was familiar to those rising through the ranks of the instructor group. Petzoldt believed in leadership development, and in many ways student education and instructor training in those early years were very similar: Everyone was learning—Petzoldt was still learning to run the school, his course leaders were learning to run courses, new instructors were learning to teach, and students were learning to lead their peers and themselves.

"The amazing thing about Paul," said longtime instructor Randy Cerf, who started as an unpaid assistant in 1967 at age 14, "was his belief in people. He would give incredible responsibility to young people with limited direction because he truly believed in people. There is story after story out there about folks with shaky backgrounds and limited educations who were very successful at NOLS. They rose to the occasion in part because Paul believed in them."

One of the first course leader instruction lists found in the archives is a two-page mimeographed sheet dated May 1973, listing classes to be taught on the basic NOLS Wilderness course, although many kept their own private notes.

Sixteen priority classes were taught in the first three days, including the purpose and philosophy of the school, pack carrying, shelters, and simple cooking. These were all to take 45 minutes to two hours. Others, such as trail technique, sanitation, practical conservation, and expedition behavior would be "continuous."

By the end of the first week, nine other classes, including first aid, litter building, and leadership, were given. In week two, emphasis shifted to such things as fishing, flora and fauna, baking and advanced cooking, and also increasingly sophisticated rope techniques such as signals and rappelling, snow techniques, and Tyrolean traverse. In the final two weeks before students headed out on survival, 17 classes were listed, including axmanship, advanced rock climbing and snow/ice techniques, astronomy and geology, and horsemanship (done at re-rationing).

At the heart of what instructors taught was Petzoldt's insistence that camping should in its own way remain fun. He emphasized that a good camper is a comfortable camper, and that once a person is comfortable in the outdoors, everything else is possible. "He is the most comfortable person in the outdoors," remembers Gipe. "He just made other people feel the joy of being in the wilderness. He loved sharing that with other people and helping them grow." What evolved was a basic core curriculum that

RULES ARE FOR FOOLS

The following is excerpted from a 2006 conversation between Cody Paulson (an instructor since 1971) and Liz Tuohy (NOLS director of education as of 2015).

Liz: What do you think Paul meant by "rules are for fools?"

Cody: Although "rules are for fools" has become a NOLS cliché, it is a reminder of the importance of developing critical intelligence and individual perspective. Paul's concept of "judgment" implies considering all the facts and making appropriate decisions. It also implies taking full responsibility for those decisions. I knew Paul to make mistakes. I never knew him not to assume responsibility and continue ahead.

I think this idea "rules are for fools" is tricky for people, because it is multi-faceted. It operates on several levels that appear contradictory. On the one hand, it reminds us of our responsibility to think critically and make our own decisions–not to be naive or lazy. We must discipline ourselves to think and not blindly follow collective opinion. On the other hand, though, if chess had no rules, the game would not make sense and, indeed, could not exist. Cultural rules are based and structured on human morality and ethics.

These apparently contradictory aspects exist together in tension. As human beings and leaders, we also live in tension. We have to understand that rules are situational and know when and how to apply them. We have to discriminate and choose and, of course, take responsibility for our choices.

Liz: How do you think "rules" apply to wilderness education?

Cody: I think we would be wrong to assume that Paul's leadership vision didn't extend beyond mere trips in the "wild outdoors." Students and instructors alike consciously take risks. Whether they are physical, due to the rigors of life and travel in the wilderness, or psychological, due to self-scrutiny and peer relationships, they are real. Managing these risks through skill and judgment develops common sense, character, and strength.

We need knowledge, technique, and practice to develop skill. The word "rule" seems to imply control, but novices need guidelines and techniques as a starting point. I had a teacher in the martial arts who would sometimes make us practice or execute one technique for hours as slowly as we could. It seemed absurd, but the next time you threw that punch, it was in your cells, almost instinctual.

In some sense, when we are learning a discipline we are "fools." When students first begin to climb, they make mistakes and take unnecessary risks. (We certainly did!) With practice and experience, the ability to accurately assess risk increases and judgment improves. It's the same with leadership. We start with the basic skills and guidelines. Through practice, discipline, and risk, we develop strength and perspective.

consisted of four essential elements. Although tweaked over the years, these have remained remarkably consistent, as shown by this 1971 list:

1. Competence with basic outdoor skills
2. Development of leadership skills
3. Expedition Behavior (EB)
4. Environmental stewardship through practical conservation

Cody Paulson climbing in Fremont Canyon. *Andy Davis*

Permeating the curriculum is the concept of judgment, and through it, safety (much later dubbed risk management). The goal of well-honed judgment in the field was what was underlying that famous Petzoldt quip, "rules are for fools."

The system envisioned and developed by Petzoldt was consistent and simple: "For Petzoldt, the only way to teach outdoor leadership was through direct experience: applying knowledge, being observed, receiving feedback on performance, and then generalizing this learning to future situations," wrote Maria Timmons in the 1989 Staff Conference Proceedings. "He believed that all teaching should go beyond the 'what' to the 'why.' If students understood why a decision was made, they could ask questions and begin to develop judgment."

Each new skill learned and practiced was a step for students toward the experience of "survival," a four- to five-day small group hike out of the mountains without rations or instructors. Course descriptions of survival mentioned "living off the land . . . off fish, vegetation, and possibly small animals" during this final expedition. It was anticipated by some with dread, and by others as a rite of passage.

Despite the description, "the objective was not that you'd really learn to live off the land in order to survive," said Dave Kallgren, an instructor for more than 40 years whose survival experience on his 1970 student course lasted seven days. Rather, "it was a way to add stress, a leadership challenge more than anything. It was a good one." Petzoldt's goal with NOLS was to create leaders, and survival was perhaps the most visible example that he believed in what he was doing; he taught students to lead in the wilderness, and then turned them loose in very challenging conditions to prove what they had learned.

To prepare for it, students gained direct experience with the various skills of leadership, including acting as "leader of the day." As the time for survival loomed, they worked on their navigation plans, scrutinized maps to work out how to arrive at a predetermined roadhead by a certain date, and also learned how to summon help in case of emergency. Any rations left over at the beginning of survival were burned.

Arriving at the trailhead after days on their own, students were visibly changed. For many students, surviving survival was a prominent memory of their experience, and a source of pride. Web Webster drove countless runs to retrieve student courses. "The thrill of being at the roadhead for a survival group pickup. That's something," he said. "Seventeen dirty, haggard, and drawn-out 'ex-students' emerge from the woods, with smiles that need no interpretation . . . to eat corn flakes as though it were a Thanksgiving feast." Many who witnessed the frequent student transformation commented on the dramatic differences in self-confidence that were evident

Tom Warren teaches axmanship, one of the skills that has disappeared from the NOLS curriculum. *NOLS Archives*

between their arrival in Lander and when they left.

Originally, it was common practice for instructors to turn their students loose on survival and leave the mountains, free for a few days to do as they wished before returning to the trailhead to meet the students. This practice yielded a host of stories of era-appropriate bacchanalia, starting with the not-infrequent practice by the transportation department of leaving a six-pack in the truck awaiting the instructors at the trailhead for the drive back to town. By 1992, instructors were no longer leaving the field ahead of their students.

Re-rations, like this via bush plane in Alaska, are frequently the first contact with the outside world for days or weeks.
Zeno Wicks

Expanding the
Instructor Corps

ACCORDING TO JIM HALFPENNY, Petzoldt led all courses through the summer of 1968. He was assisted by others—principally Andy Carson, Tom Warren, and Halfpenny—since course sizes swelled to as many as 120 people. The large courses were subdivided into patrols, with PLs and assistants for each group of 12 to 15 students. They would enter an area and disperse as much as possible, according to Randy Cerf, but with so many new PLs and assistants, Petzoldt often brought the entire group together for certain classes. In particular, he set the tone early on each course, to get everyone off to a good start.

Since the beginning, course by course, he had developed new instructors in an apprenticeship system that gradually gave a person increasing authority. "In the early, early days, you became an instructor because Paul and Rob liked you," said Haven Holsapple. "There was no instructor course. You went out, you worked, they observed. If they liked you, they would take you another step."

By 1969, Petzoldt had to rely on his senior instructors to take the role of CL and lead courses on their own without his direct oversight. "Finding myself as a course leader really had a logical and natural flow to it," recalled Carson. "After a good many courses and after having observed and partici-pated with Paul, Tap, and others . . . being 'in charge' seemed like a logical progression."

In the summer of 1970, Holsapple found himself both CL and "Super-Leader" (SL), a designation that lasted briefly while the school grappled with developing adequate staff numbers to lead the expeditions. "On my second course [that summer]," he said, "I was the CL for the Wilderness course and at the same time the SL for both my Wilderness course and the Mountaineering course that went out at the

Steve Gipe. *NOLS Archives*

same time. As the combined CL and SL, I did not have a patrol, but floated between the courses. Paul did show up at the start of those courses and gave some classes before we left the roadhead."

Instructors also scouted their students. Those with instructor potential received follow-up letters (often from Paul himself) inviting them to come back. Many did. For Gipe, who was 16 turning 17, it didn't matter that his letter said they couldn't pay him; he would get to go backpacking for free. "I was thrilled," he said. Even those who were paid received a pittance (four weeks in the field as an assistant instructor in the early 1970s yielded roughly $150, according to Tod Schimelpfenig), but it didn't matter. "You're 19, 20 years old and this is a job that's going to take me to Wyoming to be in the mountains for the summer," he remembered. "Even that by itself is so attractive. And pay me!"

In 1970, with enrollment tripling, there was no longer time to mentor new instructors via the master-apprentice system of old. The school needed instructors—fast. The need for more instructors was addressed by the school's first instructor course, in June 1970, on the Wind River Indian Reservation. "We canoed to the end of Bull Lake and started from there up Bull Lake Canyon. That's still the most difficult and wild canyon in the Winds," remembered Skip Shoutis, who was among those assisting Petzoldt on that course.

"Paul was desperate for instructors," recalled Tom Warren, who was also there as a staff assistant. "He was teaching the instructors. We had lots and lots of classes on what to teach and how to teach, and if you knew how to, say, cook, you'd teach the others. It was still very informal. Still nothing was written down. It was just what you needed to be able to do to go out into the woods." In addition to reviewing outdoors skills instruction, Petzoldt emphasized building a leader's sense for the safety of others, and ways to supervise that while teaching.

However, even this concentrated learning environment wasn't fast enough to meet the school's needs. Within a few days a summons came from Lander saying they needed instructors for upcoming courses. "So a few of us left the course and climbed out of the canyon and were picked up by cattle trucks at Kirkland Park," said Shoutis. (That day also highlights a familiar NOLS phenomenon: meeting your true love. According to Shoutis, one of the trucks was driven by Martha Hellyer's sister, Diane Newbury. Shoutis and she ended up working a course together that July, and were married in October.)

As far into the boom years as 1974, some who had taught at NOLS for years had never taken an instructor course (IC). An announcement was circulated that proper instructor certification would be required. Although he had previously *taught* the IC, Steve Gipe thus found himself as an IC student that year. "I was not happy about some of the 'instructors,' the tone, the way it felt," he said. "So we left after a couple of days." When he and his wife, Pookie Godvin, returned to Lander a few weeks later, Hellyer sent him out as course leader on two courses. "I was never asked to take an instructor course again. I guess I was kind of grandfathered in," he said.

High demand for instructors led to some meteoric rises in the organization. For example, Jon Hamren went from being a student in the summer of 1970, to being an assistant and then PL later that same summer. In 1971, after working as PL on two early courses, he was promoted to CL at age 21.

Not everyone was as "old" as Hamren. Scott Fischer, who instructed for NOLS and went on to considerable fame in mountaineering circles before dying on Mount Everest in 1996, was among the youngest to take the instructor course, at age 16, in 1972. Randy Cerf, who came to NOLS in 1967 when the school launched its first adventure course for 13- to 15-year-old boys, was a patrol leader by age 15 and, after missing a couple of summers, a course leader at 19.

Just as the PBWA scholarship program helped students attend NOLS, similar incentives helped prospective instructors, according to Willy Cunningham, who came to NOLS in 1970. "Back then [some of us] didn't have to pay up front...Once you had graduated from the instructor's course and worked three courses, then you either didn't have to pay off the loan or you got your money back. It was an incentive to work for the school and not just grab the education and go work for Outward Bound." Cunningham, who often described the weather as the "fourth instructor"—meaning the direct lessons that come with sun, wind, rain, snow, and cold—was the first NOLS instructor to complete 200 weeks of field instructing, in 1986. When he began to teach in 1971, there was enough work available that, he said, "someone made the comment that if you got off the instructor course and were still ambulatory, you had a job."

That didn't mean there weren't a few learning curves to be negotiated. For example, one 1971 student who had seen *Thirty Days to Survival* wrote, "I came looking for a challenge, a wilderness adventure, to be pushed. That was the message of 'Thirty Days,'" he said. "As an educational experience, there were a few flaws. As an adventure, it was incredible." He didn't mind the post-holing through June snowfields, he said, but the instruction seemed not to have "a lot of intentionality about it." Then one day he fell into a snow moat beside a large boulder and there was no one to help. When he was finally able to crawl out 30 minutes later, no one was there, so he followed the footprints across the snow to camp, where he discovered that he hadn't even been missed. That student was Tod Schimelpfenig, who, notwithstanding his experience, would go on to a long career with the school.

Lack of intentionality in some areas of the school contrasted with too much of it in others. When the school's second instructor course was held in 1971, some participants were surprised to learn that an effort was under way to standardize the program—for example, teaching just one knot for joining two ropes, contrary to the past practice of working through the pros and cons of knowing multiple knots. Instructors rebelled at the notion, because freedom to manage didactics independently was already becoming an embedded value at NOLS. Aside from their own notes, very little was written down for many years. Instructors knew the basic gist of what needed to happen on a NOLS course, and held one another to a very high degree of competence. As Jim Acee, an instructor in the 1970s, said, "Being part of the NOLS community of instructors was an awesome experience. The knowledge and competence of the instructors was dazzling, and the competitiveness to be the best of the best was intense and pervasive."

In this instance, instructors retained their freedom to decide what and how to teach. But the budding culture of instructor autonomy would yield recurring bouts of tension between instructors and NOLS administration many times in coming years. Visceral resistance to any perception that administration was dictating field practices would often both serve and startle the school.

Notable academic developments that came along during the early 1970s were additional opportunities for students to earn college credit, winter courses, and the development of semester programs. In the 1960s and early '70s, students could earn physical education and biology credits on select courses, but in 1973 Fort Lewis College in

Durango began granting credits in outdoor education for NOLS students. The fresh concept of outdoor education was rapidly advancing, with NOLS playing a prominent role in defining a new discipline that had lacked academic rigor until then.

After the 1970 summer season, Petzoldt asked Geoff Heath, who had mentioned doing some winter camping in Utah, to organize a winter program. They began as two-week courses in the Wind Rivers. Largely on his own, Heath said, he painted skis, canned food, horsepacked in to cache it in the high country, and developed snow clothing with Thelma Young. Others, including Steve Gipe, Randy Cerf, and Willy Cunningham, soon joined the winter instructor ranks, but Heath was the sole instructor for the first few courses. Once, after musing about whether he was okay, Thelma told him later, Hellyer's reply was, "No news is good news." Heath was just 20 years old.

The year 1974 was the advent of NOLS semester programs. Credit for the idea goes to Jim Halfpenny, who saw the need to create work for instructors in the "shoulder" seasons of spring and fall. The first semester course started that fall, and included caving, horsepacking, canoeing, climbing, hiking, camping in Yellowstone Park, and downhill and cross-country skiing. Semester programs were an instant hit, and the school ran two sections with 17 students each that year. Alaska ran its first semester in 1975, and the school

Geoff Heath, who was instrumental in founding the NOLS winter program. *NOLS Archives*

has offered semester programs throughout its various locations ever since.

With so much to manage and do because of the school's rapid growth, Petzoldt—revered and respected as he was—wasn't always easygoing. He was described as mercurial and choleric at times. His standards for himself and others were very high, and sometimes his expectations were too much. Managing the details of running multiple business affairs, especially when funds were tight (as they always were), was a constant pressure. He was famous for firing people, sometimes repeatedly. Eventually it became a certain badge of honor among NOLS veterans to boast how many times Petzoldt had fired them.

"I was fired by Paul twice," recalled Don Webber. "The first time, I was working in the issue room, with Allen Robinson and Jack Niggemyer and Rob Weller. We were working in the fishing equipment area putting line on reels. Paul was taking some people around. Thelma was with him. He looked at the line and said we couldn't fish with that line and told us to get out. Thelma was standing behind him and told him he was the one who bought the line at surplus in Cheyenne. He laughed and walked out."

Don Webber in the Lumberyard with a heap of Optimus 111B stoves to be checked. *NOLS Archives*

If Paul didn't hire the fired person back, Rob or Thelma would. On this occasion, Thelma told the boys to sit down and get back to work. But not even Thelma was immune. "Paul fired me several times because I wouldn't go on a course," she once said, referring to a time he mandated that all employees must do so. "I'd start to walk out of the building and he would change his mind. Sometimes he'd even give me a new job title because he couldn't afford to give me a raise."

Another of Petzoldt's foibles, said Jon Hamren, was "his horrible memory for names. When he finally knew your name, it was a big deal." According to Don Webber, Petzoldt might wander into the Lumberyard with some people touring the school while they were getting courses ready. "He'd walk up to me," recalled Webber, "and he knew who I was but didn't know my name, so he'd say, 'This is one of our finest instructors. Go ahead and introduce yourself.' And then he'd say, 'Great work, Don,' and wander off." It was a ploy he reportedly used often.

Whether or not he knew your name, though, Petzoldt was fierce about doing what he could to support his people. He arranged housing where instructors could stay between courses. There were gatherings at his home. If someone had a good idea, he'd say, "Go for it!" such as when John Cooper proposed the *NOLS Alumnus* (now *The Leader*). When draft notices arrived in the mail, Petzoldt returned them, since printed on the envelopes was "Return to Sender If Undeliverable Within 5 Days." His men were in the backcountry. Those letters were undeliverable as far as he was concerned.

Between courses, instructors had fun. In late spring 1970 or 1971, a group drove one early morning to a roadhead near Cold Springs. The goal: cache 10 Grumman aluminum canoes near Slim Jim Lake in the Bull Creek drainage so courses could use them.

The original idea—to make litters and carry them up— failed. The 18-foot canoes were too long and the litters too flimsy. They tried overhead carries and hauling them by the ends. "It was impossible," remembered Bill Scott, because they were post-holing most of the way. Finally, the group dragged them with harnesses across the snow up to the pass.

When they got there, the group gazed 2,000 feet down to the lake and knew they weren't going to carry those canoes down to the flats. Instead, they put the snowpack to good use and rode in the canoes down the hill. "You can't turn and you can't slow down," Scott remembered. "Essentially we had to bail out." Everyone arrived at the bottom without harm, and they hung the canoes in trees high enough that the lower end was some 20 feet off the ground. "You couldn't see them unless you looked right at them," said Scott. "Course leaders who knew where they were could go in and use them. I know they were there for years."

Equipment and Outfitting

Nancy Carson remembers being with Petzoldt in 1968 when he definitively decided against goose down as insulation. "I was camping with Paul and cooking for him. We were in a rainstorm, camped between two lakes, and we'd moved some rocks out of the way to put up our tent flies. When it got really wet, the water came up through the holes where the rocks had been. Paul's down bag got soaked, and I distinctly remember him holding it up to the light where you could see the down was all clumped and the light came through the nylon. It was after that when he decided to go strictly with the synthetic fill."

In the school's early years, military surplus supplied most of NOLS's outfitting needs, but as time went on Petzoldt began to want items that simply weren't available from surplus yards. He turned again to Thelma Young. Her ability to translate an idea into reality, paired with the lightweight, durable, and relatively inexpensive synthetic materials that were coming on the scene at the time, was a winning combination.

In 1969, Petzoldt, together with Rob and Martha Hellyer, had created a for-profit venture called Outdoor Leadership Supply (OLS). Later renamed Paul Petzoldt Wilderness Equipment (PPWE), the goal of OLS was to develop and manufacture outdoor clothing and equipment both for use by NOLS as well as for retail sales. For the two men, it was a way to make some money, since their work on behalf of the school was inconsistently compensated.

They purchased the old Safeway building at Lincoln and 2nd in December 1970 for $20,000, and Thelma and her crew moved in. The huge space was filled with large cutting tables, sewing machines, and raw materials. She was already reworking older prototype sleeping bags and parkas using Fiberfill II, a double-crimped synthetic insulation developed by DuPont that yielded more loft and was both warmer and lighter than the earlier version called Dacron 88.

Over time, Thelma's talents were credited for revolutionizing the outdoor gear industry. She developed different sorts of tents, rain flies, mummy-type sleeping bags, Dacron parkas and mittens and booties, gaiters, and expedition pack bags. The "Baja tent" was the first to have mosquito mesh interiors, a feature now common to every three-season tent.

Many NOLS instructors, including Carson, Paula Hunker, Nancy Pallister, and Anne Cannon, circulated in the off-seasons through the sewing rooms for NOLS and PPWE under her tutelage. One of Thelma's students was Concha Dias, who came from Baja, Mexico, with Cannon when she returned from instructing there in 1972. About 12 at the time, Concha was sent to Lander by her father to improve her English. Concha returned to Baja that fall and became the Mexico branch's seamstress.

Within a year, the fledgling OLS employed 12 people doing marketing, design and layout, production, purchasing, and retail sales of outdoor specialty clothes. The innovations that ribboned out from under the sewing machine needles of Thelma and her crew were a long way from butt patches and woolen double-sweaters, although those items were still used on NOLS courses for years.

Equipment was field-tested by NOLS instructors on courses, and follow-up suggestions were listened to and

Thelma flies have always proved useful—and durable—well beyond Thelma's original vision, such as on this early Prince William Sound sea kayaking course. *NOLS Archives*

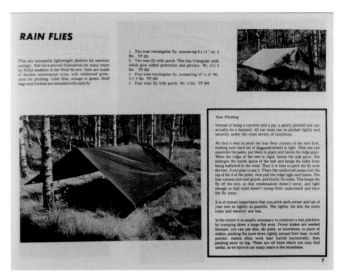

Thelma flies and words of wisdom in the first Paul Petzoldt Wilderness Equipment catalog. *NOLS Archives*

incorporated, such as when Cannon suggested that gear bag handles be sewn to loop underneath, for better strength and support. When the first expedition to Mount McKinley (now called Denali) was mounted in 1971, the team had an array of gear including flight satin windsuits and special packs sewn in Lander, as well as redesigned Baja tents with an added vestibule in front for a place to cook and put equipment. In 1973, the McKinley climbers were road testing fiberglass wand tents under development at PPWE when the tents

were buried in a small avalanche. Seven of the traditional poles broke, but the wands remained intact.

Students in 1970 were sent an eight-page Personal Clothing and Equipment List. The cover page includes the following advice: "The technique for dressing for comfort and safety is one of the important teachings of NOLS. A large percentage of outdoor tragedies can be traced directly or indirectly to ignorance in this technique." There follows a list of 51 items covering clothing, camping, personal gear such as toiletries, rock climbing (including six rock pitons and one ice screw), cooking, and fishing. Item 40 reads: "Shorts, Cotton: 2 pairs Boxer Type Necessary: Jockey type prohibited. NOLS can supply. Bring your own if you wish. Have plenty of room in the crotch (Girls, nylon underwear that will wash easily and dry quickly may be worn under cotton boxer shorts. NOLS does not provide nylon underwear.)" Item 44C, under optional field equipment, reads, "radio, small, light, transistor encouraged."

Food, Cooking, and Re-rationing

The task of cooking was new to many NOLS students, and cooking in the backcountry raised the challenge of that new skill to another level. It mattered to Petzoldt to keep things inexpensive, so whatever could serve the purpose and not cost too much was preferred. There were no fancy cooksets. Through the early 1980s, students cooked in #10 "billy cans" (the largest standardized food can, approximately the size of a three-pound coffee can), with heavy-gauge wire twisted through holes punched near the rims for handles. Also, recounted Bill Scott, in the early days students would each "get an empty beer can from the pile, cut off the top, poke a hole in the side for a string, and that was your cup." By 1973,

metal enamel cups were also being used. Eventually, the use of cookfires was curtailed for conservation reasons and sturdy Optimus 111B stoves became the norm.

Food was carried in zippered rations bags with ingredients weighing two pounds per person per day. Inside was an array of clear plastic bags filled with easily confused ingredients. The author, for instance, boiled the wheat bran thinking it was hot cereal; breakfast that day tasted like cooked sawdust. Similarly, someone else discovered that powdered garlic doesn't work too well as cream of wheat. The spice kit, or "food repair kit" as it was known, has always been the saving

Pizza-making using the Optimus 111B cookstove and a twiggy fire. *NOLS Archives*

grace for novice chefs at NOLS. (For Claudia Pearson, manager of the Gourmet Gulch since 1978, "the most challenging part of my career is the NOLS spice kit. No matter how hard I try, it's never big enough, there's not enough variety.")

"What was revolutionary about NOLS's idea for backcountry cooking was that you did not have to take special foods on the trips," said Pearson. "NOLS wanted to teach people to save money by taking basic foods and then experimenting once they were in the mountains. That's what Paul felt: take a bag of macaroni and learn how to cook it 10 different ways using a spice kit."

Summertime rations provided about 3,700 calories per day; in winter, up to 6,000 calories helped against the cold. Only a few items (such as vegetables) were freeze-dried. Nuts, cheese (often in four-pound blocks), pastas, rice, cereals, and flour, along with honey, butter or margarine, and various flavor bases were prominent ingredients. In winter, high-fat ingredients and meat were added, including bacon, salami, and M&Ms. Then there were the salt crystals; for years, everyone at NOLS ingested a large chunk of crystallized salt each day in the mistaken notion that it was nutritionally important.

"The most useful ingredient for a backcountry meal," Randy Cerf once said, "is appetite." That, along with coaching on methods for cooking good meals with the right caloric

Claudia Pearson, manager of the Gourmet Gulch since 1978. *Brad Christensen*

blend of ingredients, led to many famous NOLS recipes, such as the Whiznut, cinnamon rolls, and gado-gado.

Supplies were sometimes cached in the backcountry in the early years, in autumn, to make re-rationing easier the next summer. Food, toilet paper, matches—anything that would fit—were stuffed into #10 cans and sealed by Gulch workers. In one report to the board, Petzoldt said there were some 6,000 pounds of rations cached in readiness for the following summer.

So many recipes began to emerge, especially as instructors honed their skills, that someone suggested a cookbook

The first edition of the *NOLS Cookery*, 1974. In 2015, the cookery was in its sixth edition. *NOLS Archives*

Cinnamon rolls in a Banks Fry-Bake pan.
Tracy Baynes/STEP

FRY-BAKE LIFE

The prototype of the Banks Fry-Bake pan sits in a place where Pam Banks can look up and ponder it now and then. It's 38 years old now, crusty and blackened from use, she says, but looking at it rekindles her own memories of NOLS. A spring semester student in 1976, Banks left for the IC the day that course ended, and then went out right away as an instructor on two more courses before heading for Massachusetts and home. She almost immediately went back, arriving in time for the winter IC. She was an active instructor until 1981.

In 1977, she was camping with her family in the Utah canyonlands, schlepping a 14-inch cast-iron skillet because she refused to cook on Teflon. Her dad, whose business was making things out of metal, said, "Let's make something." By that time they were at the airport for his flight home, so they used the proverbial cocktail napkin to draw the idea.

She knew the first pan—the one in her house—was wrong right away. "It was only one inch deep, and we needed it to be two inches deep," she realized. The next run was 10 lightweight, two-inch-deep pans that were field-tested at NOLS. One arrived out of the blue where Pam was camping with a NOLS caving section. She didn't know it was coming, and couldn't believe her eyes when another instructor pulled out a pan and said, "Look at this!"

The Fry-Bake/NOLS connection runs deep, although the pans are favored by wilderness guides, school and college outdoor programs, as well as individuals everywhere for their durability and function. Most editions of the *NOLS Cookery* have featured a Banks Fry-Bake on the cover, and generations have wrought gastronomical miracles with the mysterious plastic bags of ingredients in their rations bags with it; as her website says, "The pans are excellent for frying, steaming, sautéing and baking any number of delicious recipes. Extremely durable and designed to be used with metal utensils, the pans are made in the U.S.A. of aluminum construction with an anodized hardcoat cooking surface which makes for easy clean-up after use." They're durable enough to pose as Dutch ovens with twiggy fires on the specially designed lids, and can be scrubbed clean with river sand.

In 2015 student Nathan Russell fell in love with the Banks Fry-Bake pan on his mountaineering course in the North Cascades. "I was really thankful that you always had a plan B when it came to trying something," he recalled. "For instance, if you were going to be bold and try to do some baking with the Fry-Bake over the power tower and it somehow went sideways, you always knew that you could just add oil or butter and turn a baked good into some kind of fried goodness. And there were several cake attempts that turned into cookie-like biscuits that we flipped like pancakes." When his NOLS course ended, Russell returned to his outdoor school in Montana and immediately implemented some changes. "I overhauled my entire backcountry meal approach," he said. "I'd put Fry-Bakes up there with the old adage, 'If it can't be fixed with WD-40 or duct tape, it can't be fixed,' and say [instead], 'If it can't be fixed with duct tape or a Fry-Bake, it can't be fixed.'"

NOLS RIVER BASE

On June 8, 1869, John Wesley Powell and his expedition floated down the Green River through the Gates of Lodore—a narrow, towering cleft worn in the deep red rock of what is now western Colorado. They were not the first to enter the canyon—Native Americans had lived in the area for thousands of years, and the early 1800s saw numerous explorations by trappers. But for Powell, it felt completely unknown.

Lodore Canyon has retained that magic through the present day; its 44 miles are a place removed from the world. "It feels special, like you're discovering a new place

A student getting after it on the Green River.
TC Rammelkamp III

every night," says Laura Hudecek, an instructor and former program supervisor ("P-Sup" in NOLS vernacular) at the NOLS River Base. The deep red cliffs hide ancient pictographs, and mysterious side canyons rise from the banks, devoid of footprints. "It's pristine, and that's remarkable, considering that we sleep in impacted sites most every night. Students can really see the impact of people practicing LNT firsthand" (referring to Leave No Trace, a conservation concept largely developed by NOLS).

Lodore Canyon lies within Dinosaur National Monument. A few miles from where the Green River spills from the monument's western edge lies the NOLS River Base, and the town from which it takes the name most NOLSies know it by: Vernal.

Vernal is inextricably linked with that river and is the hub for kayaking at the school. It lies between the take-out at the bottom of Lodore and the put-in for Desolation and Gray Canyons (better known as Deso). Together, those 128 miles of river form one of the best progressions for teaching novice whitewater boaters in the western United States. Deso starts out flat and smooth, then builds along its 84-mile length to a technical series of class III rapids. Courses get picked up at the bottom, spend the night in Vernal, and then drive north to the Gates of Lodore, where the whitewater picks up where it left off. Courses either canoe or take rafts and kayaks. "We're able to get students paddling class III in kayaks inside two weeks," said Nate Ostis, an instructor. "It speaks to the quality of the classroom. In rafts is one thing, but big whitewater alone in a kayak? That is a big experience for a student. We hand over a lot more independence in kayaks than in other courses. It's a dynamic environment, and while they are in the middle of a rapid they have to make consequential decisions for themselves."

Hudecek notes that the rest of the time on the river, courses travel in big groups, which provides excellent leadership challenges of a different nature. "We move as a large group. Cook as a large group. It feels almost too big–sometimes managing that many people as leader of the day feels like chaos. But it's so representative of many of the leadership situations they'll encounter in the rest of their lives."

The NOLS river program in Utah started in the late 1980s under then-Wyoming branch director Dave Neary. "At first, we didn't have our own permit, so we were subcontracting through commercial outfitters to run semester courses on the river," said Pip Coe, who ran Vernal with her then-partner Mark Donahue from 1993 through 1997. An instructor or two would go along on the trip, remembered Neary. However, the contractors didn't necessarily share the same values as NOLS instructors. In about 1990, instructor Eric Sawyer helped the school obtain its first permit, for Deso, from a commercial outfitter. About the same time, a different outfitter sold the school a permit for Dinosaur. With the ability to run its own trips, the school rented a warehouse in Vernal to store gear. Nancy Siegel oversaw the program for the first two years until Coe and Donahue took over.

In 1996 the school acquired a 40-acre property on the east side of town that houses the base to this day. After Coe left Vernal in 1997, Dave Stinson and Jhala French took over, followed by Phil Henderson in 2002. Pam Rosal took over in

A paddle raft lines up at the top of Rattlesnake Rapid in Desolation Canyon, downstream of Lodore Canyon.
TC Rammelkamp III

2013, and still ran the base as of 2015.

NOLS also has permits on the San Juan River in southern Utah, and the Yampa. "The Yampa is not only one of the largest undammed rivers in the US, but . . . the only undammed river in the entire Colorado River watershed," said Frank Preston, a senior instructor.

"To travel down these rivers is to experience the arteries and the veins of our planet," said Ostis. "Keeping those veins and arteries free from blockages has not always been easy; the Colorado River and its tributaries have been ground zero for many of the most heated conservation battles of the twentieth century, and students can easily see in the landscape examples of both wins and losses."

be compiled. Nancy Wise Carson wrote and gathered most of the recipes, but the project stalled during the busy years after *Thirty Days* aired. The unfinished work was eventually handed to Nancy Pallister. In March 1974, the first edition of *NOLS Cookery: Planning and Preparation of Food for Backpacking Expeditions* was published, crediting Pallister as editor and Beverly Holsapple as illustrator. The *Cookery* was the very first NOLS publication, predating Paul Petzoldt's *The Wilderness Handbook* by two months.

Loading a NOLS bus before a dispute with the county made the school paint them green. *NOLS Archives*

Transportation

Steve Matson could tell the state of the school's vehicle fleet when he began his 1977 student course: The bus taking them to Three Peaks Ranch broke down three times on the way. "The guy driving, after breakdown number 3, walked around, and he gave the bus the finger. That's one approach," he said. Matson took over the transportation department in 1985 when Dudley Cole resigned, and was still NOLS Rocky Mountain transportation manager 30 years later.

Early NOLS vehicles were purchased, usually from surplus yards, used and cheap. The NOLS "fleet" in 1970 included a couple of flatbed stock trucks, one named "Grunt" and the other "Groan." They had high stake frames used to transport horses, piles of packs, equipment—and students. The one-and-a-half-ton enclosed van that was mostly used for haul-ing gear required double-clutching. "Moby Dick" was a giant white ex-Air Force bus with a midmount diesel engine.

And then there were "the Geese": several four-door, Air Force blue, 1964 Dodge Power Wagon pickup trucks. According to Matson, they were named when a string of them was being driven to Lander in the mid-1970s. Those that broke down on the way were cannibalized for parts. "I'm not sure how many made it to Lander," he recalled, but people "watched that fleet of vehicles come into Lander and said it looked and sounded like a gaggle of geese."

At NOLS, and in America in general, there were far

fewer rules and regulations in the early 1970s. Students were transported clinging for dear life in the back of stock trucks up questionable four-wheel-drive roads. Breakdowns were common and tires were threadbare. Once, when Bill Scott was driving to Riverton, a front wheel came off one of the Geese and went rolling off into the sagebrush while the axle ground into the pavement with a horrifying screech. (No one was hurt.)

Another time, when Bill Scott and Rob Hellyer were trailering 20 canoes back from Utah with one of the Geese, the hood blew off and got plastered against the windshield. Fortunately, they were on a straight stretch and pulled over safely. They got out, tied the hood down, and went on their way.

"We could never get away with the stuff [now] we did back then," said Scott. There was so much transportation to be done that drivers often worked well beyond today's eight- to ten-hour limits. One relentless task, and no one's favorite, were airport runs, best described in "Welcome to Wyoming," by Jeff Woods, which appeared in the *NOLS Alumnus* in 1977:

"It's 6:30 a.m. at the Riverton airport . . . A good-sized early morning shot of Copenhagen is under my lip and I haven't had breakfast yet. I am neither coherent nor cheerful. I am the first NOLS employee students arriving by air run into—hardly the leader and musclebound mountaineer they were expecting. Instead, I stand there, a dirty, greasy, foul-smelling grub with the apparent intelligence of an anvil. I am doing an 'Airport Run.' . . . I try to break the ice a little. 'Hi' or 'howdy' is my best early morning line—not too many syllables and hard to screw it up . . ."

The (Brief) Shifting Legal Structure of the School

At the cusp of the boom years, NOLS—a registered nonprofit in the State of Wyoming—had a brief shift of legal structure. On January 2, 1970, paperwork was completed with the State of Wyoming that changed the National Outdoor Leadership School into a for-profit corporation privately held by Paul Petzoldt and Rob and Martha Hellyer.

The reasoning behind the change hinged primarily around two things. Even before *Thirty Days to Survival* was aired, the growing school needed real estate, vehicles, equipment, and other facilities estimated between $175,000 and $300,000. In addition, an unforeseen downside to the Pay Back When Able scholarship program was its impact on cash flow. Although PBWA had generated robust enrollment figures by creating opportunities for many to attend NOLS, thousands of PBWA dollars were still owed to the school. As a result, critically low levels of cash flow were jeopardizing the school's ability to pay bills.

During the early years, Petzoldt had enjoyed sturdy

support from his board members, who were mostly local men who believed in the school and wanted to help it succeed. They had frequently given money or pledged their personal credit. But the skyrocketing financial demands of late 1969 were too overwhelming to continue, and tuition revenue wouldn't be enough to manage the situation.

Petzoldt and the Hellyers pondered the dilemma and offered to the board, in October 1969, to take on the financial risks personally. With their permission, the men obtained the necessary financing and effectively bought the school, plus its existing equipment and supplies. By January 1970 the new NOLS was a private school—essentially, a for-profit corporation. In February 1970, the new corporation purchased additional assets, including the Lumberyard.

The nonprofit entity formerly known as NOLS was renamed and registered with the state as the Outdoor Leadership Foundation (OLF). It retained responsibility for scholarship fundraising, and held the receivables (largely the PBWA scholarships) and other liquid assets. Soon, however, the directors of OLF, many of whom were new, began to worry that public criticism could compromise the "public service to the causes of outdoorsmanship, mountaineering, conservation, leadership, and promotion of the highest use of mountain and wilderness areas," wrote Jack Nicholas in a letter to the local Forest Service ranger at the time, Doc Smith,

who was wondering about the changes. There were concerns about the perception that private individuals were profiting from a school that was using public lands as its classroom.

They were worried that the school risked losing its public lands access. Additional wrinkles to the for-profit NOLS/nonprofit OLF situation also came to the new board's attention. The material and equipment obtained over the years from the National Civil Defense (surplus) program could no longer be used for private or personal use. The school's accreditation and ability to grant college and high school credit were jeopardized. It was unseemly for items donated to the nonprofit (such as a $1,500 Land Rover) potentially to be used for private gain.

What had seemed a suitable arrangement in the fall proved unsatisfactory by the end of May 1970. The OLF board adopted a motion to exercise an option it had retained, allowing it to reassume control of the school's academic curriculum, provide teaching personnel, and administer the education program. However, the for-profit NOLS owned the mountaineering equipment and other fixed assets needed by the school's educational program to conduct courses. OLF would necessarily have to rely on Petzoldt and the Hellyers to provide equipment and logistics, which they agreed to do.

In June 1970, on top of preparing for the huge summer season ahead, Petzoldt and the board of OLF attended to the reconfiguration of the legal structure of the school. By September 1970, the paperwork to return NOLS to its nonprofit status was complete and recorded with the Secretary of State. By November, the paperwork renaming the for-profit NOLS to Outdoor Leadership Supply (OLS) was done; it was later renamed Paul Petzoldt Wilderness Equipment (PPWE).

Real Estate

In June 1972, after years of what Hellyer referred to as "homelessness" for the NOLS string of packhorses used for re-rationing, he and Martha came across an old ranch for sale a few miles outside Boulder, Wyoming, across the Winds from Lander. Homesteaded in 1886, the spread was only about 10 gravel road miles from the Scab Creek roadhead, where a couple of years earlier the school had obtained a permit from the BLM for a pole corral with a water source that they used for access into the Winds by their re-ration pack trains.

"Martha and I went over and looked at it, and within the hour signed the deal," he said. Hellyer wrote a check on the spot for $48,000, securing 120 acres that included irrigated pasture, several buildings, corrals, and the future of horsepacking at NOLS. They then drove straight back to Lander to discuss the transaction with Petzoldt and make sure there was enough money in the bank to cover the check.

They decided to call it Three Peaks Ranch after three major Wind River peaks: Raid, Ambush, and Geike, according to one account, although it was referred to variously as the Pinedale or Boulder ranch as well. "When we moved to the ranch, we had a great setup for access to all the roadheads for pack supplies and student take-off and returns on the west side. It was private property and we no longer had to search for temporary pasture, parking, overnight camping, or a place for staff to stay," said Hellyer. "Most importantly we didn't have to compete with the general public for camping and corral space at the end of the road. We immediately became a lot less visible to the Forest Service, BLM, general public, and other outfitters. Logistically, it was (and is) for NOLS like Gibraltar for the British Navy!"

Three Peaks Ranch became NOLS's center both for re-rationing and horsepacking education. Once WMI (Wilderness Medicine Institute) arrived at NOLS in 1999, the ranch began hosting four or five wilderness first-aid courses each year as well. The 30 horses in the NOLS herd (amplified by another 30 or more seasonally) have always been selected for their good-quality feet, conformation, and dependable personalities, and considered valuable "instructors" in their own right.

Of all the NOLS locations, the ranch was one that allowed cotton: Jeans were variously described by longtime instructor Bill Danford in his unpublished essay, "Memoirs

NOLS Three Peaks Ranch in a thunderstorm. *Brad Christensen*

of a Young Saddle Tramp" as sometimes dusty, sometimes slightly green from Bickmore saddle sore salve, or shining "from the filth and neats' foot oil, polished by the rubbing friction of saddle and chaps."

Renovations at Three Peaks started in 1978, and over time resulted in a complex that included a barn that was ret-

rofitted into a multi-room building with a tack room, a veterinary room, a bay where students assembled their gear, and an issue room. There was a classroom, a manager's house/office, a cookhouse, a shop, a bunkhouse, three staff housing cabins and one storage cabin, plus corrals, loafing sheds, a shoeing shed, and a hay barn. Most venerable, though, was the Steele house, named for the original homesteader and one of the longest continually occupied dwellings in Sublette County. The house retained its original historical form through a renovation and upgrade of the foundation funded in memory of John Avant, a NOLS student, by his family in the late 1990s.

On May 23, 1973, Petzoldt and the Hellyers, as the owners of PPWE, purchased the Noble Hotel from Don Peterson, a local rancher, for $120,000. Knowing that the bar was the social center of the hotel, they made the sale contingent on successful transfer of the liquor license, which was done in a special session of the Lander City Council on June 19. They planned to use the basement for mail-order operations and lease hotel space to NOLS to house students. An ad in the paper brought Lander's first Chinese restaurant to the hotel, and course banquets were held there throughout the summer. Later, Petzoldt, ever a dealmaker, attempted to change the original agreement with the proprietor. Watching Petzoldt negotiate with the restauranteur was Mike Williams, who had been with the school since 1966. The experience, he said, "gave me an insight into Paul as something besides a course leader." When the man refused to knuckle under to Petzoldt's hard bargaining, the restaurant closed. But the hotel bar, often with Paul's brother Curly as bartender, remained a popular watering hole for years.

Administration

The administrative effort to keep a semblance of record-keeping order was enormous. In 1971, the offices moved from Jack Nicholas's basement and other temporary offices into the Nicholas Building at 258 Main Street, right next door to the Noble Hotel. That winter, office personnel consisted of Paul Petzoldt, Jean Johnson, Skip Shoutis, and five secretaries. The strict and dour Mrs. Johnson continued to ride herd, once chastising Shoutis for clogging the files with too many staples.

Long-distance calls were pricey and reserved for emergencies, "facsimiles" (faxes) were still the province of Western Union, and no spare typewriters were in sight, so office duty included sending handwritten replies for all correspondence. "Paul's theory was that a personal hand-written letter with a real stamp on it was more likely to be opened and read," remembered Haven Holsapple. "He was totally on target with this. I consider this as part of the success of the school."

The office also housed route-planning and mapping areas, and obtained wilderness permits. Skip Shoutis often worked with Hiram "Doc" Smith at the Lander office of the Forest Service to figure out how NOLS could achieve the permitting it needed. Because the NOLS program was unique at the time, it required a fundamental shift in understanding

NORTHERN ABSORPTION

By Katie Raymond, Yukon Backpacking and Whitewater Canoeing, 1999

Reprinted from The Leader, *Winter 2000*

We rounded the last bend in the river and I could finally see our campsite. The sun had broken through the clouds and a bald eagle flew overhead, not more than 30 feet away. I looked at Sarah. Relief was in her eyes. Today had been rough. After 13 hours of paddling and 75 kilometers, it had been more than a full day. With one final burst of energy, the six of us powered our canoes to shore and collapsed on the beach, triumphant.

It was July 1999. I was a member of the Yukon Backpacking and River course, which was comprised of 45 days in the remote Canadian wilderness. We were traveling down the Macmillan River, and after six weeks in this backcountry, we were honed, sharp and skilled. In the first half of the course, we backpacked for 25 days through the Itsi Range of the Selwyn Mountains. We didn't see another soul. We bushwhacked to get above tree line, and sometimes we followed caribou paths. Our feet sunk into the soft brown sphagnum moss and crunched over stiff white lichen. One day we trekked to "snow school." Our instructors held our feet as we laid back, head first and upside down, on the snow-covered slope of a mountain. They let go and we careened down, ready to flip over, jab the ice axe into the snow and self-arrest.

On the river we shot countless rapids. We came across numerous logjams, ferrying through some and portaging around others. We learned to avoid holes and tried to surf waves. We became experts at eddying out at just the right moment, and perfected the crossbow draw.

But you can't be prepared for everything. On the river and in the wilderness you just never know what lies around the next bend, and nature was constantly teaching us new lessons. This particular day proved to be one I will always remember.

A few days before we left, our instructors began to prepare us for our independent travel days. Lawrence and I were the elected leaders, and I was psyched that my fellow students felt confident in me. We divided up the gear and marked the final "X"—our rendezvous site—on our map. It was at the convergence of the Pelly and Macmillan Rivers, 150 kilometers away. We had three days to get there.

Our group decided to make the first day the hardest so we would have time for leisure later. The plan was to cover 75 kilometers, starting at 9 a.m. and paddling into the night. In the summer, the Yukon is known as the "Land of the Midnight Sun." Night after night we watched sunsets that lingered for hours. And then at last, around 2:00 a.m., the blaze sank beneath the mountain ridges. A few hours later, it rose to circle the sky once again.

As the day wore on, clouds covered the warmth of the sun. The wind picked up and began to sting. By early afternoon, it was raining and we were piling on more layers. But we had experienced weather like this before. We talked and played games. We sang songs and just kept on going. The conditions were only a minor inconvenience.

We were pumped with adrenaline and determination,

Canoeing in the Yukon.
Deborah Sussex

absorbed in the sights around us. We paddled through wild mountains and thick boreal forest. Summer was in full bloom. The land was a brilliant green, flecked with wildflowers in every color of the rainbow. There were purple lupines and blue asters, white lilies and pink fireweed. The trees were so thick we could never see more than a few feet into the timber. Occasionally we caught a glimpse of a dark shadow moving nearby. A swaying branch here and a snap of twigs there. Possibly it was a moose. Maybe even a grizzly.

By early afternoon we could no longer ignore the weather. The rain blocked our view of the shoreline. It was difficult to tell if we were making progress at all. Strong as we were after 40 days of hard-core tripping, we certainly weren't stronger than the wind. Still, we kept going for a few more hours, confident that the weather would let up.

Eventually there was a break in the rain and we stopped to make dinner. Two hours later, we were back in high spirits and determined to go on. But as we were loading the boats to get back on the river, a hailstorm began. We looked at each other and, in some odd combination of humor and frustration, burst out laughing. It seemed that after conquering every challenge, a new one arose. We tightened the cam straps, securing all of our gear. Tentatively, we headed into the choppy water. Soon the waves were actually coming over the bow of the canoe even though we were heading downstream. Talking to each other now took too much effort. Every paddle stroke

Hiking through the Yukon's vast wilderness. *Ashley Wise*

was full of power and precision. "Three forward strokes. Now a hard back pry. Keep the boat steady. Watch that hole and avoid the sweeper up ahead," I kept repeating to myself. I was thankful that Sarah and I had paddled together so many times before. Words were no longer necessary to communicate. We understood each other in the movement of the canoe.

Our three canoes began to drift far apart. Matt and Adam S. were leading the way. Their strength far surpassed mine and Sarah's. Right behind us were Adam B. and Heidi. Heidi had begun to feel ill, and though she insisted she was well enough to go on, it was impossible to sail along at the pace we had hoped for when we set out.

Adding to my worries was the noise created by the storm. If something did go wrong, if a canoe tipped from the force of the waves, it would be hard to shout over the wind. In addition, our progress was so slow that a quick rescue would be difficult at best.

We pulled over again and discussed the merits and hazards of continuing. On the one hand, we had to complete these 75 kilometers at some point. If we didn't finish it now we'd have to add these last few to our journey tomorrow. Besides, there was no way to know if conditions would be any better the next morning.

Everyone stated their opinions and then turned to me to make the final call. It was a personal milestone. I knew they were depending on me. I saw the trust in their eyes and realized we might end up experiencing one of our greatest celebrations yet. Our fate was in my hands. At that moment I truly believed it was possible to reach our goal. It was important to our overall success as a group. The decision was easy; we had to go on.

So we set off again, pulling our pogies back over our freezing hands, bodies hunched over to block the icy chill. Much to our relief, the wind and the river soon calmed down. We finally made it into camp, and we did indeed have a fantastic celebration. We had a quick round of hot chocolate and popcorn before happily sinking into our heavenly sleeping bags for the night, ready to face the surprises awaiting us tomorrow.

The next few days made it all worth the work. There was plenty of time for campfires and storytelling, fly fishing and reading. We slept in, lingering inside the tents late into the morning and savoring the warmth of our cozy nylon bubbles. On the third day, the sun finally broke through, lifting the heavy cloud cover and our spirits as well. We spread our sleeping bags across the rocky beach and basked in the warmth of the Arctic light.

new ways for people to enjoy the backcountry. Doc Smith was always concerned and very supportive about helping develop the NOLS program, remembered Hellyer. "You have to give that man credit. He was a cool head."

Smith's NOLS introduction was a two-week winter course to Wind River Peak (where he was tactfully granted pipe-smoking privileges, since he always had a pipe in hand). "He became an advocate. He didn't call us a bunch of hippies or anything. He saw the value of teaching kids," said Shoutis. "He was a pioneer as much as we were. If you look at the first permit he gave the school, it was on a grazing form, because there weren't permits in those days for recreation."

"The Forest Service wanted specificity," said Shoutis, "but once we convinced them that we wanted to go off-trail and that we weren't going to wreck the environment, they made NOLS areas." Dividing terrain into sectors allowed NOLS courses to move into one area for a few days and then to another based on parameters that made sense, such as moving from one drainage to another. Nancy Pallister devised a system done by hand on charts showing what courses were going where and when. The basic system was still in use in 2015.

As the years went by, the permitting challenges got greater. In the early 1970s, the school expanded into five national forests in about 15 ranger districts. As of 2015, just one fall semester might run on Wyoming and Utah BLM land, a national monument, a national park, three national forests, a state park, state land, and a US wildlife refuge. Shoutis, who went on to a career with the Forest Service, helped Smith with the complicated task of creating an inter-regional permit for NOLS. In 2015, NOLS was among the biggest holders of backcountry permits in the United States, and it still took a lot of work to manage all the different players. "NOLS has always been unique and difficult to put into a 'square box' by land-use agencies," said Gary Cukjati, Rocky Mountain director in 2015.

Drascombe Longboats in the Sea of Cortez.
Ben Lester

Making an Impact on Lander

IN THE BEGINNING NOLS and Petzoldt were warmly welcomed to Lander. Many townspeople were staunch supporters of the school and its goals, according to Jack Nicholas. The founder was even graced with "Outstanding Citizen of the Year" accolades at the state convention of Wyoming Elks in May 1970.

But to most Americans, the early 1970s were an uncertain and unnerving time. For Lander residents, the outside world (featuring the Vietnam War, the antiwar movement, hippies, and the Age of Aquarius) was not only swirling across their televisions, it was also arriving in Lander—to the growing consternation of some. "NOLSies" began to be regular fixtures around town, especially once the school began offering courses year-round. Dedicated and passionate about their work, they also tended, in the free spirit of the era, to have a lot of fun.

"It was the Wild, Wild West," said Jon Hamren, echoing the sentiments of many. Living quarters tended to be communal and co-ed. People came and went with little concern for propriety. Hair was long, beards abundant. A sense of being overrun by the "longhairs" felt threatening to some in the old Lander order. As Mayor Del McOmie said in 2015, back then, "NOLS wasn't all that great as far as Lander was concerned."

"There was always a dichotomy about us in town," said Peter Simer, an instructor since 1971 and executive director of the school from 1975 to 1983. "There were forward-thinking people and those for whom any change was too different. Lots of people were on different ends of different spectrums. It wasn't that people hated us. It was more that there were people in town who hated what we represented."

Sometimes, the simmering boiled over. Neil Short recalled a time he and Haven Holsapple were in the Fremont

Hotel bar enjoying a beer before a course banquet. "These two cowboy types (I recall they were huge!) peeled off their barstools and came over and blocked access to the booth." said Short. "One pulled out a huge knife. He said, 'Gimme one reason I shouldn't cut your hair.' He was angry. They were drunk, or close to it. At that moment, the door opens and a figure comes in. He's backlit. It was Paul. He walked between these two guys, saw the knife, saw what was going on, put his arms around the both of them, jacked 'em up so they were on their tippy-toes, and said, 'Hell, I'm glad to see you're getting to know my hands. These are a couple of my good instructors. Barkeep, buy these two guys a beer!'—and he's crunching them. It was a dramatic moment. Those guys sat back down at the bar and Paul, Haven, and I walked into the banquet."

In one public exchange in the *Wyoming State Journal* in December 1970, a letter to the editor from Landerite Pluma Facinelli said, "Why can't they leave our beautiful Sinks Canyon alone? . . . We can get along very nicely without any of this Outdoor Leadership School. The way some of them was dressed this summer was enough to make you sick." A reply from Bruce Dehnert, a local man, in January said, ". . . I agree with her partially . . . but NOLS is an outdoor school which teaches students like us to love and appreciate our outdoors. Dirty clothes are part of this learning, because 30 days of mountain traveling and learning is going to make anyone dirty. I think Paul Petzoldt deserves recognition for what he has done to help us."

Fueling the fire were rumors of what was happening out on courses, how people from NOLS, so the stories went, were ruining the mountains, killing the game, having sex orgies, drinking and smoking pot, and more. Neil Short said that the response by NOLS instructors was mostly dismay for missing out on what sounded like so much fun.

Nonetheless, accusations of impropriety niggled, and were bad for public relations—something Petzoldt worked hard to maintain. He did not take the accusations passively, either, remembered Rob Hellyer. "One day I was sitting there with Thelma when this local radio show came on, 'Man on the Street,' and they were hosting Paul. As they talked, he said, 'Yes, this isn't true what you hear, and in fact we're going to have an Open House tomorrow.' Well, this was news to us. We were going to issue a course the next day! But it was the shrewdest maneuver."

The day-long open house was a great success. Three hundred visitors came. Dottie Petzoldt provided refreshments, Thelma's sewing machines whirred, and the cutting tables were also busy. "It is a mark of efficiency when a school can completely outfit 120 students for a three-week trip in the mountains and conduct a school tour amidst the confusion," reported the July 13, 1970, issue of the *Wyoming State Journal*.

Always eager to leverage publicity to benefit the school, Petzoldt made a point when summarizing the summer season for the board that the school purchased much of its food in Lander. And when two *Time* magazine reporters who had never slept outside wanted to see the Wind Rivers, Petzoldt summoned instructor John "Blackie" Bolton from Jackson. He and an assistant arrived in Lander in his 1957 Dodge Power Wagon nicknamed "Black Magic Woman," outfitted the novices, took them into the backcountry, and kept them safe. Paul knew the value of keeping the press happy.

Community involvement took on various other forms as well. NOLS teamed up with Lander Parks and Recreation to offer courses in basic outdoorsmanship in 1970, possibly in response to injuries sustained by two recreational climbers in Sinks Canyon that February. Their high-angle rescues were done by a team from NOLS.

One of the most high-visibility moments for the school occurred on February 3, 1970. Steve Gipe was working in the basement of the Nicholas Building, where they had a big table set out with maps, doing course planning. Someone came to the top of the steps and yelled down, "The hotel's on fire!" Gipe, Skip Shoutis, and John Cooper ran up the stairs into the gray, drizzly winter day.

Fire escape rescue as depicted in the *NOLS Alumnus*.
NOLS Archives

Across the street black smoke was billowing out the windows of the Fremont Hotel. "I looked up," said Gipe, "and on the top floor, there's this 16-year-old kid hanging out of the window, his right leg bent at knee, yelling 'I'm gonna have to jump!' Some merchants had gathered on the sidewalk below. One had a blanket; they were maybe going to try to catch him with it."

Then someone appeared with a garden hose. Gipe grabbed it and got on Shoutis's shoulders, reached up to the metal fire escape, and ran up. "He was 15 to 20 feet across from me, and had that near-death look on his face—freaked, but focused on me.

"I thought about wrist-to-wristing him, but didn't think that would be possible. So I threw the hose end to him, said, 'Tie it around your waist and grab the hose.' I said, 'Trust me, and swing out and hold on.'

"He swung out, and I let the hose slide through my hands so it didn't impact him too hard and brought him to a stop at the sidewalk. It was over in a minute or two. Turns out he was a runaway from Idaho. He kinda disappeared the next day."

As reported in the paper: "The spectacular rescue showed the result of the training received in NOLS. Both Gipe and Cooper are experienced mountain climbers and employees of NOLS." All three were later given golden keys to the city by the mayor. Still, NOLS had its critics: That night, Gipe was at the Safeway store on 5th and Main and overheard a couple of locals behind him. "Did you see that guy climb the fire escape?" one said. "He must have been on drugs or something."

In August 1973, the citizens of Lander who had railed against the "longhairs" of NOLS were given a dose of per-spective when the Rainbow Family of the Living Light chose the Lander area for its annual gathering. The *Wyoming State Journal* described them as "a loosely strung-together band of hippie-like 'Jesus freaks.' They typically set up large camps and romped in the nude for days at a time at their previous meetings . . . It was reported that over 75,000 invitations had been mailed out to the one for Lander."

Hellyer remembered the group swarming the town, saying it was quite a sight to see. The women were often bare-breasted, he said, and many just walked into Safeway, taking food and walking out the door without paying for it. Neil Short recalled that his clothes were stolen out of the laundromat. In the end, Hellyer credited Sheriff PeeWee McDougal and Doc Smith for keeping cool heads. "I don't believe there was one incident of fisticuffs, and there weren't any arrests," said Hellyer. "It's a credit to the town of Lander."

Peter Simer remembers that he had just come off a course. When he had showered and saw some of the 5,000 members of the Rainbow Family who had arrived in Lander clogging Main Street, "I went straight to the barber shop and had my hair cut off." He didn't want to be mistaken for one of them. In the end, NOLS came through the Rainbow Family's visit for the better, according to Simer: "Lots of people in town decided, 'We like our hippies better than we like *those* hippies!'"

Branching Out

After five years of using the Wind Rivers, the school began to scout new possibilities for courses elsewhere. No one wanted to overuse the tried-and-true areas near Lander, and instructors, perhaps weary of seeing the same terrain, were curious to explore new places and feed their sense of adventure.

Petzoldt was always open to new suggestions for the school, often saying, simply, "Go for it!" He understood the eagerness of young people to see what could be accomplished, and listened to his staff when they looked elsewhere to see where they might go.

The results were impressive. By 1974, there were NOLS "expansion" courses, as they were initially called, in New England, New York, Baja, Tennessee, Alaska, Washington State, Idaho, and Kenya. Each "branch," as it was known, had a rich and lengthy history, filled with the same wonder and pride (and sweat and struggle by many people) as the original NOLS locations in Wyoming.

Setbacks

In the course of such intensive activity in so many new environments, mishaps and more serious incidents were perhaps inevitable. Each was a chilling reminder that the NOLS classroom wasn't a normal schoolyard. On the first McKinley (Denali) expedition in June 1971, Robert Bullard, a doctor

The approach to Denali.
Dale Lescher

Landing a canoe in the Brooks Range.
Stéphane Terrier

NOLS ALASKA

After the hectic summer of 1970, Rob and Martha Hellyer and 13-month-old Jim headed 2,800 miles north in their turquoise-green '68 Chevy truck to scout what Alaska had to offer. There they met up with Bill Scott and Steve Gipe. They hiked in the Talkeetnas and on the Kenai Peninsula, and ventured out onto Prince William Sound (PWS) in Folbots (collapsible kayaks). An epic 90-mile open-water transit by Rob and Bill in a two-man Folbot from Whittier to Valdez in late October capped it: "This is great, this is real adventure, this is beautiful country," said Scott. "We'll figure out how to do this!"

NOLS Alaska set up shop the following spring. Scott returned to Anchorage and rented a dilapidated warehouse. The fleet of Folbots bounced back and forth from duty in Baja and the canyonlands, and tons of other equipment was hauled in each year by truck from Lander.

Alaska offered exquisite terrain and endless opportunity for adventure. When the resupply failed to appear on the first PWS course in 1971, instructor Tom Warren dealt with the situation in an unusual manner. "There was a big ol' bear on the edge of the stream," he said. "I didn't say anything to Dorothy [Warren, his wife, also an instructor, who was in the front of the boat] but whipped the rifle up real quiet, and boom." He took down the running bear from 10 yards. "Half of the students were horrified, but I made a class out of it—how to skin and hang him." Just out of hibernation, the bear didn't have much meat, but the group ate as many bear ribs as they could. [Note: Alaska courses no longer carried guns in 2015.]

Alaska is like that, filled with big stories. Just getting courses out the door was huge. After four years of renting warehouses and odd (but cheap) places in Anchorage, including an old church in 1974, they were in condos and a warehouse in Whittier (1975-76), back in Anchorage for two years, and then in Palmer (1979 and 1980). A horrible rental house experience north of Wasilla in 1981 spurred efforts to find a permanent home for NOLS Alaska.

Jack Niggemyer came to NOLS when he encountered a course hauling its boats to the train depot for the ride to Whittier in 1972 (there was no road then). He inquired about what they were doing. Since there was a spot open on the course, he went with them on the spur of the moment—and stayed for many years. It was Niggemyer who later found the 40-acre farm in Palmer and showed it to then-branch director

Oceans and mountains make Alaska special.
Michael Hosken

Jim Ratz and his assistant, Molly Doran. With funds raised largely by board member Joan Chitiea, NOLS bought the farm in the fall of 1981. An old colony farm, the original farmhouse is listed in the National Register of Historic Places and serves NOLS as a communal staff living room. The barn was the first passively heated dairy barn in the state of Alaska. The NOLS team discovered, when they went to clean it the following spring, that this meant it had troughs in the floor where the manure landed and decomposed, creating heat. "We spent the first week pickaxing and shoveling cow shit out of the barn," recalled Niggemyer.

After Bill Scott started the branch in 1971, the Warrens took care of things in 1972. In 1973, there was no one named director, but Ken Clanton and George Hunker led Denali while Bill Scott and Willy Cunningham led courses to PWS; the following year, Clanton was in charge of Denali while Dave Slovisky and Willie Cunningham led kayaking courses. Together, they somehow managed the various in-town tasks until they left on their expeditions. That's just how it was in those days. Haven Holsapple took over in 1975, followed for two years by Dave Slovisky. John Elliot arrived in 1978, and in 1979 Jim Ratz took over, staying through the spring of 1984. John Gans soon arrived and stayed until 1988, when Don and Donna Ford came on board until their retirement in 2012. At that time, Janeen Hutchins moved into the role.

The Fords' long tenure at NOLS Alaska is remembered fondly by many. "Don was someone that made you want to be better," remembered Katie Baum Mettenbrink, an instructor and former program manager in Alaska, "a better leader, a better teammate, better for our students and for the school. A branch *is* NOLS to the instructors who work there a lot. It's home for a group of people who don't have another home or a regular workplace. Don was very intentional about trying to create a sense of community that made people want to come back to Alaska year after year, while still making choices that he thought were best not just for NOLS Alaska, but for all of NOLS. He always pushed me to think beyond the bubble of our branch to prioritize the best interests of the school."

Eventually, NOLS Alaska operations extended across the huge state. Wilderness and mountaineering courses explored the Talkeetna, Wrangell, Chugach, and Alaska Ranges. NOLS also went north after Cunningham and Slovisky scouted the Brooks Range in 1974. Canoe courses started on the Sheenjek River around 1985. "Above the Arctic Circle seasons are quick: snow melts literally while flowers bloom, fall approaches and colors change again while plants wilt, and snow starts—all in just over eight weeks," said instructor Tre-C Dumais. The range sprawls across the north of the state and includes the Gates of the Arctic National Park, an area larger than Connecticut, with no roads. "It feels like you might be walking somewhere where no one has walked—few places feel this remote," she said. Two Brooks Range courses found mammoth tusks melted out of the permafrost where they had been since the ice age. Truly, the Brooks Range was wilderness beyond description.

The school's Denali expedition, ongoing since 1971, saw its share of epic situations. Robert Bullard died on the first expedition in 1971. In 1979, Scott Fischer was flown off the mountain with high-altitude cerebral edema; in 1984 the expedition was pinned down by high winds and rapid accumulation of snow for three days at high camp at 16,300 feet. In 2002 another course was pinned down for six days at 17,200 feet. In 2013, Expedition Denali, the first attempt by an all-African American team, was turned back by a lightning storm at 19,600 feet. More happily, in 1988 John Gookin, soon to

Making dinner under cloudy skies in the Talkeetnas. *Wilson Yandell*

become the school's longtime curriculum manager, proposed to Mary Butler from the summit, by radio. She said yes.

The branch also took to the water. As of 2015 the Alaska branch ran sea kayaking courses on Prince William Sound and also in the rugged fjords of southeast Alaska, a region rich in marine life, rain forest, and Tlingit history and culture. The latter originated from a smaller base in Petersburg, which was opened after the Exxon Valdez oil spill caused a reduction in sea kayaking operating areas in PWS.

Rivers, too, were a tough challenge for backpacking courses to cross safely, and NOLS Alaska has seen several scary unplanned swims when eddy lines washed out. Since 2011, packrafting courses turned that hazard on its head. Students embraced the rivers—and stuffed ultralight individual rafts, paddles, and drysuits into their packs. The new technology allowed them to cover immense distances in a way impossible before. The first packrafting course traversed the Talkeetna Mountains, 120 miles on land and 120 miles by river, and in 2013 another course traversed Wrangell-St. Elias National Park from north to south. "The result is total expedition independence where anything is possible," said Ashley Wise, Alaska program manager in 2015.

In addition to regular field expedition courses, Alaska hosts much more. Between short courses and semesters, WMI programs and Pro courses, in 2015 Alaska hosted 692 students on 63 courses, totaling 18,344 student days—all in the shortest operating season of any NOLS location.

who was there to study high-altitude physiology, stepped just beyond the marked safe zone on the glacier and fell 130 feet to his death into a snow-covered crevasse. His was the school's second fatality. Radio communications failed, so George Hunker and Randy Cerf hiked 18 miles, including a horrific crossing of the McKinley River at high water, for help. The body was sent out with the famous bush pilot Don Sheldon, who had been flying airdrops for NOLS.

The school's third fatality occurred in 1972 on the Green River. A canoe carrying student Gary Hall capsized about 20 yards from the riverbank. Hall was wearing mountaineering boots, and one of the big boots got wedged between underwater rocks. As Anne Fadiman, another student on the course, wrote years later in the *New Yorker*, "Thirty seconds passed, maybe a minute. Then we saw the standing wave bend Gary's body forward at the waist, push his face underwater, stretch his arms in front of him, and slip his orange life jacket off his shoulders." He drowned while the members of his course, exhausted from multiple rescue attempts, watched.

Hall's brother was on the first night of a different course. His instructor, Skip Shoutis, who barely knew the boy yet, had to find him in the darkness and tell him. The incident highlighted the need for better preparation for crisis situa-tions. In addition, instructors needed better training about river safety. Shoutis, who grew up whitewater canoeing in the eastern United States, began including a river component on instructor courses. "I took them for three or four days canoeing on the Wind River to Boysen. We'd run rapids and sink canoes. They learned light years about rivers," he said.

On January 16, 1974, the school experienced its single largest incident when an avalanche struck a Teton Winter Mountaineering course. The course was moving up the face of the Teton glacier when the avalanche hit. Instructor Mike Moseley was swept off a 300-foot cliff and died. Four students were buried. Bart Drodsky and David Silha died, but two others, including Don Webber, were found and recovered from beneath the snow in time. "I was buried for 10 or 15 minutes," recalled Webber, who later became an instructor and was still working for the school in 2015. "Just as I was running out of oxygen, I heard people above me."

And there were some other significant incidents as well. In the summer of 1970, there were two that required helicopter evacuation. In 1971, students on an instructor course were climbing near Jenny Lake in Grand Teton National Park. One of them, Van Yancy, took a groundfall when a piton failed, and was paralyzed instantly. A quadriplegic, he sometimes returned to Lander in a specially outfitted van the school arranged for him to speak with students about his experience.

On June 12, 1974, disaster of a different sort visited the school when the main building at the Lumberyard burned to the ground, along with about $500,000 worth of supplies and equipment. Discovered by Lander police at 6:45 a.m., the fire department was able to prevent the fire from spreading to the rest of the complex. No one was hurt, but the destruction included several hundred pairs of $50 mountain boots, enough fly fishing equipment for 500 anglers, all the winter gear, plus $20,000 to $30,000 worth of summer food rations. Students (including the author) and instructors on courses came back to town to discover that whatever they had left in storage was gone.

A couple of months later, the school received its insurance money, which only came to $150,000. To make matters worse, half of that went to taxes because the property was held by the for-profit PPWE. But people rallied and managed to send courses into the field on schedule. And in July, a group of 16 climbers joined Petzoldt on his beloved Grand Teton. Once again, he stood on the summit, surrounded by friends, longtime NOLS staffers, and his brother Curly, celebrating the 50th anniversary of his first climb up the mountain.

Paul and Curly Petzoldt joking on the summit of the Grand Teton. *NOLS Archives*

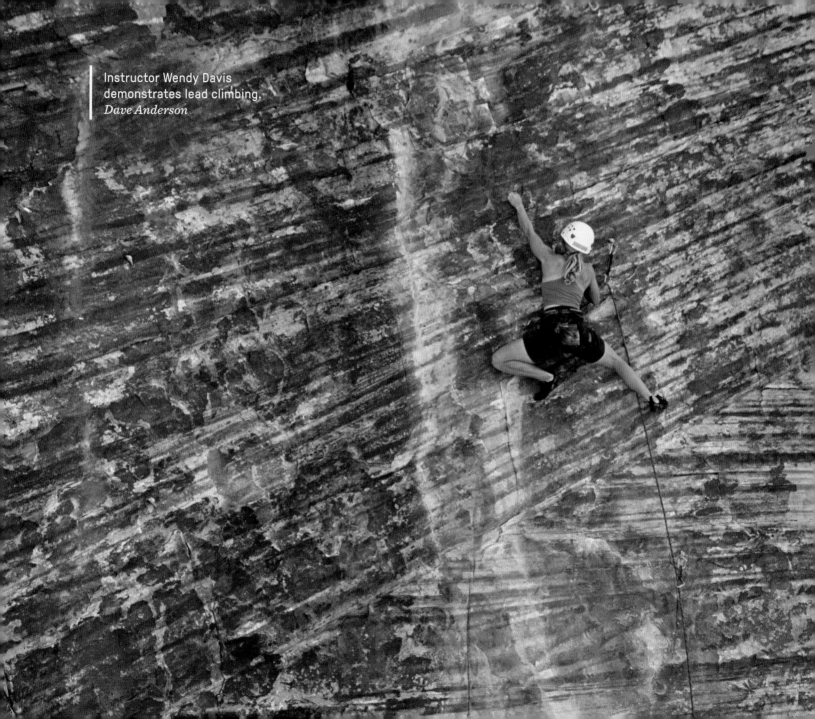

Instructor Wendy Davis
demonstrates lead climbing.
Dave Anderson

Trying Times

DESPITE THE VARIOUS SETBACKS, the school seemed to be humming right along. There were more courses, students, and instructors than ever. But inside the NOLS office, out of the view of most people, an array of business problems were growing to proportions that would eventually test the very existence of the school and the people central to its start.

Although he was very well read on many subjects, Paul Petzoldt had never obtained a traditional education. An astute if somewhat unconventional businessman, his business savvy was honed at the School of Hard Knocks early in life, when he was often broke and had to live by his wits and his engaging personal style. He was a master dealmaker who intuitively knew all the angles, and was renowned for winning at the poker table and elsewhere. This approach had served him well for selling used cars, running a bar in Dubois,

building his guiding business in the Tetons, and even on the golf links around England's Windsor Castle.

But his freewheeling approach to finances led to friction at home with his wife. Much of the early funding of the school came from Dottie, who was a successful business owner in Lander and a careful steward of funds. Paul's handling of money had never meshed well with her own approach to financial matters. For example, Dottie was always astonished when Petzoldt admitted forgetting about the $20 bills she sometimes found in his pocket. "She couldn't understand how he could do that," said Nancy Carson. "She'd never forget a $20 bill." In time, Dottie opened her own private bank account and began to keep her finances separate. They were divorced in 1973.

Petzoldt spent the Christmas holidays that year with Mike and Jill Williams at the NOLS branch in Driggs before

An iconic African savanna landscape. *Michael Schmertzler*

embarking on a successful New Year's climb of the Grand Teton. He left in February for an extended scouting trip in Tanzania and Kenya with the Williamses to help establish the inaugural Africa courses.

When he returned to Lander in May, he discovered that a new, stricter climate of accountability had been established. Jim Halfpenny was managing the office, and bookkeeping was being done by another former instructor, Janet Jahn. They told the previously unfettered Petzoldt that he needed to provide receipts for his expenses.

By then, tracing and documenting the line between the nonprofit NOLS and the for-profit PPWE (and some other businesses Petzoldt owned) was increasingly difficult. Partly that was because Petzoldt had never separated intention from structure. To him, it didn't matter if PPWE paid for some things and NOLS others. He and the Hellyers had taken on enormous personal debt to build PPWE and buy assets, largely for the benefit the school. Every effort was for the greater good of the school, whether that was promoting NOLS on a public relations trip that PPWE paid for or using the PPWE pack string to take curious journalists into the field to see a NOLS course in action. But the government was starting to see things differently.

On the afternoon of August 27, 1974, chairman of the NOLS Board of Directors, John Walker, and Petzoldt traveled to Laramie to meet with IRS Exempt Organizations specialist George Granato. The IRS had identified 22 distinct concerns in the relationship between NOLS and PPWE, including billing and ownership of assets (including the pack string), how employees of one were also employees of the other (at one time, Mike Williams said, his salary was paid half by NOLS and half by PPWE), and handshake agreements instead of properly written contracts. According to Granato, the available records "made the school look like a brother and sister operation set up to profit Paul Petzoldt."

Minutes from the NOLS Board meeting three days later show growing concern: "All business conducted from this point forward shall absolutely conform to the IRS regulations." Petzoldt agreed that all irregularities would be "cleaned up immediately," and that "henceforth NOLS would operate on sound business principles." There was a call for transparency of all records, and for weekly progress reports and monthly profit and loss statements to be provided to the board by Halfpenny, who was formally named the school's business manager. An organizational chart was drawn and approved. Travel was to have prior approval and an allowance of $35 per diem—once expense receipts were turned in.

––––––––––

It was a good start, but significant issues remained, and others kept popping up. Questions about the legality of the sale of the Noble Hotel by PPWE to NOLS bubbled up when a title issue involving a preexisting mortgage arose. The school's lawyer bemoaned the lack of proper documentation regarding the transaction. The loan by NOLS executed in 1971 when reversing the NOLS/OLF situation was deemed improper, and the paper trail was confusing; it appeared that as of October 1974, PPWE had overpaid on the loan by several thousand dollars.

Not only was the financial situation a complicated mess, but the minutes of another board meeting on October 25-26, 1974, also reflected a growing issue of eroded morale among personnel at the school. Feedback had been solicited and compiled that showed the need to "develop policies governing personnel upgrading the salary, vacation pay, etc., so that we can assure ourselves of high-quality, permanent employees at the school. Motion carried."

The rising turmoil spurred the board to increase its level of involvement in the operations of the school; a motion was also passed that no new courses were to "be started or explored without the Board's approval." By November, much of the hubbub was under better control. Petzoldt wrote a letter to the board using contrite language and explaining how systems had been put in place so that NOLS could operate according to the IRS code. He promised to consult attorneys and accountants should further questions arise. "Mistakes made in the past are being terminated—as fast as possible," he wrote, and then, ever optimistic, he added, "We will try our best to continue the service we are doing for our country, our youth, and our educational system while still observing the letter and spirit of the regulations that govern our school."

Petzoldt returned to Africa that winter and was due back in mid-March. Halfpenny resigned January 1, 1975, after only a few months on the job so that he could finish his PhD. His replacement, Janet Jahn, sent an update letter dated March 4 to the board. The good news, she indicated, was that income and bookings were good, and instructor pay had been raised. (The base pay per course for a CL was $700; for a PL, it was $475; and for an assistant, $200). But the school was still waiting to hear about the final results of the IRS examination of the school's records.

When the results arrived, dated April 23, 1975, four questions remained. They largely stemmed from the effort in 1969 to 1970 to convert the legal status of the school, the lack of competitive bids for services rendered by PPWE to NOLS, the fact that the nonprofit had loaned money to PPWE in 1971 in attempting to resolve the NOLS-OLF situation, and certain real estate transactions. The letter warned against recurrence of any of the infractions noted, saying, "It is emphasized that the Board of Directors should exercise its authority in overseeing the operations of the school."

Although nothing much seemed amiss to the field troops, according to Andy Carson, they could sense the tension as the board took a far more active role in the everyday affairs of the school. But the worst was yet to come. When Petzoldt returned from Africa in the spring of 1975, he brought a new face to Lander: his new wife, the former Joan Brodbeck. In his May 17 report to the board, Petzoldt wrote about the need to engage in some fundraising for the school, and that "I think Joan Petzoldt, my wife, [a former business woman] has special abilities and experience which will help NOLS in fund raising." Given that the NOLS Board at the time included relatives and loved ones of his former wife Dottie, Petzoldt could be given no points for diplomacy for that comment.

Welcome news that the IRS was not going to alter the school's nonprofit status arrived by mail on May 29, 1975. But still not all was well between the founder and the board. On June 24, John Walker wrote a letter to Petzoldt in which the opening sentence reads, "This is to try to clear up some of the doubts, misunderstandings, untrust [sic], etc., concerning you, PPWE, and NOLS." Much as they wanted an arms-length relationship with PPWE to keep the IRS happy, the fact was, the school could not mount courses without the logistics, support, and equipment held by PPWE. The two were inextricably linked. The second-to-last sentence states, "Paul, ask us for help and be honest with us . . ." Clearly, some amount of distrust and blame remained.

The problems proved insurmountable. On July 11, 1975,

the board met at the Royal Inn in Salt Lake City. At 8:30 a.m. it was moved and seconded that "Paul Petzoldt be removed as an officer of NOLS and that he no longer serve in any capacity with NOLS." Severance pay would be $2,500. The reason given in the minutes: Petzoldt's ongoing conflict of interest between his role in PPWE and NOLS. To John Walker fell the unenviable task of informing Petzoldt of the board's action. With that, a motion was made and seconded that they adjourn for lunch.

Paul Petzoldt. *Skip Shoutis*

Dirty Devil Canyon, Utah.
Jamie O'Donnell

1975-1983

ROCKY TIMES AND THE POVERTY ERA

Seventeen dirty, haggard, and drawn-out 'ex-students' emerge from the woods, with smiles that need no interpretation . . . to eat corn flakes as though it were a Thanksgiving feast.

– Web Webster, instructor

In the middle of July 1975, many NOLS courses were in the field when news started trickling across the landscape that Petzoldt had been fired. The telegraph of the wilderness, thanks to re-ration horsepackers and backpackers, hummed. The conversation might have gone something like this:

"Have you heard the news?"

"No, what?"

"They fired Paul."

"What?! How can that be?"

"Dunno. That's just what I heard."

"They can't do that! Who could do that?"

"I don't know, man. All I can tell you is that Paul's been fired."

As surprising as the firing was to the instructors and staff, it was also "a total surprise to Paul," said Bill Scott, who came in from a course to discover that all hell had broken loose in Lander. "Paul didn't see it coming. He knew there were issues, but he didn't think they would do that."

Few people had been privy to the financial problems or the exact nature of the build-up of tension between Petzoldt and the board over the prior year. The firing brought the conflict into the open, but didn't necessarily provide clarity on what had happened, or what would happen moving forward. As more and more field staff returned to town, anxiety increased, both for the school and for the members of the NOLS community. As George Hunker recalled, the previous five years had been intense and heady: "From 1970 to 1975, everything was happening. All we did was eat, sleep, and drink NOLS. We didn't care if we made any money. We were doing new things. It was all exciting and new and really good."

And now, it was all up in the air.

Jon Hamren in a snow cave. Diane Shoutis and George Hunker in the background. *NOLS Archives*

The fateful board meeting in Salt Lake City actually got under way on the evening of July 11, but the vote to fire Paul came when the meeting resumed at 8:30 a.m. the next day. One final straw, according to Halfpenny, was that Paul had missed a crucial meeting with the IRS and the board in June—just didn't show up, after promising to be there—which rocked the board's willingness to support him. Certainly, Petzoldt's history of financial wrangling, lingering family issues (relating both to Dottie and his first wife), and the board's mounting lack of trust in him were all factors. When the meeting reconvened at 5:00 p.m. that day, two new faces were at the table: Janet Jahn, the school's business manager, and Jon Hamren, who had most recently held the title of chief instructor in charge of staffing courses.

Hamren had been in Lander 12 hours earlier when his phone rang at 5:00 a.m. "It was the first I knew about the firing," he said, "and they wanted to ask me, 'do you want to be executive director?'" He was surprised by the offer, but not the news. "There were rumors of trouble, but I never thought it'd be me. I was by no means in the inner circle," he said. It turned out that others, including Rob Hellyer and Skip Shoutis, had also received calls, but had declined the offer. "I was the last man standing. I was hired and named."

Hamren came to NOLS as a student in 1970 and started working courses right away. His father's family were cattle ranchers in Jackson Hole and had known Petzoldt since 1924 when he first climbed the Grand Teton. Hamren's aunt, Geraldine Lucas, had given Petzoldt his first job in Teton Valley, and family members had climbed in the Tetons with Petzoldt during his guiding years there. Now, Hamren, age 25, found himself quite suddenly succeeding Petzoldt as executive director at NOLS. His appointment was announced on July 14 at an all-staff meeting in Lander by the newly formed executive committee of the board consisting of John Walker, E.J. Breece, and Joe Kenney.

Meanwhile, July was high season at NOLS, and students were arriving in Lander for their courses. Walker asked Hamren if he could get courses out the door. "The situation was," said Hamren, "that NOLS had no way to put people into the field or resupply, because that was all PPWE." The only way to carry on would be to hire Petzoldt back and cut a deal with him and the corporation's co-owners, Rob and Martha Hellyer, for PPWE to provide logistical services. Forced to backpedal on relieving Petzoldt of his duties entirely, the board gave him the title of "Senior Advisor." In an agreement he signed July 14, Petzoldt's role was to act "in a non-administrative capacity and primarily concerned with public relations . . ." The document reserved the right to terminate the contract should Petzoldt "act contrary to the written instructions of the Director."

George Hunker. *NOLS Archives*

Tod Schimelpfenig. *NOLS Archives*

The NOLS community was unsure from one day to the next that summer whether or how the school would go forward, but they got through somehow—essentially by the good graces of Petzoldt and Hellyer, who continued to supply and resupply courses. It was an intensely emotional and uncertain time. Instructors who left on courses didn't know whether they would get resupplied, or picked up at the trailhead, or what they'd find when they came back.

"I was a recipient of some of that chaos that summer," said Tod Schimelpfenig, who had been an instructor since 1973. "I had a course in the Beartooths where a re-ration was two days late. It was a scheduling glitch, but when you have seventeen 14- and 15-year-old boys who are hungry . . . well, we went right into the same mode you'd go into at the end of the course: survival, except, we said, 'It's going to happen now.'"

Founding of the NOLS Instructor Association (NIA)

The instructor corps had been floating the idea of forming a NOLS Instructor Association (NIA) for some time, but the firing of Petzoldt galvanized them. A unified instructor voice was needed, said Bill Scott. "There was a lot of pressure on the board, because instructors were threatening to walk out, and Paul, of course, was just livid. It very nearly could have just fallen apart—which nobody wanted to happen," he said.

They convened quickly. An early NIA document lists

Peter Simer as chairman, with George Hunker, Randy Cerf, George Newbury, Mike Guillaume, Bruce Hampton, Kim Fadiman, and Jon Hamren (as "Director, NOLS") in attendance, but many others were also involved.

On July 22, 1975, Hamren received this letter:

Dear Jon:

We, the undersigned, are members of a committee duly elected at a meeting of interested NOLS personnel and alums July 21, 1975, to organize an association of NOLS instructors. At this meeting the committee was instructed to convey to you, as director of NOLS, our unanimous support. This vote of confidence reflects our dedication to the continuing strength and ideals of the National Outdoor Leadership School. Please convey this pledge of support to Paul Petzoldt, Senior Advisor, and John Walker, Chairman of the Board of Trustees. [Note: the surviving copy is unsigned.]

Until that summer, no one among "the troops" had really questioned the NOLS/PPWE connection. But as rumors and information filtered through the people coming and going on courses, the NOLS community began to separate into factions.

"Looking back on it now," said Bruce Hampton, "I think basically there were a lot of people that didn't want to believe what was going on and were loyal to Paul, and there were a lot who were the first to say, 'Yeah, he's wrong and let's get rid of him,' and there were a lot of people in the middle who loved NOLS and wanted to keep working there and didn't know what to do."

Quite a few early members of the NOLS community who felt loyal to Paul left the school in 1975 (although some subsequently came back), including Skip and Diane Shoutis, Bruce and Molly Hampton, and George and Paula Hunker. Hellyer stopped being involved with NOLS on a daily basis at the end of that summer. In September, Thelma Young left her sewing machine, citing "personal reasons," returning in 1977. Remembering those days, Hellyer said, "They shot him out of the saddle, but they hit the rest of us in the gut."

Between July and October, the board, Hamren, and the newly hatched NIA struggled to resolve the school's critical immediate future while still coping with "business as usual" as courses came and went from the field. Negotiations were further pressurized because the school's service contract with PPWE was slated to expire after the fall semester ended. One idea was to buy out Petzoldt and the Hellyers, and merge PPWE with NOLS. A twist on that idea that Hamren proposed was to create an employee stock ownership plan (ESOP). "If the instructors owned the old PPWE," he said, "it could be self-sustaining and give instructors their own means to be self-sufficient over time. It was a naive idea, but I wanted people to be able to be there a long time." The board rejected the idea.

At the end of August, Petzoldt agreed to sell PPWE as long as the board first signed a three-year service contract—but the board wouldn't sign a service contract without a sales agreement in hand. The deadlock eroded what little spirit of cooperation remained. Petzoldt finally made another offer in October, but the board felt the price was too high. Petzoldt rejected their counteroffer and launched a plan to start his own school.

The cover of the PPWE catalog from about 1974.
NOLS Archives

He had quietly been looking into the feasibility of starting a new school in Lander for much of the summer, according to Skip Shoutis, who wrestled only briefly about whether to stay or go after the firing. "I supported Paul," he said. At the time, "I was his assistant director. I handed in my resignation fairly quickly once I knew he was really out. Rob and Paul and I had some meetings and started another school. We called it the College of Outdoor Leadership," or COOL. Although a syllabus and curriculum were penned, incorporation papers for the proposed school were never actually drawn up, according to Shoutis.

One of the reasons was the NIA. The members of the NIA believed that Lander and the already overburdened Wind River Range weren't big enough for two outdoor schools. A war was brewing in which everyone would lose. On October 23, according to an NIA document, "the Governing Board of the NIA talked with Paul for the better part of a day to discourage him from the plan. We told him that we had unanimously decided to work only for NOLS and not for him separate from NOLS. Paul understands that running the [new] school without the cooperation of many instructors is impossible."

Meanwhile, out in the field that October, the semester course was unusually challenging. Logistically, according to Herb Ogden (a student on the course, who later became the NOLS medical advisor), "they couldn't get us out the door, couldn't pick us up—of six sections, we got picked up right only a few times. It was a crazy semester." The weather wasn't helpful, either: At one point, the course was slated to do its biology section in Yellowstone, but early-season snows left them post-holing through drifts while they probed for the canoes. The instructor team of Ken Clanton and Bruce and Molly Hampton was overwhelmed. Molly remembered calling Lander and begging, "Don't make us go back out!" George Hunker, in disbelief, got in the school's Buick (known as "Go Fast"), went to Yellowstone, and, seeing the general situation and desperation, relented. The course went to a hotel in Jackson to warm up, and the climbing section was moved to Sinks Canyon.

On October 25, the NOLS Board met again and agreed on a bylaw change to increase the size of the board to nine members. Two familiar NOLS faces were then seated: Jim Halfpenny and Bill Scott. (One operations proposal made at that meeting by Halfpenny and supported by Walker was that "NOLS instructors shall not encourage, condone, or impose, nor will they allow other individuals on courses to encourage, condone, or impose their views on nude bathing on other individuals on the course. Motion passed.")

On November 7 and 8, the board meeting was held in Denver. Ten instructors made the six-hour drive to urge approval of a reasonable offer to Petzoldt. Their agenda also included trying to reestablish a sense of unity in the NOLS family, and to voice support for a by then beleaguered and exhausted Hamren. At that meeting the board agreed to allow a member of the NIA to sit in on its meetings from then on.

Several deadlines were looming. Petzoldt confided in Walker that he was reaching a critical financial state—in his words, "going under." The first winter course was scheduled to leave for the field on November 24. And there was still no service contract or resolution to the impasse. Complicating matters was the news that board chairman John Walker had approached Colorado Outward Bound to request instructional, logistical, and administrative assistance if needed—and to inquire whether Outward Bound might possibly be interested in buying NOLS.

The NIA dug in, renting its own warehouse on November 10 to begin preparations for the November 24 start to the winter season. Hamren and Scott met again with Petzoldt, and left with a sales offer in hand that included a request from Petzoldt for a seat on the board. They urged the board to accept the contract during its conference call meeting on November 11, but the first vote failed and the offer was rejected. Then, according to the NIA document, "Jon suggested that he and the instructors might be unwilling to fight a war they felt was unnecessary." The idea of a school without instructors caused the board to reconsider, and in a 3-2

Early mountaineering, probably Alaska. *NOLS Archives*

vote (with one abstention and another member not present) it agreed to accept the offer.

There was jubilation! NOLS appeared united—for two days. On November 13 the board rescinded the vote, saying that 3-2 with one abstention did not represent a majority on the still six-member board. Everything was back in limbo. Although no proper strike vote was taken, the Lander-based NOLS instructors and most of the staff, outraged by what seemed to be a technicality and feeling their trust had been violated, walked off the job in protest on Friday, November 14.

Meetings that weekend resulted in calls for the resignations of several board members. Walker was especially reviled, and even more so once news of his discussions with Outward Bound were discovered. In its November 18 issue, the *Casper Star-Tribune* quoted him as being "jubilant as he relayed [the] news 'that . . . we have the upper hand.'" Built like a stovepipe, the husky track coach from the University of Wyoming had been with the school since about 1966, but, in the perception of most instructors, Walker had done little over time to ingratiate himself with the notoriously independent and opinionated group. According to Bruce Hampton, Walker never said, for example, "This is what happened, we found Paul with his finger in the till and we're going to lose our nonprofit status, so we've got to separate ourselves." Instead, said Hampton, "Walker came to us and spoke down to us with a very condescending attitude. You know this is an individual group. There are a lot of people who went through the 60s, the war, civil rights, and they weren't going to take any shit from anybody, especially this guy who represented the establishment and was so outrageously rude to everybody in the instructor group. That created a lot of animosity."

The Strike

Q Belk, a NOLS instructor since 1972, was bicycling to Wyoming that month to work a course and saw a newspaper "with headlines that NOLS was melting down," he said. He called from Laramie and spoke with George Hunker, who was trying to keep things running in the office.

"I remember Hunker distinctly saying, 'No point in coming. We don't even know if we can put a course in the field'," Belk said. "'Oh, you're in Laramie? Might as well come then and join the fun.'"

Belk arrived in time for a meeting on Sunday, November 16, at Petzoldt's house. "There were probably 75 people crammed in his living room. The majority of us still idolized him," he said. At that point, Petzoldt was still trying to recruit instructors for his new school, but his overtures were rejected.

Over at the NOLS offices, Hamren and his assistant director, Hunker, were working with Janet Jahn, Larry Higby Sr., Bruce Young, John Osgood, and Walker, trying to hold things together without the regular staff. Charley Fiala, who breezed back into town two days before the strike, found himself, Steve Goryl, and Bruce Young driving a borrowed flower van to Boulder, where they bought skis and boots and other equipment for a winter course. On the drive back, Young asked Fiala if he would work the upcoming winter course. "We were considered 'scabs'," said Fiala, but since he hadn't gotten any contracts the previous May after his instructor course, he was fine with that; he was just eager to work.

Meanwhile, the Lumberyard was locked with chains on the gate, and being guarded. No one knew what was going to happen.

Perhaps it was the constellation of circumstances—no one supporting the new school, equipment and supplies being brought in for the winter course, people agreeing to work despite the strike, students arriving—but to everyone's surprise, on Friday, November 21, Petzoldt and Walker finally signed a sales agreement: NOLS would pay PPWE $225,000 over three years; about $30,000 of debts owed by PPWE to NOLS would be negated; and NOLS would assume the Small Business Administration (SBA) loan of $197,000 for the Lumberyard, the Noble Hotel, and all non-horse-related outfitting equipment and vehicles. In the end, said Petzoldt in *On Belay*, "Whatever happens, I am not going to see my life-work in building the finest and

Summit shot, probably in the early 1970s. *NOLS Archives*

most motivating educational system fail. Our school shall continue and I will be part of that school until I am sure it is in trustworthy hands—then I'd like to retire and go fishing."

Two days later the NIA met again at Petzoldt's house, its fourth general meeting in nine days. The sales agreement depended on qualified instructors completing the remainder of the fall semester, and the strike was putting that contingency in jeopardy. The group identified two alternatives: continue the strike and potentially invalidate the sales contract, or return to work. At some point in the evening, according to one eyewitness, the students from the course that was to leave the next day had filed into the back of the room and were listening. Belk stood up and said, "NOLS is not Paul Petzoldt." Pointing at the students, he said, "That's NOLS. I'm working tomorrow."

The vote went in favor of continuing the strike, but after sleeping on it overnight, many instructors reconsidered. According to an NIA document, "At 6:30 the following morning, a half an hour before the first winter course of the season was to begin, the instructors reevaluated their position and returned to work."

After the 6:30 a.m. decision, said Belk, who was 20 years old and about to be a winter course leader for the first time, instructing with Jim Acee and Charley Fiala, "I stormed out, got my students in the lobby, and walked down Lincoln Street to the Lumberyard. It had been locked for days, but it was open. We walked in and started issuing students. . . . Nobody stopped us."

The end of the strife also signaled the end for Hamren. Exhausted and sick, he resigned after four months on the job. Life between the battling wills of the board and Petzoldt, even with instructor support, was too much. Looking back in 2015, he said, "I was 25 years old, I hadn't finished college, and I didn't like the board any better than I liked Paul. It's a very hard group of people to please."

Others remember the end of his directorship differently, claiming he was fired by a board tired of what appeared to be his taking sides with Petzoldt. In the end, said Hamren, "what we're really loyal to is NOLS because of what it meant."

School lore has sometimes defamed the board and administration for their actions in 1975. The three power centers—Petzoldt, the board, and the instructor corps— each had a major stake in the game, fueled by passion for the work of the school. But the story has more than one side. In 2005, NOLS long-timer Kathy Dunham reported a telephone conversation she had with a somewhat wistful Walker. From his perspective, many people deserved praise and recognition for their behind-the-scenes, good-faith efforts to keep the school going. Walker credited Janet Jahn for helping the board understand the complexity of the financial crisis, and Jim Halfpenny for preserving the school's nonprofit status. In addition, he said, many on the board, including himself, made personal decisions to take time away from their own jobs to serve the school, and some even mortgaged their own homes to lend the school money at times. While Paul was the inspiration for the school and should be recognized as such, he said, the school would not—could not—have survived by continuing the way it was going; it quite possibly would have lost the IRS investigation, and almost certainly would eventually have been bankrupted.

As winter descended on Lander in 1975, the leadership school found itself without a leader. The board called Haven Holsapple to see if he was interested in being executive director, but he had returned to the University of Wyoming that fall and refused the offer. Whether queries were made elsewhere is unclear, but by December 13 the board had appointed a new executive director: Peter Simer.

Instructor Clair Parrish teaching leadership. *Lucy Rogers*

NOLS INDIA

By Annalise Grueter staff writer, and Manohar D'silva, instructor

A line of giants stretches across Kashmir and Jammu, Himachal Pradesh, and Uttarakhand, the three northernmost states in India. In northern Uttarakhand, where NOLS courses explore the Kumaon Himalaya, Nanda Devi (25,643 feet), the Bliss-Giving Goddess, rises in her circle of defenses. One of the two tallest peaks in India, she dominates the northeast skyline as students on Himalaya Mountaineering courses make their crux move over the Dhana Dhura at 18,400 feet, the high traverse that separates the Milam and Pindari Valleys.

Those valleys, though, are not just wilderness. People live there as well. Instructor Prasad Gadgil explains, "This is one of the most unusual classrooms compared to the other areas that NOLS operates. This is one of the only classrooms where students can interact with locals who live here and have been living here for centuries, and also at the same time have an experience of a remote wilderness setting." NOLS India came to this area starting in September 1991, after instructor Krishnan Kutty convinced the school that it should run courses in the Himalaya. What started with one mountaineering course per year for the first three years grew to one each in the two operating seasons of spring and fall. Backpacking courses began in 1998, WMI courses in 2001, and alumni trips in 2004. A semester program was added in 2007, and a combo course of hiking and culture—the Himalaya Cultural Expedition—was inaugurated in 2015.

The India program has always been supported by NOLS Pacific Northwest in Conway, Washington. Until 2014, all courses met in Conway and flew together to India, finishing in New Delhi so those who wanted could continue exploring the region afterwards. Over time, some courses flew directly to India to start.

Until 2001, Kutty lived at his home in Bangalore, in the south of India, meeting up with students and faculty farther north in Delhi to stage their expeditions from the home of Mr. Sarabjit Singh, an old NOLS friend. Eventually, Kutty moved with his family to Ranikhet, a small town in the Kumaon region where the NOLS India base has been housed ever since. The exposure to cultural components in all courses had a long-lasting impact on students unaccustomed to witnessing how human settlements can coexist with wilderness. In addition, many courses had the chance to hike on historical

trade routes over mountain passes as high as 15,300 feet. Some mountaineering courses camped above 17,000 feet and crossed 18,400-foot passes.

From the outset, outreach programs were a branch priority. The first local outreach course, in November 2000, was named Trip Leader India and geared toward outdoor professionals. Four years later, an outreach course for local 15- and 16-year-olds named Young Leader India began as well.

In May 2009, Kutty retired from his NOLS position, and Ravi Kumar took over as program manager. In addition to being involved in the process of registering the branch as a legal entity in India, he applied skills from his 20 years with the school to ensure active involvement with government bodies regarding outdoor policy and best practices, and memberships with various Indian outdoor space organizations.

Despite many changes in the 25 years since inception of NOLS courses in the region, the outdoor classrooms in the shadow of Nanda Devi still provided an incredible opportunity to participants. "My favorite parts about this course area are the interaction with the locals, interviews with the shepherds, playing with school children, the high alpine meadows, the biodiverse ecosystem, overcoming language barriers, as well as the spectacular views of the Himalayas," said Gadgil. And the Milam Valley continues to be entrancing; according to program supervisor Vinay Sirsi: "[It is] a magical place with migratory herds of sheep and shepherds . . . who have been trading with Tibet for centuries."

In India, culture and the wilderness exist side by side.
Shawn Stratton

Llama packing in the Winds.
Brad Christensen

The Simer Years

"THEY DID SAY THEY'D LIKE ME to be director and I thought about it and figured if nobody does it the school will be out of business, so I'll do it. It wasn't like I applied or anything . . . I think they thought taking someone from the NIA was reasonable," recalled Simer in 2011.

His appointment wasn't without controversy. Simer, who had been chairman of the nascent NIA, had a reputation as a bit of a wild man in the instructor corps. He had read about NOLS in *Life* magazine while living in a commune in Santa Monica during graduate school at UCLA, and arrived for his student course in the summer of 1970. A member of the 1971 instructor course, he joined the first McKinley climb that same summer. In 1975, Peter Simer was 28, one of the older instructors. When he walked into the crowded NIA meeting with Petzoldt on November 16, he had just arrived from the canyonlands with the semester course and "looked for all the world like a cross between Che Guevara and Frank Zappa," remembered QBelk.

By December, "the hair was gone. He came to my course's banquet and politely asked me to lead the Winter Teton Climb . . . All I could think was, 'What's happened to the wild man?'" Belk added, "To his everlasting credit, he stepped into a leadership vacuum and pulled it off, completely changed overnight, and literally saved the damn school. There probably would not be a NOLS if Simer hadn't taken over."

According to Bill Scott, who was on the board at the time, "One of the reasons Peter was hired was that he came across very businesslike, very objective, very professional. That's pretty much how he ran the school. I think he did a good job getting things back on a solid footing. Before that it hadn't been. It was run out of a shoebox, basically, in Paul's style. Peter was the kind of person people could like. The instructors and board respected him, and he was able to work in the community. He was absolutely critical. He was the right one for the job." This sentiment was widely echoed with the perspective of time.

Peter Simer. *NOLS Archives*

For Simer, it was a time of change from his more carefree NOLS days to one of responsibility for a cherished institution. Succeeding Petzoldt, even with the interlude of Hamren's tenure, could have been daunting, but, he said, "I didn't think of it that way. Paul was an innovator and a leader, and he started the school. What I did was make that school [work for] the future." Simer's first two goals were to run the operations of the school well, and pay off the debt.

It was a mountainous task. "What I remember about the purchase agreement was that Jan Jahn, me, and John Walker personally guaranteed the SBA note to buy NOLS, buy the stuff, and get NOLS going. At the time I owned a sleeping bag and a van. I thought 'What do I have to lose?'" he recalled.

Without going into great detail about the shake-up, a carefully worded announcement appeared in the December 1975 issue of the *NOLS Alumnus*:

The National Outdoor Leadership School has undergone an administrative and logistical transition recently. Last July, the Board of Directors of NOLS made Paul Petzoldt Senior Advisor. He was replaced as director by NOLS Director of Field Operations, Jon Hamren.... In mid-November PPWE sold its outfitting division, the Lumberyard, the Noble Hotel, all NOLS related equipment both in Wyoming at [sic] at branch schools, to the National Outdoor Leadership School. Late in November, Peter Simer became Director of NOLS. Peters [sic] has been with NOLS since 1970 and has served as course leader, Assistant General Manager and Course Planner. Until accepting the Directorship Peter was Chairman of the Steering Committee of the NOLS Instructors Association. NOLS is the same school it has always been. Our logistical problems are well under control. Our new Director has our utmost support and confidence. We, the instructors of the National Outdoor Leadership School, are more confident than ever in the positive direction our school is taking.

With that, it was time to move forward. By January 1976, an air of control began emanating from the NOLS office. A letter from Simer to E. J. Breece of the board indicated efficient attention to the various departments of the school and included reports from the heads of those areas. Paul had signed the sales agreement, wrote Simer, and NOLS had "taken over everything." The letter was optimistic (despite the crushing debt), citing the acquisition of two new buses,

and included encouraging reports about outfitting and the branch schools.

In his progress report from the planning department, Randy Cerf wrote, "All is going quite smoothly so, I am afraid,

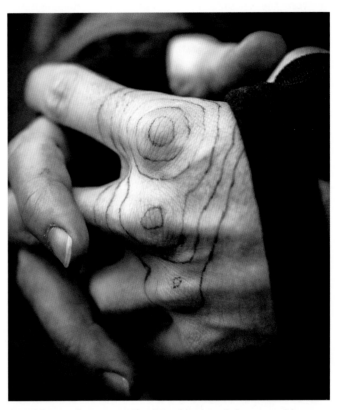

Knuckles make an excellent tool to teach topographic map reading. *Alex Chang—Cornell Leadership Expedition*

the progress report will be less interesting than the last one." Permitting applications and processing for the 1976 courses were well under way; re-ration planning and other logistics were in hand. Routes for the summer were largely planned, as were the upcoming instructor courses. Although the school's finances were still deeply concerning, the school was finally on a smoother track.

They called 1976 to 1979 "the Poverty Years." Debt hung over the school like a dangling sword. It didn't help that economic conditions in the wider world were also a mess. When the Vietnam War ended in April 1975, the nation slumped into a severe recession, and by March 1980, inflation levels had swollen to 14.8 percent. That same month, home mortgage interest rates averaged an astonishing 15.28 percent.

Sometimes, Simer recounts, cash flow was so tight that paying the loans for the purchase of PPWE and from the SBA occasionally meant that certain people had to vouch their personal property. But the bills got paid, and eventually things started looking up.

One improvement that had a significant impact was a concerted effort to fill courses. A study of course enrollment had shown that on average courses were only 82 percent filled. Further study showed that if that figure could be boosted to 100 percent, the result would "enable us to pay off our debt within a year, hold tuition at present levels, create a scholarship fund, and do the many other things necessary for NOLS to realize its potential," said Simer. In the Summer 1977 issue of the *NOLS Alumnus,* he put out a plea:

> NOLS enters its twelfth year in 1977. We have grown from a small unknown school into a leader in teaching outdoor leadership, practical conservation, and outdoor recreation. In 1975 with the change in administration, we assumed a $425,000 debt for equipment and facilities. We were able to reduce this by almost $150,000 in 1976. During this time, inflation has resulted in significantly increased costs. We want to establish a permanent scholarship fund for students and make available advanced educational opportunities for graduates and instructors.

He asked the NOLS community to get the word out—do slide shows at colleges, speak to organizations in their hometowns, anything to promote the school by word of mouth. It was an era of transition, from the school's start-up days driven directly by Paul's work and charisma, to increasing organization and systems development in every department.

The demands of maintaining tight control over every dime in order to survive the Poverty Era required a firm hand, and did not always win popularity points for Simer. His personal style was sometimes off-putting; some remember that he could be downright caustic or snobbish. "He was unbelievably bright and could out-think almost everybody," remembered Charley Fiala. "He was the Cheshire cat, with a grin on his face, smarter than everyone else, a step or two ahead—very confident, verging on arrogance." If abrasive at times, Simer was effective nonetheless at implementing the changes the school needed.

Simer accomplished much in his first four years. "He held the place together when it could have fallen apart. He held it together by pinching pennies and by making financial decisions with almost no money," said Tod Schimelpfenig, who rode those roller-coaster years. "He kept managing the school and kept his nose to the grindstone." The school teetered on the brink of bankruptcy throughout the late 1970s, but by the end of 1979, the debt was finally dissolving. It would be paid off within five years.

People stayed at NOLS in those difficult times because, despite the grinding lack of money, the school was a lot of fun. "You're doing stuff you love, you're out with a bunch of people you're helping to love the same stuff you do, and seeing them develop from picking up 12 bags of mystery powder and wondering how to eat it," said Simer. "Those first days of the course, the instructors know everything and the students look like Siberian prisoners of war . . . 25 days later, they were on their own to go on Survival and meet you somewhere and not get lost."

"Sometimes the instructors look at each other and say, 'Thank god no one died today,' and then some days, it's, 'I can't believe someone's paying me to do this,' and also days when it's, 'They are not paying me enough to do this,'" observed Cyndy Simer, who arrived at NOLS in 1976 from a teaching post in Washington, DC.

Beyond the fun, NOLSies witnessed, again and again, the changes wrought by the wilderness. One who saw it was Kevin McGowan, who estimated in 2015 that he had fit upward of 25,000 pairs of hiking boots over his 35 years in the Rocky Mountain issue room. "NOLS instructors are not camp counselors or trip guides. They're teachers," he said. "There's a difference.

"It is truly amazing to see a course leave and then come back," he continued. "I can tell whether the course was successful or not immediately after they get off the bus, because of the enthusiasm, the way they're organized, the spirit that they have, the way they treat each other. It's incredible. Ninety-eight percent of the courses that come back are out of their minds because they're, like, 'Oh my gosh!' Those things? That's why I'm still here. It changes people's lives. That's the simplicity of a NOLS course."

Kevin McGowan fitting boots in the Lumberyard.
NOLS Archives

Board Matters

To comprehend the board's role in the early history of NOLS, it helps to go back to the start. The first NOLS Board, formed in January 1965, consisted of a group of eight personal friends and influential people that Paul and Jack Nicholas felt could help promote the school, such as Petzoldt's mountain guide concession partner, Glenn Exum. Although most of the first board members were from elsewhere, three—Nicholas, E.J. Breece, and Dr. Bill Erickson—gave local legs to the new idea of NOLS. Many other Lander people gave crucial support to the school as well, but Breece's commitment was both nota-

ble and long-standing (he was on the board through 1977). Not only was he Dottie Petzoldt's brother-in-law and co-owner with her of the local radio station, but he also became a political powerhouse in Wyoming, serving under several governors and as chair of the Wyoming House Ways and Means Committee. As Jack Nicholas said in 2015, "You need to realize how much a new undertaking like NOLS importing dozens of unshaven long-haired young people to a small western town would be received without the unspoken natural assurances that accompany the active participation of a prominent recognized 'town father' such as Ed."

Board composition fluctuated over time—normal for any start-up moving from its pioneering days toward maturity. In 1966, after the school started offering college credit, board representation broadened to include academics: Robert Boles from Kansas State Teachers College; Joseph Pease from Fort Lewis College in Durango, Colorado; and John Walker from the University of Wyoming. Then came the stutter-start of altering the school's legal structure in 1970, which caused some resignations. Despite reestablishing nonprofit status later that year, enthusiasm for board positions dwindled, especially as tightening finances led to waning goodwill to continue donating money to the school.

By 1974, the board consisted mostly of friends and members of Dottie's family. Until the IRS raised the alarm about

Tyrolean traverse. *NOLS Archives*

the school's financial situation that year, the board had generally given Petzoldt free rein with the affairs of the school while they supported him from the background. However, the threat of IRS involvement led the board to sit up, take notice, and start asking questions—actions that one source described Petzoldt as saying were "uppity." And then he had the lack of foresight to suggest that his new wife—Dottie's

successor—have a role at NOLS. For his part, Petzoldt often later reflected how he rued the decision to set up the school as a nonprofit that would make him beholden to the dictates and constraints of a board of directors.

Few, if any, of the young instructor corps would have known that nonprofit corporations such as NOLS are technically governed by their boards of trustees, and that executive directors serve at the pleasure of the board. Pet-zoldt had never seemed subordinate to anyone, so it's no wonder the NOLS Board had operated off to the side for most of its history until then—and why his firing was such a jolt to Petzoldt's troops.

Another jolt came in February 1978, when Petzoldt was fired again, this time for good. Petzoldt, in violation of the 1975 agreement that had named him senior advisor, cashed for himself a $1,700 royalty check made out to NOLS without authorization. The board used the action as cause for dismissal. There was no repeat of the firestorm of 1975, but it was a terribly difficult time for those close to it, especially for Simer, who was still unwilling to revisit those days in 2015. Former instructor Neil Short, by then an attorney and a member of the board, penned a statement on February 2 tendering his resignation from the board. He was, he wrote, "unalterably opposed to modifying or terminating Paul Pet-zoldt's contract." There followed four pages summarizing the greatness of the man's vision and accomplishments, and how perhaps others—including the board—were "fattened and strengthened from living off Paul's power" and then failed to help him with his weaknesses regarding monetary matters. "I don't care what he has done," wrote Short. "The fault lies at the feet of everyone, including myself, who came in contact with Paul and neglected to give counsel."

In coming months, the wound festered, as shown in a board conference call on October 19, 1978. The board was considering their options regarding what they perceived as unfair business practices by Petzoldt in the aftermath of his departure. Despite a non-compete clause, Petzoldt was reportedly setting up several new organizations, one called the Wilderness Youth Education Association. Petzoldt also appeared to be bad-mouthing NOLS (an Idaho newspaper quoted him as saying, "NOLS was doing a fair job but not good enough"). Disparaging comments he made at the Outdoor Education Assembly in Indiana were also cited. Possible damages to NOLS were discussed, and a motion to prepare a lawsuit was approved. (The suit was never brought.)

By then, a big shift in board dynamics was in the air. In August 1977, a 37-year-old man named Homer Luther from Houston, Texas, took a 30-day mountaineering course in the Winds. He was by far the oldest student on his course and already an avid climber in Arizona, the Tetons, and Yosemite. He came to NOLS because he heard it was the place to learn how to do big mountains (he completed two more NOLS courses within the year: Advanced Winter Mountaineering and Denali).

A successful and well-connected businessman with years in the political swirl of Washington, DC, Luther had served on diplomatic missions to over 25 countries (including China and Russia) under presidents Nixon and Ford. In addition, he had a background of serving on nonprofit boards, mostly related to the outdoors and wilderness, and for a private school.

Luther's course leader, Dave Hubbard, knew enough about Luther's background by the time they returned to Lander to go speak with Peter Simer. As Luther and his coursemates were hanging out in the lobby of the Noble Hotel after dinner, Hubbard approached with Simer at his side. Simer got right to the point: Would Luther consider joining the NOLS Board of Trustees?

He would. Luther was voted onto the NOLS Board at the December 2, 1978, meeting, when, as it turned out, John Walker resigned his position after nine of the school's most tumultuous years.

By then, Simer was frustrated by his relations with some members of the board, and Luther quickly discovered that the group wasn't functioning the way an effective board could or should. He was the only person from well beyond the world of Lander, Wyoming. It was, he mused, like arriving on an island. "The school in those days was tiny," said Luther, "and I knew nothing about the existing relationships or allegiances."

Quietly, the two men began to strategize ways to craft a new board consisting of people with specialties—finance, business, law, insurance, medicine, and such—whose expertise would be helpful to the school. Despite the work on the debt Simer had already begun, Luther said, "It was clear the school in all fairness was in bankruptcy and just didn't know it." The real costs of courses had never been figured out, so despite improved enrollment, the school was still actually losing money. They had a brochure for marketing, he said, "but it wasn't much. No one was familiar with the importance of that sort of thing. And we needed someone strong financially to meet with the banks and make this thing work."

Luther began to recruit some fresh faces by tapping friends and business associates. Joining the board in December 1979 were Charles "Reb" Gregg (a Houston lawyer), Mike Raoul-Duval (from Washington, DC, with helpful governmental connections), Bob Hoffman (a financial expert from Chicago and colleague from Luther's Harvard Business School days), and Bob Stewart (a Houston physician). Others with different specialties followed in the years to come.

At the time, and Bob Hoffman was the Chief Financial Officer of FMC Corporation, one of the 100 largest corporations in America. He discerned that the three most obvious and immediate problems facing the school were that liabilities far exceeded assets, that the school was in arrears with its SBA loan on the increasingly shabby and rundown Noble Hotel, and that the equipment—all of it, ropes, tents, backpacks, vehicles—was dangerous and in desperate need of repair or replacement. "When you looked at transportation," he said, "it was scary. Those things were waiting for an accident to happen."

The specter of risk was all too real: In July 1979, 22-year-old student Matt Strominger had died after falling about 400 feet while unroped on third-class terrain during an ascent of Sloan Peak in the North Cascades. The tragedy was the seventh fatality in the school's history. Although the investigation of the incident found no negligence on the part of NOLS, the board was anxious to begin addressing more deeply the various issues surrounding safety.

On his second trip to Lander, Hoffman walked across the street from the Noble Hotel to meet Tom Davey, president of Central Bank & Trust, which held the school's $197,000 SBA loan and other debts. He introduced himself, presented his credentials, and laid out a plan. Whether foreclosure had been threatened is unclear, but certainly the bank had every right to be considering it, given the situation. That, said Hoffman, would simply put the school out of business, and the bank would then have an empty, dilapidated hotel on its hands. Instead, he asked for forbearance to give the new board time to rebuild the school's financial outlook. Davey agreed.

An early NOLS bus in its natural habitat. *NOLS Archives*

"It was major," said Hoffman. "We still had to do the job, but now we had some time. Nothing was put into writing . . . but we had his word that he wouldn't pull the plug, and he had my word that we'd get this thing fixed." By the end of 1980, the bank's gamble worked out and the loan was paid off, according to Simer.

The arrival of Luther and his team meant that "you finally had people who got what being a board member meant," Simer said. "Without Homer, we wouldn't have been able to start the process of having really good board members who were useful for donations, for leadership, for setting strategy—all the things the board does now." But the changes didn't come without a cost. The old-guard members of the board saw the new faces at the table, and meshing the two worlds did not happen without friction.

"When we went on the board and the school's problems became apparent," said Hoffman, "they felt we were accusing them of doing a bad job. We weren't trying to do that. It's just that their skill set was not what was needed. They were not bad guys. They were honest, and wanted to do the right thing—but the problem was that none of them was really a sophisticated businessman who understood the challenges and objectives you have to have if you are going to run a growing nonprofit company."

Over time, Luther said, "Other members began to feel we were taking control." In fact, that was the plan, he said, "Eventually, we had to get control." There followed several challenging meetings as people took sides. Things finally came to a head in late 1981, and after some boardroom drama resembling "the showdown at the OK Corral," according to Hoffman, enough new members were seated on the board that the balance of power finally tilted to Luther and his group.

Fresh Wyoming powder.
Tony Jewell

The Administrative Team Settles In

WHILE THE NOLS BOARD was sorting itself out, Simer continued to run the school. He knew he couldn't do it alone, so he surrounded himself with a great team. At the start, he had help from Dave Slovisky, Kevin Hildebrandt, Rob Clarke, Dave Gipe, Willy Cunningham, and others. "I'm not claiming all the credit—and Paul wouldn't either—but heads of organizations create the teams they surround themselves with, and that's a big part of leadership," said Simer in 2015. "I'm not claiming to have done everything right. But I got my team right."

But it was a fluid administration. Department responsibilities and titles changed, people came and went, roles shifted. The backcountry pulled some of them back into the field instructing; for others, graduate school beckoned. Things morphed. In the second half of Simer's eight years at the helm, for example, Steve Gipe did course planning through 1983, then left. Molly Hampton was hired to plan routes for the Wyoming branch until Drew Leemon took on the job in January 1985. Molly moved over to work on permitting and access issues, but then eventually shifted to staffing/HR when Linda Ellis resigned. Leemon moved into running the program department, and so it went. Many have held numerous positions in the school over time—too many to allow easy tracking of their trajectories.

When he started in 1975, Simer also had complete responsibility for the various school locations in addition to general administration. "I picked great branch directors, gave them broad strategies, and I didn't interfere," said Simer. "They fulfilled the broad strategy we had. The board wanted to shut down Africa, so I sent Mary Jo and George [Newbury] to make it a break-even proposition, so that's what George did. I had little to do with the actual decisions in Africa, but by picking George and giving him the challenge and knowing he could do it, I knew Africa was safe." In addition, Simer selected Jim Ratz to go to Alaska as branch director, and Wes Kraus to try to clean things up in the Cascades. "Up until then, the Cascades was the hippie commune of NOLS," he chuckled.

Beyond the well-founded school departments such as course planning, staffing, and transportation, Simer's administrative team also needed to begin placing emphasis on marketing and communications. He asked an old college buddy, John Sullivan, to come from Los Angeles to Lander in 1978. "I always had done communication/PR/marketing, writing-based work. He couldn't pay me, but he asked, if he flew me up and gave me a free course, would I take a look at their marketing efforts and write a brochure or report," said Sullivan.

One of Sullivan's legacies is the school's logo, which remained in use through 2015. "I was 31 years old, and had never been camping," he said. "It was a whole new world—a great experience." After getting a feel for the school on his NOLS course, Sullivan sketched out a logo idea and sent it to a friend in Los Angeles, graphic designer Jack Marquette. Marquette brought the familiar rectangle with the sun rising from behind a stylized mountain to life. The reinvented look of NOLS served to separate the post-Petzoldt school from the school's original blue and white triangular logo showing a series of sharp mountain peaks with the word "NOLS" superimposed, and also from the smaller red, white, and blue

NOLS logos over the years. *NOLS Archives*

shield found on the earliest NOLS garments.

Sullivan also co-wrote with Simer the first edition of *The National Outdoor Leadership School's Complete Wilderness Guide*. Intended to present the basic NOLS curriculum to general readers, the book was published in 1983 and later updated by Mark Harvey in 1999.

In those lean years, Simer looked for savings wherever he could. He had discovered the welcome news that non-profit groups did not have to pay property taxes. The county assessor objected, Simer said, and they ended up at the Wyoming Supreme Court. The court ruled in favor of NOLS, and the county, reportedly piqued by the loss, pointed out that according to the law, only public school buses could use the yellow and black livery. So the NOLS buses went from school bus yellow to green.

It was at his very first meeting, in December 1978, that Homer Luther made a motion to change the title of the NOLS "Board of Directors" to "Board of Trustees." The motion passed. It was also at that meeting that Simer's team produced at least two reports investigating where to place their energies as the school moved forward. Sullivan had drafted "An Initial Analysis of the Communication Needs of the National Outdoor Leadership School." The 16-page report analyzed current challenges, noting that the school lacked external communication in the form of public relations and other outreach efforts. NOLS had a "fuzzy" image nationally, and what little existed was still enmeshed with the powerful persona of Petzoldt. If people had heard of NOLS at all, they often remarked, "Oh, you're like Outward Bound."

The report also noted that communication with NOLS alumni (and their parents) was sorely lacking, and that while the emerging advent of wilderness studies as an academic field had positioned NOLS superbly, the school had not yet leveraged that position.

The report identified specific goals:

1. To establish NOLS as the nation's most respected educator of wilderness leaders.
2. To establish NOLS as the nation's major source for improved minimum impact techniques and personal wilderness ethics.
3. To establish the new management team as well as the NOLS instructor core [sic] as competent, experienced, and well able to develop the aggressive and forward looking program of the school.
4. To gain a much clearer and more comprehensive indepth [sic] understanding of NOLS among the more sophisticated and influential members of the national academic wilderness community.

The report concluded with several recommendations. One was to seek improved publicity and press relations beyond a history of occasional, usually unsolicited articles in magazines and newspapers. It also called for an effort to spread improved understanding about NOLS through greater local involvement in Lander and at the branch locations.

Simer's recent membership in Lander's Rotary Club was cited as an example of a step in the right direction.

The final recommendation was to develop support from the NOLS alumni community—a significant departure from past practices. Simer had sent a plea out to alumni in 1977, but in general there was a hands-off attitude toward graduates—the result of Petzoldt's insistence that graduates be well-enough trained that they should never need to come back to NOLS. Improved alumni relations and outreach were initiated in the spring of 1979, beginning with a letter: "Dear Graduate: NOLS wants to be a continuing part of the educational process in your life . . ."

Until this time, graduates had rarely been wooed by NOLS. An alumni fund had been established in 1971, but that year it brought in just $304. There was much room for improvement. An early element in the alumni outreach program was the introduction of two-week "special skills seminars" for NOLS graduates on such topics as wilderness photography, fly fishing, climbing, and caving.

———————

Another report to the board was drafted by Rob Clarke. Its purpose was to scrutinize the possibility of decentralizing NOLS in the manner of the Outward Bound system.

The growth model at Outward Bound had created totally separate schools with different administrators and boards of directors, resulting in system-wide duplication of overhead that ultimately became financially overwhelming. In addition, the different OB schools essentially became like franchises that were competing for the same student base, and that could provide little ability for staff to move laterally within their system. The NOLS Board decided to retain the NOLS structure with a centralized administration. Over time, this model proved its worth financially and systemically for NOLS by creating a strong base of consistency in staff hiring, training, core curriculum, public relations and outreach, risk management, purchases, vehicle procurement, and more. And since NOLS has just one central staffing office, instructors who want variety can easily teach in different locations for NOLS.

The school's basic survival seemed relatively assured by about 1980. For the administrative team, according to Simer, the biggest remaining challenges became improving the quality of the curriculum and instructor life. That meant examining procedures and formulating policies, and beginning the process of professionalizing NOLS.

Developing a business model approach to the school's forward progress wasn't always popular. By 1979, there were some 157 NOLS instructors (140 in summer and 35 in winter, with some of them working both seasons). The average age of a NOLS instructor was mid-20s, with a range of 19 to 39. While they opposed formal curriculum standards and policies, the instructors themselves had always demanded very high instructional standards among their own ranks, a culture of excellence that had persisted even during the Poverty Era when the school had few resources to put toward instructor development. The instructor course curriculum had grown into an intensive four weeks, including a climbing section, and the winter instructor course was two weeks long, including a three-day avalanche seminar with the American Avalanche Institute in Jackson.

Some of the changes, though resisted, eventually became unquestioned, such as wearing a helmet while rock climbing. As other safety measures were put in place across the school, it wasn't hard to understand the need, but it was sometimes a challenge to alter the habits of people unaccustomed to such rules. In addition, instructor evaluations were instituted and, as of 1978, instructors were required to have first-aid certification (although it wasn't until 1983 that it had to be current).

Experiments in course design were encouraged. In June 1976, Paul Link and Bruce Barrus led a traditional backpacking course with an added focus on geology. That same summer the first all-female course—both instructors and students—was run in the North Cascades.

Bruce Barrus, who taught geology clinics on some 1970s courses.
NOLS Archives

Don, Donna, and Ryan Ford. *NOLS Archives*

Another instructional experiment was to bring in various experts who could provide focused instruction in specific skills. For example, Don Peterson, a respected climber and former NOLS instructor, would go out and meet up with different courses, then provide "super rock-climbing classes," as they were known, to courses. A similar initiative was done for fly fishing by expert Robby Garrett. Bruce Barrus joined various courses in 1977 to do a day-long clinic on canyon geology. It was a cost-effective way, said Simer, "to strengthen the program without having to make some of the financial commitments we'd have to do otherwise."

In addition, some of the historical precedent of hiring only NOLS-trained instructors started to erode. An instructor exchange program with Outward Bound was pilot-tested in 1978, an initiative that hinged on love: Don Ford, who had been with Outward Bound Minnesota since 1975, met Donna Dick, who had worked for NOLS since 1976. He contacted the directors of both institutions, and both Simer and OB director Derek Pichard agreed to allow an instructor exchange. In August 1978, Ford participated in the NOLS instructor course, and NOLS instructors Willy Cunningham and Eric Hosek did a staff training trip with OB Minnesota. By about 1981, it became more accepted for outsiders with strong outdoor resumes to take the NOLS instructor course.

Shifts in NOLS Culture

Maybe it was the changing times, or maybe it was that the school was emerging from its pioneering days, but some of the more questionable behaviors common at the school began to slow down in the late 1970s. Still, antics were tolerated, as long as they weren't totally irresponsible or dangerous. As always, they have to be viewed within the context of their times or, as Hamren put it, "what is considered safe and appropriate evolves with the times."

But social mores were still far different than they would become in future decades. The 1975 board resolution disallowing nude bathing aside, there was still plenty of skinny-dipping in lakes. Getting naked was widely regarded as okay, a fun and natural thing. Saunas were frequently constructed and enjoyed. The sexual "revolution" was under way, and it was a time when birth control was readily available and AIDS wasn't yet an issue. With the average age of staff and students roughly college age, NOLS was similar to most US college campuses, where some couples formed and had casual relationships, some met their soul mates and lived happily ever after, and most just went about their business without hooking up with anyone.

Likewise, alcohol use was viewed differently. The legal drinking age in Wyoming was 18 until July 1988, when it became the last of the 50 states to raise its drinking age to 21. With 18-year-olds being able to drink legally, alcohol-fueled parties at the completion of courses were the norm. And despite the limitations of very heavy packs, taking some alcohol on courses was still fairly typical—though having good judgment about drinking was expected as much as with other activities such as rock climbing. (In May 1976, Simer expelled seven semester course students from the spring semester course. In his report to the board he wrote, "These students after celebrating a birthday party had returned to the mountains and climbing practice. They were discovered by Jim Huntley to be drunk while they were climbing. Due to this misconduct they were dropped from the course.")

By the early 1980s, efforts to slow the unfettered use of alcohol were increasing, according to one source, but drinking was still done with a bit of a wink. When supplies of beer at a spring climbing camp in 1981 were excessive, though,

Rob Hellyer's dog, Yogi, on a Tyrolean traverse from *Thirty Days to Survival*. *NOLS Archives*

the administration started to push back harder. It took until 1986 for the practice of imbibing on courses to become clearly unacceptable.

In the school's early days, even dogs went on courses, famously including Rob Hellyer's German Shepherd/lab mix, Yogi, who is shown harnessed into the Tyrolean traverse in *Thirty Days to Survival*. Unfortunately, Bruce Hampton's border collie dog, Spreck, was surprised when Petzoldt appeared suddenly at dusk to visit a course, and bit him on the leg. When George Hunker tried to suggest the blood was from a thorn bush, Hampton remembered, Petzoldt said,

"George Hunker, I've been a mountaineer for 65 years and I know a goddam thorn bush from a dog!" The edict came down the following week: no more dogs on courses.

If behavior in the backcountry could get raucous, it was worse in town once the responsibility for students was off the shoulders of the instructors. The itinerant life of an instructor inevitably led to communal housing, with people constantly coming and going. In the early 1970s, groups of up to 20 people might be staying at the various houses in Lander that owners dared rent to NOLSies—the Cliff Dwelling, the Wash Shack (on Washakie Street), Big Pink over on Lincoln, and the Barrus Mansion. Everyone kicked in a few dollars for rent (totaling $50 or $75 a month).

Once the third floor of the Noble Hotel became available as in-town housing for instructors in the early 1980s, other antics ensued. In the depths of the winter of 1981-82, severe cabin fever set off the Noble Hotel Wars. At the time, there wasn't much winter work, and for several nights a week for several weeks ("until the cease and desist orders came down," said Herbie Ogden), a dozen or more cooped-up mountaineers divided into teams after beers. Then they waged guerilla warfare throughout the hotel—in the rooms, the fire escapes, elevators, elevator shaft—using dart guns and soft pellet guns. According to Ogden, "When you got hit, you went to the lobby and drank more beer."

NOLS TETON VALLEY

Backcountry ski-touring in Grand Teton National Park.
Jared Steinman

As conscientious objectors to the Vietnam War, Tom Warren, Geno Forsyth, Haven Holsapple, and Dave Polito were required by the draft board to demonstrate gainful employment. NOLS counted as an "approved" employer since it was a nonprofit, so in the fall of 1971, Petzoldt sent the men to build a bunkhouse and later a lodge on some lots he owned in a subdivision called Targhee Town, just outside Alta, Wyoming, on the west side of the Tetons.

The NOLS winter program in the Tetons began there in November 1972, once Geoff Heath had proven the feasibility of ski mountaineering courses in the Winds during the prior two winters. Tom and Dorothy Warren served as managers and hosts in Alta for the next several years. When the lodge was finished in late 1974, room rates for NOLS grads were $2 a night ($3 for non-NOLS visitors), plus $1 for breakfast or lunch and $2 for dinner. By the 1973-74 season, there was enough interest to schedule five Teton Winter Mountaineering courses.

When Petzoldt was ousted in the summer of 1975, he held onto his property and the lodge. Without a local base, the school started trucking winter courses into the Tetons from Lander. Petzoldt ultimately gave the lodge to his longtime friend and former Noble Hotel barkeep, Pete Petersen.

Thirteen years later, in 1988, Tony Jewell arrived to start a new base in Teton Valley, and was surprised when an old-timer told him about the lodge. The years of bussing back and forth from Lander and the chaos that followed Paul's ouster had wiped out institutional memory of the lodge and bunkhouse. "No one at NOLS Wyoming told me about it . . . We thought we

Winter courses offer unique opportunities for building the perfect camp. *Lindsay Yost; Matt Burke*

were starting something new," recalled Jewell. He operated the winter base as a satellite location for the Wyoming branch (as it was then called) out of a leased building at Cottonwood Corner, on the south side of Driggs, Idaho. It operated seasonally, with courses running over Christmas and wrapping up in March. Courses explored the west side of the Tetons, but more commonly headed for the Wyoming Range and Absarokas, or the Snake River Range for outdoor educator courses.

The old train depot in Victor—frequented over several winters in the 1930s by Petzoldt and his first wife—became the NOLS winter base in 1991. In 1993, the school purchased an old Mormon church with five acres at the head of Darby Canyon, between Victor and Driggs. Most recently the building had housed a Jazzercise studio, but when NOLS moved in, it had been vacant for years. The new manager, Ben Hammond, remodeled the church and built a barn for storage. In 2013 the school purchased an adjoining farm with 10 acres plus a giant barn and a mobile home that were turned into raft/vehicle storage and staff housing, respectively.

In September 1999 the base was formally renamed NOLS Teton Valley, but everyone at NOLS called it "the TVB." By that time, telemark skiing was the rage, and the school moved away from winter mountaineering toward pure backcountry skiing and winter camping.

By 2015, Teton Valley was busy most of the year, according to branch director Abby Warner, who stepped into the role in 2002. The bulk of the branch activity in summer was "Adventure" hiking and rafting courses geared to 14- and 15-year-olds, and supporting rafting and climbing sections of Rocky Mountain semesters. In winter the focus shifted to backcountry ski and snowboard courses for older students.

And, said Warner, "we're the biggest branch for seminars on winter skills and river skills. We run a third of all seminars for teaching instructors skills."

The TVB also supports the school's Salmon River program. The Salmon is the longest free-flowing river in the continental United States and has been protected since the signing of the Wild and Scenic River Act in 1968. "The Salmon is the quintessential venue to witness the 'multiple use doctrine' in practice," said river program supervisor Rick Richter. "On this canvas, instructors share lessons ranging from fire ecology, endangered salmon habitat, free-flowing versus dam-controlled rivers, and introducing students to the art of compromise that build a community to support land protection and preservation."

Continued Richter, "All of this occurs in a rigorous technical environment as students decipher the art of river running, acquiring an eye for the construct of a river drainage, its rapids, its features, its never-ending dynamic nature, which rises and falls with snow melt and precipitation. The unobstructed river will continue to provide a classroom unique within the school's operating areas."

Canoeing on the Salmon River. *Adam Swisher*

The Noble Hotel Wars crew. *Herb Ogden*

The caving instructors discovered the fun of exploring the air ducts, sometimes emerging in the staffing office, where it wasn't unheard of to alter course assignments. One night, Kevin Hildebrandt, who was doing staffing at the time, walked into his office at 10 p.m. and reportedly found one of his friends sitting at his desk making long-distance calls.

Then there was the time Steve Lawrence's birthday cake was wheeled into the party on a projector stand with a note that said, "Hope you get a bang out of this." Then the cake exploded, the two M-80s (equivalent to a half stick of dynamite) triggered remotely. Cake and frosting splattered everything and everybody. Very luckily, no one was hurt, although the projector stand was permanently bent and

frosting blobs decorated the ceiling light fixtures for years.

In those days, the elevator at the Noble did not function. Although the common story was that it was broken (and had been for years), another version from a well-placed source says it was purposely disabled when elevator surfing was at its height of popularity.

"The stuffed marlin [that was mounted on the wall] was often found in someone's bed, before they solved that problem and shipped it to Mexico," remembered Drew Leemon. When the Coke machine disappeared, the manager of the Noble Hotel, Frank Berch, looked everywhere in the hotel and around Lander, eventually involving the police. Finally, a cryptic note appeared on his desk: "It's in the elevator"— and there it was, in the defunct elevator.

And who could forget the coneheads? Dan Aykroyd, Jane Curtin, and others on the cast of *Saturday Night Live* brought their highly popular comedy sketch "The Coneheads" to life in January 1977, and it swept popular culture even as far as Lander. Simer was having dinner one night in 1978 or 1979 when a local lawyer called. "I understand a bunch of your people just got arrested," he said. "Want me to bail them out?" As it turned out, a group of instructors, feeling silly (and perhaps not completely sober) had been walking up Main Street when they saw a bunch of traffic safety cones, put them on their heads, and passed the police station with enough vigor to get themselves arrested. Simer had them bailed out, and then had a chat with all the coneheads the following day.

Some of the best antics, however, occurred as backlash to well-intentioned efforts by Berch to clean up and professionalize the image of the Noble Hotel. He (somewhat bravely) said he was going to "modify behavior, lay down the rules," said Dave Kallgren, but soon discovered that the idea was very much at odds with the interests of the restless instructors.

"Frank Berch was beside himself over what to do," remembered Ogden. "He was telling Simer he never wanted us to work again, he wanted us thrown out . . . it was a little 'us versus Frank.'" The group tried to settle down, he said, but couldn't. Instead, Berch's efforts spawned pink flamingos.

Karl Weller is credited with finding them at the hardware store in Lander, and suddenly pink flamingos started showing up in NOLS offices, hotel bathrooms, on the roof of the Noble, and on lawns throughout Lander. They were everywhere. Those that were removed were replaced. One instructor climbed the 20-foot vent pipe for the plumbing system outside the hotel, stuffed the feet of a plastic flamingo through a straw hat for a nest, and put a drywall anchor on its leg so it couldn't be pulled up out of the pipe. It wasn't removed for years.

Soon, there was a T-shirt sporting a pink flamingo with the word "modification" streaming off the back of its head, mocking the concept of reining in the fun. Everyone seemed to have one. A flamingo painting hung in the lobby of the

The Pink Flamingo goes to Alaska. *Herb Ogden*

hotel. Even the course catalog the following year had a flamingo on it. A pink flamingo was fastened on the front grill of the NOLS equipment bus to Denali for the trip up the Alcan Highway, and went to the summit wearing glacier glasses and zinc oxide, according to Ogden. In 2015 the pink flamingo still enjoyed an honored role as the NIA's official mascot.

Over time, more and more NOLS folks gained reliable year-round employment, and lifestyles began to change. People started getting married, having kids, settling in. The concept was a shock to many people who had lived with the Petzoldt-infused idea that they shouldn't rely on NOLS for a career.

Tod Schimelpfenig was working in the issue room and doing field work when his first son arrived in 1977. A second son arrived a few years later. Being a father with kids to raise, he said, separated him from the mainsteam NOLS employees of the era. "I remember people saying flat out a career with NOLS and having a family were incompatible," he said. "Instructors without kids thought you were contagious."

Before long, many others transitioned to the world of parenthood and the increased responsibility it represents. The first of Peter and Cyndy Simer's three children arrived in 1981, and many other NOLS kids were also soon born: Cunningham, Hunker, Lindsey, Ratz, McGowen, Shoutis. There were mortgages to qualify for, banking and other services to support, elections and health care to worry about. For some, there were faith communities to join. Sports pro-

grams began to evolve, including a vigorous swimming program and Nordic skiing.

As parents increasingly found themselves holding little hands and taking their children to preschool, then elementary and middle and high school, NOLS families discovered a sense of belonging. Many others settled in or near Lander after leaving regular involvement with NOLS even if they didn't have a family to raise. In addition, people born in Lander took jobs at the school and developed a sense of belonging there; by 2015 many members of old Lander families had worked for the school for decades in various capacities. Not only were emotional ties built, but the NOLS community was also a financial hedge against the downturn in the 1980s, when the mine closed and other economic woes beset Lander and the surrounding area.

Simer's Legacy

In 1983, Simer had been executive director for eight long, hard years. He was ready to begin a new phase in his life. On May 10, he resigned his position.

"I left because I had done what I wanted to do," he said in 2015. "I wanted to do other things. I'd originally planned to be director for five years, and I'd been director for eight." He headed for Stanford Business School that fall. Others were likewise ready for a change (for example, Jon Hamren and Randy Cerf both went to Stanford, Ben Toland to Yale and

Instructors and students play cricket in India. *Nick Storm*

Stanford, and Herb Ogden to University of Pennsylvania Medical School). The exodus at the end of the Simer years was the second wave of instructor departures the school had experienced, and it would not be the last. Often, changes in leadership are simply the outward sign of more fundamental shifts in organizations like NOLS, a natural turn in the ebb and flow of human institutions.

During Simer's watch, the school found better financial footing than anyone could have dared hope. The branches were strong. Alumni relations were beginning to evolve. Simer had a knack for picking the right people for the right jobs. From his point of view, "The three greatest accomplishments in my tenure are 1) paying off the debt and keeping [the school] alive, 2) creating a professional staff who could work year-round, and 3) changing the board."

Luther agreed in 2015, saying, "Peter Simer deserves great and special recognition for the work he did, for his vision and his successful effort in keeping the NOLS family and its board working together. He did a great job. Think about it. He was a kid on an island with tension from the Petzoldt episode still very fresh. But we connected and he did a great job of keeping it all together."

Instructor Pablo Miranda teaches rappelling class.
Jared Steinman

THINGS SETTLE DOWN

I first came into contact with NOLS in 1988 when I was hitchhiking in Botswana. Jim Chisholm and Molly Doran were in the vehicle that picked me up—they were on a scouting trip for NOLS Kenya.

– Jon Kempsey, instructor

Jim Ratz arrived in Lander to begin serving as the school's fourth executive director in March 1984. A 10-month gap between executive directors had been filled by interim director Charley Fiala, who was Simer's assistant director during his final year, enabling the board to conduct a more deliberate search for good candidates than when Simer was hired. After careful consideration, they gave the nod to Ratz.

Most recently, Ratz had been branch director in Alaska. The board was impressed with his management there, where a highlight achievement was building a permanent home base for the branch in Palmer, which was dedicated in August 1983.

Ratz had been with NOLS since 1970. He was best known as a caver and rock climber, and had joined instructors Scott Fischer, Peter Simer, and Taylor Lumia and board member Homer Luther in 1975 for a climbing competition in the Caucasus Mountains behind the Iron Curtain. Ratz would need his organizational skills from the Alaska branch, as well as the courage from caving and the tenacity of rock climbing to lead NOLS during the upcoming decade.

Within days of taking his seat at the director's desk at the Noble Hotel, Ratz wrote a letter to none other than Paul Petzoldt. It was so soon after his arrival that the NOLS letterhead still listed Peter Simer as executive director. Dated April 10, 1984, it reads:

I'm sure you don't remember me, but I was a student in 1970 . . . There are a lot of new faces around NOLS and there are few of us left who remember NOLS when you were director. Nevertheless, your influence here is still very strong, and thanks to your visionary thinking, the

School's philosophy rings as true today as it did 20 years ago. We owe you a tremendous debt of gratitude for that.

... I hope that it is not too late to regard you as a friend and ally of NOLS. Many of our instructors have not had the benefit of hearing you speak, nor do they fully appreciate your central role in the founding of NOLS. I would like to explore the possibilities of correcting this regrettable situation.

If you have the time, I would very much like to visit with you and get reacquainted.

"Jim [believed that] Paul needed to be brought back into the school, as well as other people," said Molly Doran, a longtime instructor. "He realized that to move forward, we needed to do that."

It was time to acknowledge and embrace the school's past. Petzoldt did, indeed, return to NOLS in late August 1985, for the school's 20th anniversary party, the first time the school had hosted such a formal gathering. The celebration was dubbed "20/20 Vision" both to look back over the school's first 20 years and also to scan the horizon to try and see what the future might bring. The keynote speaker for the 300 attendees was Dick Cheney, then Wyoming's lone con-

Jim Ratz and Paul Petzoldt. *NOLS Archives*

gressman (later, the 46th US vice president), speaking on the topic of acid rain. Paul Petzoldt gave "an anecdote-filled speech which brought back many nostalgic memories for many instructors," according to *The Leader*.

"When Jim brought Paul back to the 20th anniversary in 1985, while that was only a first step, it was a *big* one," said John Gans, who became an instructor in 1981. Although

NOLS TENNESSEE

"There is a school in the Upper Cumberland which uses 37,000 acres of genuine wilderness for a classroom. The daily luncheon menu for this school has been known to include copperhead snakes and jewel-weed salad," wrote Joe Farris for the Cookeville, Tennessee, *Herald-Citizen* in July 1972. The school was NOLS.

Shortly after *Thirty Days to Survival* aired in 1970, Harold Sims called Paul Petzoldt. Sims wanted Petzoldt to know of some great caving opportunities near where he lived in Tennessee. His son, Jeff, was a very good caver, and was familiar with the area.

Caving was already on Haven Holsapple's radar in 1969, when he wrote a proposal titled "The NOLS Speleological Expedition," hoping to see caving included in the NOLS curriculum. Sims's call was the nudge Petzoldt needed to send Ken Clanton to scout the area in early 1971, and Holsapple joined him there later that spring.

The first course, with Holsapple and Jeff Sims instructing (Clanton had gone to the first Denali climb), started June 7, 1971. "Jeff was instrumental," said Holsapple. "He and I developed the whole program and explored the caves together. The first course, we only had two students, which was terrific, because we got time to explore things and figure out how the course would run."

A second course that summer was larger, and in 1972 the two courses were filled. In addition to caving and cave biology, the students learned the usual NOLS outdoors skills and leadership curriculum, ending with a four-day, 50-mile aboveground "survival" experience: walking back to base camp over the rugged Cumberland plateau mountains and forests of central Tennessee.

The courses were offered through cooperation with Tennessee Technological University, which chose to end the partnership after the second season, effectively bringing NOLS Tennessee to an end.

1970s NOLS caving group, with some equipment no longer carried on courses. *NOLS Archives*

it took another few years to formally bestow the title of "founder and president emeritus" on Paul, "it was clear that in that beautiful summer evening in Sinks Canyon in 1985, when Paul engaged with the NOLS community, there was no turning back," he said. "Paul was back . . . For new staff it was a chance to meet an icon. We didn't know all the history, but it was neat to shake his hand and hear Paul stories. So while the rift didn't instantly get fixed in '85, it was clearly going to be fixed."

Systems and Processes

Ratz had a different style than Simer. He was generally well liked and widely acknowledged as a creative visionary, though he was not always an easy person to work for, according to various sources. Described as an introvert, Ratz "didn't really like to public speak and was not a gregarious back-slapper," said Rich Brame, who spent several years in the outreach department under Ratz. "He was a smart guy with big field experience, a thinker. He was bright and he could see out to the future, and wanted to take us on some pathways."

Priorities for Ratz included improving administrative systems and processes, providing better support for instructors, focusing on matters of curriculum and safety, building upon the longtime NOLS value on conservation, and delving further into improving alumni relations.

First, he needed to build his team. Administrative structure at the growing school was in flux. Titles were shifting, as were the responsibilities captured by those shifting roles. The goal was to create a logical, manageable administrative flow, since many jobs were being either invented or redefined in scope and mission. NOLS was by then running dozens of courses in a variety of skill types throughout the Rocky Mountain region, Alaska, Baja California, Kenya, and the Pacific Northwest. This required amped-up infrastructure for student intake, course planning, permitting, staffing, transportation, rations, and outfitting. The difference was an evolving matter of scale. There were 157 instructors in 1979. In the 10 years from 1986 to 1996, NOLS more than doubled in size from 181 instructors to 375 (and from 65,000 to 131,000 annual program days).

One benefit when he came into his position was that Ratz had someone to handle the crucial job of staffing; by then, the school had reached a size too large for the executive director to handle that level of detail. For his first two years, Linda Ellis was staff director. Ratz recognized, too, the folly of attempting to manage the daily operations of the Wyoming branch as his predecessors had done, even though it was right there in town. He hired Dave Neary in May 1984 to return to NOLS as the Wyoming branch director, and he also recruited Molly Hampton to work at the branch doing

Kenya offered a wholly different experience to the NOLS of Wyoming. *NOLS Archives*

route planning, relations with government agencies, and permitting. Both were returning faces to NOLS. Neary had spent eight years with NOLS before leaving in 1979. Hampton had come to NOLS in 1974 and moved to Driggs, Idaho, after the troubles in 1975, but by 1984, she and her husband, Bruce, were ready to return to Lander.

Within just six months, the job of planning manager demanded yet another set of hands, and Neary hired Drew Leemon to assist Hampton. When Ellis left her position in 1986, Hampton moved to headquarters to take on overall planning, except they started calling it human resources, focusing on staff-related details. "Of course, I had no expe-rience in law or personnel," remembered Hampton in 2015, "but that was how we did things back then. [Ratz] believed that I was resourceful enough to figure out how to manage the area, and . . . the chair of our board then was Reb Gregg, who was . . . very experienced with personnel issues. As part of hiring me, Jim allowed me to hire Mark Cole as field staff manager and Tod [Schimelpfenig] as safety manager so that I could focus on labor laws, in-town staff, compensation, and general personnel stuff."

Ratz also knew coming in that the school's finances, especially cash flow, were still a big concern. The budget shortfall in 1983 was $40,087, and the next year it spiked to $100,361. Good enrollment, plus years of dogged attention to the bottom line that began with Peter Simer's firm hand continued under Ratz with the board's watchful backing. In 1985, those efforts led finally to the school's first non-negative year in a very long time: $45,000 in the black. No more would board treasurer Bob Hoffman and the school's finance manager, Chuck Smith, have to stack the school's bills in a drawer, sifting them each month to decide which were most pressing. There was enough extra to pay down the mortgage and start replacing equipment. "Having two nickels to rub together allowed these sorts of things, and Ratz was willing to spend those nickels," said John Gans in 2015.

One investment the board was eager to make was hiring a finance manager with a professional background. Ads were placed in various journals, but Gladys LanTien Chu remembered that it was the ad in *Outside* magazine that she saw. A graduate of Yale and the Wharton School of Business, she had worked for four years as a merchant banker in London, Singapore, and Chicago. She answered the ad from her position at the First National Bank of Chicago, and had an interview there with board member Bob Hoffman. She told him that she was ready to get out of the

Jim Ratz and Gladys LanTien "LT" Chu. LT brought a new level of financial acumen to the school in 1985. She and Ratz were married in 1988. *NOLS Archives*

city and do something different. Going to Lander, she said, sounded like an adventure.

"NOLS was ready for a bona fide financial director," recalled Herb Ogden. "LT had an MBA, with huge portfolio experience, and she had worked in finance." When Chuck Smith suddenly quit the position, LT, as she became known, was hired. She arrived in the summer of 1985 and served as the school's director of finance until 1990. LT instituted proper accounting methods in an era when the books were still handwritten. Among other initiatives during her tenure was the start of what became the annual "State of the School" report that included extensive financial information for all to see.

Throughout the worst of the "poverty years," NOLS staff had learned to operate on a shoestring, and continued to endure the necessarily tight purse strings into the early 1980s. When the chance for innovation and expansion finally arrived, it took time for old habits to change, according to Tod Schimelpfenig. He recalled how board member Tom Sharp said "that we spent money like Depression kids. He was right—because we grew up at NOLS in the 1970s, when you had nothing. You made $700 a month if you were CL, you worked in the Lumberyard and put a rain fly over your desk because of the leaks in the roof." For many years, that theme remained an undercurrent at the school, although by 2015 the virtue of frugality, he said, seemed faded. But "being tightwads was what got us through those tough years," he remembered. "When we started spending money on a few things, we started to take off."

For example, when Dave Neary walked into the Lumberyard on his first day as Wyoming branch director in May 1984, he saw that rainwater was dripping off the eaves along the pathway from the bike shed into the issue room. His return after a four-year absence was another of those engineered by Ratz to bring people back to NOLS. Part of what Ratz asked of him, he said, was to try to rebuild morale.

Neary mentioned to the staff how silly it seemed to him to have water dripping where people were walking. "Let's just get a couple of three-foot pieces of gutter," he said. "We'll need three of them, and that'll get the water off the path." The reply was, "We can't do that. We don't have money. It's not in the budget, we can't spend it."

Thelma Young was sitting in the back corner that day, watching. "She was grinnin' and laughin', and I went back there. Thelma and I always had a very good relationship, and I asked her what she was laughing at," recalled Neary in 2015. "She said, 'Well, things are gonna change around here, aren't they? I've been waiting five years for something like this to happen.' That [refusal to spend a few dollars on some plastic gutter] was an example of the mindset that was really embedded at the school at that point." The gutter was in place by the end of the day.

————————————

Much to the credit of those who came before, many systems devised early on continued to work effectively as the school grew, such as the "pinboard" admissions used to keep track of students and the courses they were taking. Literally a large sheet of paper on the admissions wall, it was a grid of columns, each containing the three-letter course code with rows for student names. Each resulting square represented a student spot. Backing up the information on the wall were paper files set up by course, plus an alphabetical file with a card for every student.

"We had straight pins that went into the board," said admissions director Bruce Palmer, "pink pins for the girls, and blue pins for the boys. . . . And yellow pins for reservations" to hold spots until applications could arrive by mail. As a season blossomed, the pinboard would take on the look of a multihued porcupine. In honor of its legacy, the school's computerized student-tracking database was long referred to as "the pinboard" as well.

The staffing system was likewise elegant in its own way. As they had for years, instructors eagerly awaited postal

Joe Austin picking blueberries in Alaska. *NOLS Archives*

delivery of the print copy of the staff newsletter three times a year (summer, fall, and winter/spring); it contained the "dream sheet" (renamed WRAP sheets, for Work Request and Plan, in the early 2000s), with its tantalizing list of course offerings for the upcoming season. On it, the instructor could indicate dates available to work, how much work was desired that season, and what friends or relatives he or she wished to work with.

But meshing dreams with reality was a different matter. With hundreds of instructors eager for work as the school grew, the staffing office was—and still is—tasked with finding the right mix of experience, geographic availability, and

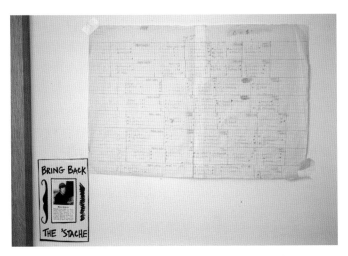

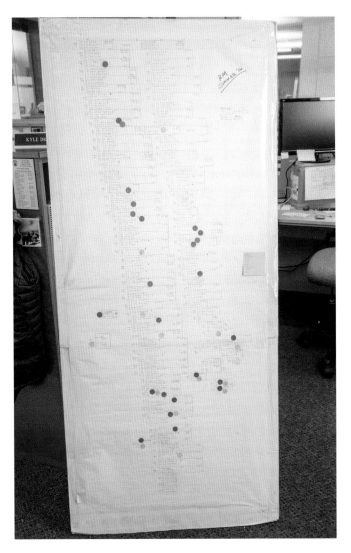

Rocky Mountain staffing boards from 1989 and 2016. Though the school has grown, the same system still works. *Brad Christensen*

more. Staffing was always tricky. Sometimes, a course might have more applicants than needed. In 1985, a new course offering was the Gannett Peak Winter Expedition. Fewer than five contracts were available—and 29 people said they wanted to work it. On the flip side, it was only slightly in jest that staffing office folks would sometimes drop to their knees and beg instructors to take unfilled courses, said Joe Austin, who recalled several years (before pay scales were adjusted) when, for instance, qualified CLs for the Denali climb were hard to find.

"You were always going to disappoint a certain number of people," said Austin, who as of 2015 still held the record for the longest stint—nearly 10 years—of anyone working in staffing. "You're giving (or not giving) work to your friends, and all of a sudden a lot of those friendships become strained. That was hard, for sure."

The age of electronics eased staffing's load somewhat, according to Marco Johnson. In 2015 he had served as staffing director since 2011, coming in from the field after accruing over 600 weeks instructing. But what hasn't ever changed is the inevitability of last-minute changes. "When an instructor cancels, it doesn't really matter the reason, the effect on you is the same: you *have* to replace them," said Austin. "It's not an option to go with one fewer instructor."

Filling openings could be a challenge. "In finding replacement staff at the last minute, you invariably have to ask other people to change their lives around," said Austin. "It was rarely the case you could just ask one person and that solved the problem. More often than not, it's a domino effect." Asking one person slated to depart on a course in three days to fill in right away would only buy breathing room; someone would still need to be found for that other course. And so on. "You have to be creative and come up with different options and try to solve them without creating bigger problems," said Austin.

Instructor Support and Development

In the 1980s, the instructor course (IC) was still the standard entry point for aspiring instructors, and a respected barometer of competence throughout the outdoor industry. John Gookin, who came to NOLS in 1981, was originally planning to work for Outward Bound, but when the people at OB mentioned the high caliber of the NOLS IC, he changed his mind. He was one of a handful of non-NOLS graduates in that era able to gain admission to the IC based on his resume of outdoor experience.

Those years also marked the beginning of a concerted effort to attract more woman instructors. It was a tough task; 2015 marked the first time that ICs were split 50/50 male/female.

The life of a NOLS instructor always relied on a heavy dose of passion. As with all educators, it seems, pay is never commensurate with the value of the service. For John Gans, gaining traction as a NOLS instructor was a matter of being flexible and persistent. "You'd do anything to get by. There were times I thought it was a stupid mistake," he recalled in 2015. "There were times I was so broke I didn't have a chance to leave. There was barely enough money coming in.

"And then, you piece things together. Once I got through that first year wondering 'can I survive?', I didn't have any desire to be anything but a field instructor. Summers in

Alaska, winters in Mexico, spring and fall in Lander or the Black Hills caving . . . once I got on that circuit, it was a sweet couple of years. Very seductive."

Knowing how few resources the school had been able to apply toward instructors in past years, Ratz was determined to do something about it. He established the Instructor Development Fund (IDF) in 1984. Its purpose was to support continuing education for NOLS instructors. Instructors could apply annually for funding to do a variety of things, such as attend an avalanche conference, take a rock rescue seminar, or even help fund a personal trip that expanded the instructor's horizons. For example, in 1989 the IDF awards included funding for an all-woman expedition to Nepal's Pumori (23,580 feet), two different Denali expeditions, and a project to improve the quality of student field journals.

For many years, in the absence of such resources as the IDF, the instructor group pushed itself to hone its skills and knowledge. Because researching topics within the limitations of a remote place like Lander was a challenge, one of the first initiatives of the NOLS Instructor Association when it was formed in 1975 was to establish a resource library for instructors that was housed at the Noble Hotel. Many spent in-town time studying topics of interest and sharing what they learned. Their efforts were frequently published, in both the staff newsletter and the *NOLS Alum-*

River crossing in the 1980s. *NOLS Archives*

nus (later, *The Leader*). Each issue contained a variety of contributions, often recaps of trips and adventures (such as Vince Fayad's description of climbing Mount Kenya) or in-depth information (such as Dave Slovisky's comprehensive article on "Marine Mammals of Prince William Sound"), both in the Summer 1975 issue of the *NOLS Alumnus*. There were articles about how to build a sauna, how to silently signal the presence of predators (helpful for hikers in Kenya), ways to be a "Wilderness Watchdog" or a better instructor, how to ice climb, or any of a hundred topics for this generally information-thirsty group.

"This was the great appeal of NOLS for instructors," said Drew Leemon. "We had a curriculum, [so] some things were standard to NOLS, but we had the freedom to read about topics to add to our classes, especially on natural history topics."

By the 1980s, there was a dawning realization that NOLS instructors were top-notch in the eyes of the broader world of outdoor education. There was some justifiable swagger. The growing reputation of the NOLS IC brought with it a rising sense, at least among some, for the need to act like a group of professionals. That change, which started in the Simer years, ramped up during Ratz's years at the helm. Many discussions on the topic ensued at the primary gathering place for staff at the time: the dining room (known by some as "Chez Reagan") at the Noble Hotel.

It didn't always feel so positive. Board members showed up more than a few times to try and reason with the instructor group over antics that had increasingly worried them. The gist of their comments, remembered Tod Schimelpfenig, was that NOLS instructors were a "bunch of adolescents" and they needed to "grow up, and do it fast." The school until that point had operated relatively free of writ-

ten policies, but that was about to change—a trend that was viewed as horrific by many instructors. They had no desire to be told what to do, and certainly not in written policies.

One such early policy barred instructors from sleeping with students. Instructor pushback was loud and clear. Many had met their spouses on a NOLS course. Others saw it as a "perk" of a low-paying job. Either way, it was not an uncommon occurrence for people who were in the backcountry for a month at a time. While some could see the merit of eliminating this inappropriate power differential and potential PR and legal liability, anyone who agreed knew it was smart to keep quiet if they didn't want to be shunned, according to some instructors.

For the better part of a decade, the board and administration were sometimes at loggerheads with the instructor corps on that and other issues. Part of the challenge, according to Molly Hampton, was the awkward fact that many of those in the administration, including Ratz, herself, and others, had come from those very instructor ranks, and had behaved in ways that they were now telling others they could no longer enjoy. "We had to do it," she said in 2015, "both from a legal and reputation point of view. It was the way the world was going."

Early NOLS whitewater boating.
NOLS Archives

Programming and Curriculum Initiatives

IN THE FIRST YEARS, NOLS was a mountain-centric school, even though sailing, sea kayaking, and other non-mountain activities had coexisted since Tap Tapley went south to Baja in 1971. For many years, every instructor (whether they worked climbing courses or not) was required to lead 5.6 rock climbs (a moderate degree of difficulty), and a rock-jock mentality prevailed. Well into the 1980s, the traditional 30-day mountain course remained the mainstay of the school's programming.

With time came the resources and interest to explore adding different sorts of outdoor activities and locations to the mix. "Expansion was actually bringing some excitement back into the school," said Neary. "My take on it when I came back was that the school was sorta bouncing along with the status quo, without a lot of energy and excitement, and people had a sense of constraint as compared to possibility." The rising sense of expansion and possibility was reenergizing, and

wrought many programming changes, largely driven by faculty excitement and interest in pushing their ideas forward. Paddlers helped enlarge the water-based program to the Rio Grande and elsewhere. Cavers scouted new locations in Great Basin National Park in Nevada (called Lehman Caves National Monument in those days). Climbers promoted the idea of Red Rocks, in Nevada, and Cochise Stronghold and Mount Lemmon in Arizona. Sailing was added in the Pacific Northwest. Canyoneering, in the course mix since the 1970s, expanded to more areas. It suddenly became a delicious era of "saying 'what do we say no to.' It was opportunity after opportunity," said Molly Hampton.

To help make the right choices, the school was careful to keep its mission at the forefront of their deliberations. The wording in the original articles of incorporation was "to develop and teach wilderness skills and techniques, to develop and teach wilderness use that encourages minimal environmental impact, to develop and teach outdoor leaders." The mission was reworded, but essentially unchanged, in 1987: "The mission of the National Outdoor Leadership School is to be the best source and teacher of wilderness skills, minimum impact, and leadership."

At the same time that programming was mushrooming, an effort began to identify more clearly what NOLS instructors actually *needed* to teach, and why. At the core of the school's curriculum since inception are what Petzoldt called the "must-know" skills: the knowledge and ability to protect the individual, the environment, and the equipment, plus the correct use of judgment. As Petzoldt wrote, "The teaching of techniques without judgment can be dangerous." In his view, it all began with learning how to minimize discomfort in the backcountry. As Rob Hellyer explained, "The difference between NOLS and Outward Bound was that sometimes at Outward Bound, the concept was that you have to have hardship to get the message that you can overcome difficult things. Paul's thing was, 'yes, you do, and you're going to use the outdoors as the medium for this, but, actually, you can also have fun at the same time.'" For one thing, he knew that a person enjoying the wilderness would want to be more careful with it.

But that core tenet says nothing about how to impart those ideas to students, and figuring out the nuances of NOLS curriculum remained an ongoing process even 50 years after the school's first students walked into the Winds. As far back as the early 1970s, some instructors began to write down their versions of the curriculum. But trying to build an intentional curriculum was hampered by the variety of approaches in the instructor community—some backed by research, and some not. Eventually, people began to recognize the value of a system. In 1987, the core curriculum was delineated into seven main threads. An instructor from 1965 would see the same topics they had taught, overall:

- Safety and Judgment (basic first aid, safety and accident prevention, hazard evaluation, heat/cold related injury prevention and treatment, rescue techniques, emergency procedures)
- Leadership and Expedition Dynamics (small group expeditions, human psychology, "leader of the day" opportunities, leadership styles, expedition planning, outdoor teaching techniques)
- Minimum Impact Camping and Resource Protection (campsite selection, shelter, stove use and care, firebuilding, sanitation and waste disposal)
- Environmental Awareness (ecosystems, flora and fauna identification, geology, weather, anthropology, astronomy, history, foreign languages, cultural exchanges)

- Outdoor Living Skills (cooking and baking, nutrition and rations, climate control, high-altitude physiology, equipment care and selection)
- Travel Techniques (energy conservation, map-reading and compass use, time control plans, route-finding and navigation, backpacking, kayaking, horse packing, sailing, fishing, telemark skiing, caving, climbing)
- Public Service (local and regional environmental priorities, multiple use theory and practice, land management issues, and wilderness ethics)

An overriding question was whether students were getting correct and consistent information from one course to the next—in other words, standardization of programming. According to John Gookin, who in 1989 became the school's second curriculum manager (Vini Norris held the position in the mid-1970s), "The NOLS emphasis on judgment meant that the trick at the management level is to insist on enough standardization to serve the students well without going overboard to the point that instructor judgment is impeded when they have to . . . figure out what to do that day."

Efforts to bolster the curriculum arrived with the 1985 publication of *NOLS Grizzly Bear Practices,* by Steff Kessler; the *Wilderness Educator Notebook,* which debuted in 1989; and the *NOLS Sea Kayak Instructor Notebook,* by Tim Conlan in 1990. Actually predating these publications was *The National Outdoor Leadership School's Wilderness Guide,* written by Peter Simer and John Sullivan and published in 1983. However, its introduction was somewhat subsumed by the timing of its release, which coincided with Simer's departure from the school.

In September 1989, instructors came together for the first educational conference, called the Staff Conference. This annual event continued through 1996, although in some years it was called the Wilderness Education Conference. It was an opportunity both to bring in outside experts on certain topics, and hear NOLS instructors address topics about which they were already expert. As Ratz said in his opening comments, "The instructor conference is important to me because it symbolizes progress toward a goal. It demonstrates that we are finally getting serious about this thing of educating people in the wilderness. We aren't simply relying on guesswork or what we learned on the Instructors Courses or from books . . . NOLS must be thinking about and experimenting with what will become the wilderness leadership methods and philosophy of the future."

Interestingly, the keynote address that first year was given by Charles Houston about his 1953 expedition to K2.

By 1989, he was a physician and respected researcher of high-altitude physiology. But in 1938, he was also the leader on the K2 expedition where he and Petzoldt had clashed. Houston did not refer to the 1938 trip in his keynote comments, except to indicate that, to him, it had been an "enjoyable expedition." Instead he focused on the intense drama of the 1953 journey, when a single, heroic belay held six tumbling climbers during a dramatic (and ultimately futile) rescue attempt of Art Gilkey, who had fallen seriously ill high on the mountain.

Attention on Safety

In the preface of the first edition of *NOLS Wilderness First Aid*, Ratz wrote, "On my student course in 1970, [Paul] began his first aid class with the observation that we would be better off spending our time learning how to avoid accidents. The rest of the class was short on detail . . . and long on common sense. Paul had his priorities in order: good judgment, prior planning, and an appreciation for accident prevention."

But many years had elapsed since 1970, and despite the persistent emphasis on prevention, the school had experienced many injuries and illnesses, and seven fatalities. Basic incident information was part of every NOLS Board of Trustee report since the 1960s (one 1965 report cited "three injuries, two shoulder dislocations and one broken arm, probably due to a lack of instruction by the school"). But the time had come to pay closer attention to the information that could be derived from those incidents.

For the frontcountry, an operations committee was formed to focus on institutionalizing the school's safety practices. Compliance with OSHA requirements, fire systems in buildings, and defensive driving got serious attention. The first written transportation protocol was developed after the Exxon Valdez tanker ran aground in Alaska's Prince William Sound in 1989. In addition to a requirement for defensive driving training, a "bottle to throttle" rule was enacted to address alcohol and driving. Concerns about transportation of students in cattle trucks had been among the first priorities of the Luther-era board, and had long since been addressed. In addition, vehicle maintenance procedures and systems were well established by Dudley Cole after he came to NOLS in the late 1970s. "He and Willy Cunningham established the foundation for the whole vehicle service procedures we use today," said Steve Matson, Rocky Mountain transportation manager in 2015. "We've changed and adapted it, but the foundation was laid by them."

Driving in different terrain, as NOLS does, sometimes demanded extreme measures; in 1984, Matson was in Mexico when a dually pickup truck went halfway over a small

Steve Matson, NOLS Rocky Mountain transportation manager for over 30 years. *NOLS Archives*

cliff. Since NOLS was a climbing school, Matson was put on belay as he attempted to save the vehicle in case extrication measures failed and the truck fell. (It didn't.)

As for operations in the backcountry, the committee reviewed such topics as fasting during "survival" and radio communications capability from the field. It also inaugurated a series of audits of field programs by outside experts from the American Mountain Guides Association (AMGA), the American Canoe Association (ACA), as well as safety personnel from Outward Bound and other outdoor programs. Partly as a result of these audits, NOLS developed long-standing relationships with many organizations in an effort to promote inter-organizational support and dialogue. As an acknowledged industry leader, NOLS was interested in knowing how the practices of different associations and professional groups might influence its own views, and vice versa.

It was always clear to NOLS that the wilderness environment cannot be made risk-free. From the beginning, the goal had been to minimize potential liabilities to the school, both in terms of the impact on the morale of staff and students, as well as on school finances and legal exposure. In 1987, the board established the position of safety director, with oversight from a newly formed safety committee of board members. (These roles were renamed in 1994 to risk management director and risk management committee, respectively.)

The school's first safety director, Tod Schimelpfenig, was an EMT who had demonstrated an ongoing interest in safety for years. He actually recorded incident data from the field beginning in 1977, but wasn't able to get data from everyone at the school until his appointment as safety and training manager formalized the process.

One motivation for his work was a desire to test myths floating around the school. For example, there was a perception that hypothermia was a major problem in the mountains. That turned out to be false, at least at NOLS; very few became hypothermic on courses. According to the data, poor hygiene was actually having a far worse impact, a fact he could prove with the numbers from his growing database. After consulting with some physicians from Vanderbilt University, he said, "We realized we don't wash hands in the mountains, and there are instructors telling students they don't have to wash their hands because the water is pure and that the grease build-up on their hand is a natural disinfectant. It's crap."

"When I started my role," said Schimelpfenig, "[I was] walking on really thin ice. The instructor body would push back, and it seemed like it was one step forward, two steps back." For example, shortly after his appointment, a policy requiring instructors to disinfect drinking water resulted in what he described as "frank disobedience. People thought it was nonsense." In some cases, instructors made students disinfect, but still refused to do it themselves, often because they didn't like the taste or were worried about long-term health effects of ingesting iodine. It was challenging for him to help instructors understand the impact of poor behavioral modeling on students, who wanted to be just like their instructors. It was left to office staff, said Schimelpfenig, to field the phone calls from parents whose kids came back from a NOLS course with unnecessary diarrhea.

According to Herb Ogden, who admitted he was one of the troglodytes, the problem wasn't defiance so much as

River courses eat together as one big group, and in 2015 were known for great food and strict hygiene.
Brad Christensen

denial. "The mountains—especially the Winds—had always been pristine, pure and beyond the contamination of the rest of the world. To disinfect crystal clear mountain water, flowing from isolated alpine slopes, was a disconnect. Intellectually, we all knew that there had been cases of giardia reported, but not from *this* stream, not from *this* lake, never on *my* courses. I think that many instructors simply did not want to accept or acknowledge that. We weren't being contrarian or purposefully recalcitrant—we just didn't want to let go of the ideal in the face of reality."

In 1989, the data showed that the school's highest illness and injury rates were occurring on whitewater courses, so Schimelpfenig went on a river trip. He saw two explanations for the high incident rates. He saw passionate instructors who, in their enthusiasm, were pushing the students too hard—plus no one was washing hands. Both were taking a toll. So he recruited the preeminent river safety expert in the world, Les Bechdel. The man, regarded by many as a legend, came to NOLS and did a river audit. "They listened to him," said Schimelpfenig. "They wouldn't listen to me. I was just a NOLS administrator. But they'd listen to Les!"

While data collection was helpful, it was useless if it was

Branch directors of the 1990s. Back row from left: Fred Roberts, Don Ford, John Gans, Dave Kallgren, John Hauf, Willy Warner. Front row: George Newbury, Drew Leemon, Les van Barselaar, Michael Lindsey. *NOLS Archives*

not accurate and complete. This meant developing an incident reporting structure, forms, definitions of reportable incidents, and a process for managing the information. It also required a culture in which instructors were comfortable disclosing events. That culture evolved at NOLS over time, in large part, said Schimelpfenig, due to the efforts of Drew Leemon, who succeeded him as risk management director in 1996, and who created a bond of trust with the instructors regarding incident reviews.

By 2015, the NOLS field incident database was the largest and longest continually running dataset anywhere regarding injuries and illnesses on organized wilderness educational expeditions. From 1984 through September 2014, there were 3,885,117 student days on expeditions (not counting frontcountry classroom programs, such as wilderness medicine courses), almost 78,000 students, and over 14,000 incident records covering medical incidents, evacuations, plus non-medical and behavioral incidents.

On July 24, 1989, at 5:00 p.m. the school's first fatal incident in just over 10 years occurred. Student David Black, 24, was three weeks into his Wind River Mountaineering course, descending the northwest buttress of Mount Warren (13,722 feet, the third-highest peak in the range). He was with one instructor and two other students when he was hit in the head by a watermelon-sized rock. He was wearing a helmet, but sustained a severe skull fracture.

The immediate response by the course was complicated by a prolonged thunderstorm that began at 7:00 p.m., just as they were mobilizing a rescue that entailed a 1,500-foot ascent across difficult terrain to Black's location. They reached it at 6:20 a.m., but he had died at 5:10 a.m. without regaining consciousness. In those days before radios, a messenger team of one instructor and one student had left as soon as possible, completing at mid-morning the 14-hour, 25-mile hike to the trailhead to notify the school.

While Ratz and others in Lander contacted families and dealt with the media and legal matters, Drew Leemon and John Kanengeiter (then Wyoming branch director, and field staff and safety manager for Wyoming branch courses, respectively) rode a helicopter into the backcountry to provide the course with support, update everyone about what was happening externally, and gather further information. Drew and John debriefed the incident with the students and instructors for almost an entire day. The helicopter returned that evening with the runner party, and Drew and John got a ride back to Lander. The debriefing helped the students make the decision to spend the remaining four days on a student expedition and use that as a way to grieve for David and end the course on a positive note.

———

Overall it was a vivid reminder that the NOLS classroom is unlike any other. Fortunately, a specific crisis management process that had been used in years past had recently been refined. In addition, the top management team had just done some in-depth crisis management training—lucky, since none of the team members had handled such a devastating event before. The training had provided invaluable tools for both the NOLS executive team and some branch directors, a procedure to follow, and contact information with crisis experts. When the call came in, Ratz and key board members were put in the loop immediately, internal communications and logs were begun, and, while Ratz notified the young man's family, others contacted the media, the school's insurance broker, and the parents of the others on the course. Letters were also sent by foot or with re-rations to all courses currently in the field, and frequent updates were sent to the branch locations. Later, Ratz, John Kanengeiter, and several board members attended Black's funeral in Connecticut.

The inquiry and incident reviews included some suggestions: improve staff safety awareness, carry certain emergency gear, do more cliff rescue training, use climbing guidebooks, and continue efforts that had already begun to provide radios for emergency communication on remote courses.

The school's radio initiative was particularly spurred by Black's death, and at last it became a priority to find the capability for workable radios. Historically, efforts to use them, hearkening back to Robert Bullard's death on Denali in 1971, had been hampered because mountains block transmissions between ground stations. In 1990, a radio communication consultant advised the school to consider using ground-to-air radios. These would allow courses to send Mayday messages to aircraft flying overhead. Pilots receiving a Mayday message would, in turn, relay the message to air traffic control, which would then contact NOLS. This system went into effect in the summer of 1990, and was used numerous times until satellite and cellular phones became available.

Just three months after Black's death, on October 22, 1989, semester student Rachael Cox got lost in South Dakota's Wind Cave, which NOLS had explored in its caving program since 1980. Wind Cave is a convoluted mess of underground mix-up acknowledged as among the most complex in the world, with over 53 miles of surveyed passages. (By 2015 there were over 140 miles of surveyed passages.) With a history of 2,722 caving students, this was the school's first lost caver.

Exploring Native American cliff dwellings.
Adam Swisher

NOLS SOUTHWEST

The Rio Grande in the Big Bend border country of Texas was a welcome change to winter when Drew Leemon, Del Smith, and Dave Neary went looking for potential new NOLS classrooms in the late 1980s. NOLS was growing, enrollment was good, and Jim Ratz had sent his scouts to see where the school could expand. They checked out the hiking in the Gila Wilderness in southwestern New Mexico. The rock climbing opportunities at Cochise Stronghold in the Dragoon Mountains in southeastern Arizona were outstanding. Rich Brame and Mike Bailey told of the caving available near Carlsbad in New Mexico, and they later heard about Lehman Cave at Great Basin National Park.

But it was the permit they obtained in 1987 for the Rio Grande that got the NOLS river program going in the Southwest. A 23-and-over rafting course in Big Bend National Park led to more, and by the fall of 1988, Leemon and Smith worked together to concoct a semester. The first, in January 1989, started and finished in a motel parking lot in El Paso. But it was successful, so they did it again the next January, that time from a parking lot of a Tucson motel. In June 1990 the school leased a property in Tucson. "We called it the Bent Gate Ranch in honor of bent-gate carabiners," recalled Judd Rogers, the equipment manager from the early 1990s. Located in a mesquite grove, the "issue room" was a shipping container, staff and student housing were Eureka four-person tents and Thelma flies, the rations room/kitchen was a shed with an awning and some picnic tables, and the office/commons was an 800-square-foot bungalow.

By July 1991, there was enough momentum to make NOLS Southwest the seventh full-fledged branch of the school. The area offered abundant course opportunities, including terrain for an instructor course. Abby Warner instructed that IC for 10 years and worked to disprove a stereotype that the Southwest environment was too easy for new instructors to show their mettle. "We had help from Mother Nature," she recalled, "when it snowed on us. And we had one high-melt year when river crossings were not possible."

Record winter precipitation in the winter of 1993 led to extreme flooding in Arizona, and Bent Gate Ranch was not spared. The board convened its winter meeting there the following month; between the flood damage and the looming end to the lease, it was time to go shopping. By April, Leemon, operations director John Gans, and board member Tom Sharp found the perfect location for a campus in the former Mystic Plains horse ranch, a 10-acre site 15 miles east of downtown Tucson. The ranch sold for $350,000, and an additional $550,000 from the Next Step Expedition capital campaign transformed the place into a NOLS branch. The existing horse barn and tack room were cleaned out to become a rations room, and a 2,900-square-foot, open-sided staging area (called "the Ramada") and 1,000-square-foot equipment room were built. The new location greeted its first students in September 1994.

One course innovation in 2007 was the Sonoran Year, an expansion of the Sonoran Semester that ran from 2000 to 2006. Inspired by the successful Patagonia Year, the 135-day program ran for four years. It started in the Southwest for backpacking, rock climbing, and either canoeing or caving, then students traveled to Mexico for sea kayaking, sailing, and a cultural section.

The Southwest also became a hub for the school's lightweight backpacking program. That program evolved in Lander under the guidance of Mike Clelland and Ryan Hutchins-

Cabibi at the Rocky Mountain branch. When Ryan's wife, Janeen Hutchins, took the director's seat in the Southwest in 2006, she said, "We started the lightweight backpacking course, and we also started having the instructor course include a lightweight backpacking section, to get that lightweight backpacking knowledge out there."

NOLS Southwest Directors:
1991: Del Smith
1991-1996: Drew Leemon
1996-1997: Terri Watson
1996-2000: Daryl Burnett
2000-2002: Judd Rogers
2002-2006: Scott Robertson
2006-2009: Janeen Hutchins
2009-2015: Lindsay Nohl

Canoeing the Rio Grande. *Ashley Wise*

It was 3:15 p.m. when course leader Tom Hafnor called to report the missing student, and the evacuation coordinator on duty, Kevin McGowan, set the NOLS crisis management process in motion. When word came at 6:30 p.m. that the hasty searches had produced nothing, response efforts ratcheted up. People from Lander and elsewhere prepared to go to the scene to assist. NOLS tapped semester students and instructors in the field to aid in the effort, including some remote caving sections that sent their underground gear to South Dakota. In addition, within hours, cavers and search experts from Denver, Wyoming, Montana, and elsewhere began to arrive by car, truck, bus, and chartered airplane. Bill Pierce, who ran Devil's Tower National Monument and was at the time president of the National Association for Search and Rescue, was summoned to be incident commander. Eventually, the search involved 132 people, including 110 searchers—at that time the second-largest cave search in US history.

At 10:22 p.m. on October 23—32 hours after she went missing—a team of searchers heard someone pounding a rock. They quickly made verbal contact with Rachael via an "impossibly tight" vertical chimney about 40 to 50 feet long; they could communicate with Rachael, but not actually reach her. After a call for more rescuers and tools to enlarge the passage, instructor Rich Brame was able to squeeze through the fissure to reach her. When Rachael saw him, she asked, "Are you God?" to which Brame responded, "No, ma'am, I'm just a NOLS instructor." After a medical survey and some food and water, she was assisted from the cave at 2:30 a.m. on October 24, dehydrated and cold, but essentially unharmed.

An early NOLS caver in a squeeze. *NOLS Archives*

Sunset over the mountains of Baja California.
Alisha Bube

Lessons Learned from Tragedy

EVERY PROGRAM AREA OF NOLS saw changes over the years, either in response to incidents, because new technology changed the way an activity was performed, or because new information changed decision-making. Talking about the school's approach to risk management in 2015, Leemon said, "We're proactive, but we can't always anticipate every eventuality. We always sought ways to do things that were appropriate for achieving our outcomes; we anticipated situations to the best of our ability while still embracing risk and the need for students to learn experientially. After an incident we learn that maybe we hadn't been able to anticipate certain things, and the incident leads us to refine our practices."

As time passed, stoppers and cams replaced pitons, avalanche transceivers replaced avalanche cord, and radios replaced evacuation runners. The earliest NOLS winter courses were essentially backpack trips on surplus wooden Army skis with mountaineering boots and rudimentary bindings, which limited skiing to slogging along until the advent of fiberglass metal-edged skis, touring boots, and three-pin bindings. Those advances plus a resurging interest in telemark turns transformed backcountry skiing into a quest to find powder instead of just traveling from point A to point B. As skiing blossomed, NOLS risk management practices necessarily put more emphasis on avalanche science and advances in avalanche rescue technology.

Petzoldt himself claimed that there wasn't a right or wrong way of doing something—instead, there was a practical way. He believed in learning through experimenting. "If I have more information tomorrow than I have today, I'm going to change my mind. I've always been experimenting," he said.

In this vein, program changes were fed by collective experience and a consistent desire to do things better. One such change came as an outgrowth of Black's death: the

In the early years of NOLS, backcountry skiing gear was fairly rudimentary. *NOLS Archives*

concept of "industry standards." During the investigation, recalled Schimelpfenig, an attorney for the family flipped open a Colorado Outward Bound manual, which showed approaches to avoiding rockfall and other procedures that were different from those used (and mostly as-yet unwritten) at NOLS. At that moment, Schimelpfenig said, he realized that industry leaders "need to talk to each other. We can't, as an industry, have wildly conflicting standards." It was time to fix that.

"I picked up the phone and called Lewis Glenn [NOLS grad and former instructor and then vice president for safety at Outward Bound USA]. I'd never talked to the guy. He was my counterpart over there, and I'd never had a conversation with him."

David Black's was the school's eighth fatality: Arthur Saltus in 1966; Robert Bullard on McKinley in 1971; Gary Hall on the Green River in 1972; instructor Mike Moseley, and students Bart Drodsky and David Silva in a Teton avalanche in 1974; Matthew Strominger in the Cascades in 1979; then, David Black. From each tragedy, however, lessons were learned. As Ratz wrote in *The Leader* in August 1989, "A death prompts us to reexamine our lives and why we do what we do . . . We can try to minimize risk but it can't be done away with entirely."

Although it took some time to coordinate, one positive outcome of Black's death was the creation and inauguration of the first Wilderness Risk Management Conference, held at the NOLS Pacific Northwest branch in Conway, Washington, in 1994. NOLS took the lead, along with Out-

Advances in gear opened up new possibilities for winter courses. *Brian Fabel*

search and rescue methods, crisis management, and emergency procedures, to ethics, pre-event preparedness, causes of accidents, and rescue technique updates for whitewater, sea kayaking, and rock climbing. The keynote address was by Tom Hornbein, MD, an anesthesiologist and mountaineer who summited Mount Everest in 1963. The conference grew every year, and in 2015 the 22nd annual edition in Portland, Oregon, drew 477 people.

Survival

For the first 25 years of NOLS, most wilderness courses typically culminated in "survival." Having learned their lessons well, students headed off in small groups for an instructor-free hike out of the mountains. A 1974 paper titled "NOLS Instruction: Subjects and Priorities" advised instructors to prepare students for the expedition behavior and leadership challenges they would experience, saying, "It's a chance to prove themselves. A final test of the quality of judgment they have learned at NOLS."

In those days, survival started with the burning of all remaining food. "We were 16 and completely dumbfounded as the food was gathered. They burned it in front of us," recalled instructor Steve Goryl of his student course. Leslie van Barselaar, another longtime instructor who passed away in 2015, conceded that the burning ritual was the only

ward Bound, the American Alpine Club, the Association for Experiential Education, the Wilderness Medical Society, American Mountain Guides Association, and Nantahala Outdoor Center, to bring together 200 people from 60 different outdoor programs. The stated goals were 1) educate wilderness practitioners in risk management and practical safety skills, 2) share field and administrative techniques in risk management, and 3) raise risk management standards in the wilderness adventure industry. For two days, participants discussed and heard about everything from

Assessing snow conditions is a vital part of minimizing the risk of avalanches. *Jared Steinman*

way they were going to get her out of the mountains anyway, saying, "I remember thinking, 'Well, I guess I'll have to leave 'cause they just burned all the food.'"

Van Barselaar and her coursemates, and Goryl and his coursemates, successfully lived off the land for the next several days before reaching the trailhead. "Still one of my favorite dishes is putting rocks in the bottom of a frying pan with water and some spices, laying a bed of bluebells,

and then fish on top of that, and steaming it," van Barselaar shared. She said that Petzoldt made the reasoning behind survival very clear: "The idea was not to suffer. The idea was, well, sometimes you do run out of food in the mountains or on an expedition. It's not the end of the world. You can actually function, read maps, keep your group together, keep safe, keep warm, and do all of that and make it out and not have it be an epic." Van Barselaar faithfully passed down that reasoning to many students of her own. Van Barselaar and Dave Kallgren would later honeymoon in the Amazon, living almost solely off the land. "We always had the confidence it would be fine," Kallgren reflected, "because we'd done a few days without food previously."

Not every grad found survival to be so tolerable in the moment, however. Goryl wrote, "[We] could not seem to catch any fish . . . We were *very* hungry . . . I thought I was going to die." Nonetheless, he classified those low days in his young life as "some of the most character building."

More often, fellow alumni reflect on the lessons of survival with a certain reverence, remembering more than the hunger. The experience was about fasting and challenge, yes—but just as profoundly about novices practicing independent leadership with real consequences. Gary Cukjati became an instructor in the 1980s. He used to say to his students before sending them off for the final leg of their course:

Dave Kallgren. *Melissa Hemken*

"This is an amazing accomplishment that is all yours. You will learn about yourself, and you will draw on it forever." Cukjati fasted for the first time as a young instructor and described it as, well, "boring." Nonetheless, he came away from the experience with a similar perspective to that of van Barselaar and Kallgren. "For me, it took away this concept that food mattered—I didn't care as much about food," he explained. "Food is often the largest stress on courses, and people have all these viewpoints about needs and what they're entitled to. Fasting got rid of that."

By the late 1980s, some of the aspects of the survival experience were losing momentum. By then, many courses were being conducted in harsh conditions and on technical terrain, where fasting was not done for risk management reasons. In addition, there were increasing numbers of instructors who had not had the survival experience themselves as a NOLS student. They began to question the contrived nature of the experience, and also the possible health impacts of multiday fasting under heavy exertion.

In 1988, these questions reached the board level. A medical doctor on the board came out with a strong statement about the effects of fasting, and Schimelpfenig, as safety director, was hard-pressed at the time to rebut the concerns. The practice of fasting was suspended for several years, and "survival" was renamed "small group expedition" (SGE). In 1993, fasting was reinstated by the board based on a proposal written by instructor Dan Posel in May 1992. Fasting would be limited to a total of 76 hours and only allowed on backpacking courses (except adventure courses), was voluntary, and groups would carry tightly packaged emergency rations. At the same time, a decision was made that instructors would stay in the field during SGE to be available for emergency support if a group needed them.

By 2015 fasting had mostly disappeared, but the focus on independence and small group leadership had not faded. Many wilderness and some sea kayaking courses still

Horsepacking in Wyoming. *Hadley Warner*

executed what had come to be known as student expeditions. Those days remained uniquely challenging, student-led adventures that provided culminating opportunities for student teams to plan and execute real mini-expeditions. Though they continued to carry—and eat—normal rations, students could still experience the self-reliance upon which survival was founded. "It's still a real surprise to some, and still a great thing about NOLS courses: It's hard and there's an element of suffering," said instructor Andy Blair. "Students always reference the student

expedition as one of the peak experiences on a course . . . expanding their sense of the possible."

Other Emerging Opportunities

In March 1986, the school's first two computers—early IBMs, both 125K of RAM, with floppy disk drives and green text-only CRT monitors—were installed in the NOLS international administrative offices at the Noble Hotel. "They sat in storage in the finance office in the hotel for a year or so because no one knew how to turn them on, let alone use them," said Bruce Hampton. "Jim Ratz asked me to investigate, saying 'get 'em working, or trash 'em.'" No one really knew what they could do or how to use them. Little did anyone know then the immense capabilities computers would provide to NOLS compared to the days of handwriting letters to prospective students for lack of a typewriter.

Marit Sawyer and Rich Brame, who were presidents of the NIA in that era, saw that the newfangled machines could be helpful tools, even if only used as word processors. Despite the fact that a computer cost several thousand dollars then, they pooled their meager NIA assets, purchased one for the instructors, and had it installed in the Noble Hotel library.

Hampton then returned to the school after a several-year absence to become the school's first technology director, although the real story, he said, was that no one else wanted the job. He was viewed as the *de facto* computer expert primarily because he had a computer at home, where he had just written a book on it.

With the computer, Hampton would write another book, published in 1988. It was a seminal publication in the canon of conservation writing called *Soft Paths: How To Enjoy the Wilderness Without Harming It*. His co-author, David Cole, was a noted research biologist with the US Forest Service. In it, they articulated the case for minimum impact on the wilderness and described methods for achieving that in deserts, on rivers and lakes and coastlines, on alpine and arctic tundra, and in bear country.

Soft Paths was the outgrowth of more than a decade of nascent efforts to articulate important conservation methods. Since the mid-1970s, NOLS and the US Forest Service had partnered on various minimum impact conservation projects; the October 1974 board minutes approved a motion "to permit the US Forest Service to publish the conservation practices developed by NOLS in their literature and permit them to say that these conservation practices were developed by the National Outdoor Leadership School and the United States Forest Service." The result was publication of various pamphlets and brochures by the Forest Service, National Park Service, BLM, and others during the 1970s, with such titles as "Wilderness Manners," "Wilderness Ethics," "Minimum

Don Webber with the school's very first computer, alongside modern servers and routers in the NOLS HQ Network Operations Center. *Brad Christensen*

Impact Camping," and "No-Trace Camping." In addition, for a number of years NOLS self-published its "Conservation Practices" as a pamphlet-sized curriculum piece for courses.

Soft Paths became the definitive clarification of practical conservation skills, and a major resource for what was soon to evolve into the widely recognized Leave No Trace movement. In 1991, a video containing its message was released and shown at 250 locations within the National Wilderness Preservation System.

Alumni Relations

By 1980, NOLS had graduated over 12,000 students, but no effort had really ever been made to keep track of them. Petzoldt had been adamant, as Jon Hamren remembered: "He wanted you to take your lessons from NOLS and move on with your life." Although star pupils were often invited to stay as instructors, the majority finished their courses and left Lander, done, finished, gone.

Part of the problem was the traditional link between alumni and fundraising. Although he was often in debt himself, Petzoldt never liked becoming beholden to anyone, so asking people for money to him meant it came with strings attached. He didn't want any of that, and the precedent became a long-standing institutional habit. "The ethos was 'when you take a NOLS course, we train you well, and you really shouldn't ever come back,'" said Rich Brame, who was in charge of alumni relations in 2015. "It was a naive, idealistic viewpoint. If someone came back for another course, we felt we had failed, because we didn't teach them well enough the first time."

The flaw of ignoring alumni began to be acknowledged during Simer's years. As early as the Spring 1978 *NOLS*

Alumnus came a somewhat eyebrow-raising change of tune: "Dear Graduate: NOLS wants to be a continuing part of the educational process in your life . . ."

Efforts to reconnect with alumni ramped up under Ratz. Buoyed by the success of the school's 20th anniversary in 1985 and the reflections it inspired as people remembered what NOLS had meant to them, he asked Paul Calver, admissions and marketing director at the time, to reach out to alumni. "A NOLS course does not end the last day of your course," Calver wrote in *The Leader* in November 1985. "This is a realization we are making at NOLS." By that time, the school had more than 20,000 alumni, and Calver was the perfect package of positive energy to develop an association of NOLS graduates. His initiative was an effort to reverse the decades of alumni neglect. For example, this message appeared in *The Leader* in May 1991:

> NOLS relies heavily on its alumni to recruit new NOLS students. If you are interested in helping in any (or all!) of the ways listed below, please complete this form and mail it to: Jane Grussing, NOLS, PO Box AA, Lander.

Options included serving as a reference for geographically nearby applicants, representing NOLS at local summer opportunity fairs or outdoor career expositions, and/or helping plan a NOLS reunion.

An early user of the school's new computer resources, Calver worked with Bruce Hampton to build the first database. He did what he could to gather information, including beginning the enormous project of transcribing decades of handwritten information from student files. Then he began to schedule NOLS alumni reunions. The very first was in Chicago on November 14, 1985. Five more were held the following year. One that occurred in around 1987 with board members and some New York alumni was to paddle kayaks around Manhattan. "Don Ford and myself hauled kleppers and gear from the Alaska branch," recalled instructor Nene Wolfe. "It was very interesting and unusual to be on the water, low down, and see the city from that perspective."

In 1988, Steff Kessler took on the task of heading up the school's Annual Fund. The next season, donations rose by $50,000, and individual donors increased from 66 to 898. As outreach logistics and processes smoothed out, the Annual Fund became more successful, and when the 25th anniversary of the school was approaching, a goal was set to raise $250,000 for the 1990 Annual Fund. That goal was exceeded.

Fundraising offered the school the opportunity to move forward with various initiatives that revenue from tuition dollars could not support: scholarships, outreach, research,

David Brower, founder of Friends of the Earth and first executive director of the Sierra Club, and Paul Petzoldt at the NOLS 25th anniversary party. *NOLS Archives*

facilities improvements, and equipment. The Annual Fund was an excellent start, but more fundraising was needed. The executive director of organizations like NOLS is typically at the forefront of the work of fundraising and promoting the school by traveling to meet alumni groups. Although Ratz's personal style was not naturally outgoing, he knew the value of being the face of NOLS and embarked on outreach trips to speak about the school and his recent initiatives. He could be impressively dynamic when he had to be, according to Brame.

The 25th Anniversary

On Labor Day weekend 1990, 320 NOLS staff, friends (including David Brower, founder of Friends of the Earth), and alumni gathered for the school's 25th anniversary.

NOLS TV. *Matt Burke*

NOLS had survived some difficult years, and was growing in ways its founders could never have imagined when the first course trudged away from Sinks Canyon laden by the three-bag-system backpacks of 1965. In fact, the school was thriving. It was a time of reflection about the past and recognition of achievement, as well as a chance to preview what was to come. As reported in *The Leader* (November 1990), "What NOLS is today surprised some early instructors, according to Kevin McGowan, who watched the old-timers wander wide-eyed through the new Wyoming branch facility. For them, the glitter and polish were a radical change from the days when an old, ramshackle lumber yard served as a student staging area . . . Down the street at the Noble, the laughter and music which used to pour out of the first floor bar has been replaced by the hum of computers and the buzz of telephones."

Paul Petzoldt had once again returned, and was honored by the board, which bestowed on him the title of "founder and president emeritus." Special tribute was also paid to Rob Hellyer, Tap Tapley, Petzoldt, and Thelma Young "for their contributions in establishing the standards and practices which continue to shape NOLS today." Thelma was given a tape recorder, in hopes she would record stories about the early days at NOLS. Peter Simer was cited for his leadership, and the scope of his efforts during the school's darkest days was acknowledged with the creation of the Peter Simer Scholarship for instructor course students.

Several awards were inaugurated that weekend as well. Instructors John Gookin, John Hauf, Lucy Smith, and Del Smith were "recognized for their dedication, enthusiasm, versatility, and initiative"—what became known as the "Instructor of the Year" Award. The first Alumni Award was presented to Mark Samuels, a teacher and coach committed to outdoor education. The first recipient of the NOLS Stewardship Award for land managers who exhibit "exceptional leadership in the care of the wildlands under their jurisdiction" was Robert Seibert, the South District ranger for Denali National Park and Preserve.

The gathering was also a chance for education. Several circus tents set up at the University of Missouri Field Station in Sinks Canyon became classrooms for two days of lectures on wilderness management, leadership and ethics, and wilderness skills. Roderick Nash, author of *Wilderness and the American Mind*, gave the keynote speech on "Evolution of the Wilderness Idea in America." Author and cultural anthropologist specializing in the indigenous cultures of Alaska, Richard Nelson, closed the proceedings with a stirring speech on ethical and spiritual relationships with the land. In between, some 32 people, including Petzoldt and Tapley, gave presentations and classes.

One remnant of the school's more radical days arose during a moment of disruption when:

> . . . The Personhood of the Cod, a reincarnation of the Strahmekians, the Flamingos and the Gang of Eight (or was it the Gang of Six?) staged a coup during the closing ceremonies, reminding the crowd that subversion lives on at NOLS. Jim Ratz was tied to a chair and forced to drink while zucchini-waving, garbage-bag-clad rebels listed their demands—tacky polyester at board meetings, hats made of tropical fruit, and scotch at debriefings—before releasing him (*The Leader*, November 1990).

Notwithstanding the Strahmekians, overall the hair in pictures from the reunion was shorter, people wore nametags, and the atmosphere had a somewhat dignified air of celebration. By 1990, the school had over 28,000 graduates. At the celebration, there was much commentary, both wistful and hopeful, about how the school had met the need to change, to grow up, and to move forward.

Instructors Aaron Devine and Madhu Chikkaraju bringing up the team during Expedition Denali.
Hudson Henry

NOLS MATURES

I am the lucky one. In the last 10 years of my life I have slept outside more often than not. I have seen the sun rise and the sun set, oftentimes before I am home. I have climbed some amazing peaks. I have seen Orion hanging upside down in the southern sky and eaten pork chops deep in the heart of the northern Wind Rivers. There were times when things were exquisitely clear to me; there were times when I didn't have the foggiest idea what to do. I have spent countless days in the mountains and in the desert. I have seen the moon reflecting off of a frozen draw draped in tamarisk while walking back to camp amid big sagebrush and sandstone. I have eaten beans and rice for dinner every night for 26 nights. And I would do it again. I have taught, learned, and grown. I have cried, grieved, and lost. I have made mistakes and I have failed. I have lived, laughed, and loved . . .

—Jared Spaulding, instructor

The adventure of NOLS has always attracted students and staff as surely as steel to a magnet. For many, the opportunity for a 30-day expedition in the wilderness was adventure enough, but there have always been those who sought more. For mountaineers, there were multiple winter attempts of the Grand Teton (13,770 feet), beginning in 1965. There was at least one annual climb, sometimes two, on Denali (20,322 feet) via the difficult and rarely used Muldrow Glacier route beginning in 1971, with biennial climbs after 2011. Together, students and instructors reached the sub-summits of Mount Kenya (17,057 feet) starting with inception of the Africa branch in 1974, and later, Kilimanjaro (19,341 feet). In 1985, Baja courses tackled Pico de Orizaba (18,750 feet), the highest peak in Mexico and fourth highest in North America. Argentina's Aconcagua (at 22,837 feet the highest peak outside of

A NOLS semester atop Mount Kilimanjaro. *Joshua McFee*

Asia) was on the course list from 1985 to 1991. Then there were the various rugged peaks of British Columbia's Waddington Range and Washington's North Cascades, not to mention the 18,000-foot traverses in the Garhwal Himalaya.

Adventure on the oceans and along rivers also beckoned students and instructors, starting with Tap Tapley and his attraction to Baja's Sea of Cortez in 1971. Canoeing the wild rivers of the Yukon and the Brooks Range was a goal for many, and the activity was also popular in New England, Utah, and elsewhere. The Folbots of NOLS's early days carried paddlers in Baja, Lake Powell, and in the far north along the challenging coastline of Prince William Sound; with modern kayaks, water-based adventure expanded to southeastern Alaska, the Pacific Northwest, Patagonia, Australia, and beyond. Rafting the Green River, the Yampa, the Salmon, the Matanuska, and others came along as well.

For instructors, the opportunities provided on courses whetted many an appetite for more intensive and challenging adventures—so many that *The Leader* began including a section titled "Expedition Update" in the 1990s. Many instructor expeditions were supported in part by the new NOLS Instructor Development Fund. By 1992, the IDF had disbursed over $55,000 to 60 endeavors, including 11 seminars, six research projects, and 40 expeditions. The funding in 1996 to 38 staff members supported 21 expeditions ranging from Newfound-

Shari Kearney. *NOLS Archives*

land to Pakistan, plus caving in Honduras and boating in Alaska, Utah, and Honduras.

In the 1980s, many NOLS climbing parties tackled the Himalaya. The 1980 American Women's Expedition to Dhaulighiri (26,795 feet) included Shari Kearney, Lucy Smith, and Cyndy Simer among its eight climbers; the death of another expedition member in an avalanche at Camp IV (24,500 feet) led to the end of that effort. Kearney and Smith returned to the Himalaya, successfully climbing the south ridge of Ama Dablam (22,349 feet) in 1982, the west ridge of Everest to within 1,000 feet of the summit in 1983, and to the summit of Pumori (23,494 feet) in 1989. In addition, they were part of the 1986 expedition to Annapurna that also included instructors Polly Fabian, Craig Seasholes, John Trainer, and George Van Sickle, with Kevin McGowan managing base camp.

In 1988, instructors Mike Collins, Dan Heilig, Rob Hess, Mal Miller, and Phil Powers were the first Americans to summit Pakistan's Gasherbrum II (26,362 feet). In 1994, Greg Collins and Gary Wilmot climbed Denali, Mount Foraker, and Mount Hunter, making them the first to climb Alaska's "big three" in a single push. That same year, John Hauf, Krishnan Kutty, and others climbed the eastern summit of India's Nanda Devi massif. In 1999, Cristina Prieto was the first South American woman to climb an 8,000-meter peak (Cho Oyu, 26,906 feet). Joining her on that climb, and also two years later on the summit of Everest, was Patty Soto. Soto later became an instructor, and was the first South American woman to reach the Seven Summits—the highest points on each continent. On a different expedition that

year, instructors Georgie Stanley, Supy Bullard, and Kathryn Miller Hess summited Cho Oyu (26,906 feet); Liane Owen and Caroline Byrd came close, but were thwarted when a weather window closed. Theirs was the first American all-women's ascent of an 8,000-meter peak without supplemental oxygen or Sherpa support.

Remarkable instructor expeditions were not confined to the mountains. One adventure, mounted long before the IDF, was a 1971 trip to "The Pit" in central Mexico. Properly known as El Sótano de las Golondrinas, it was at the time the deepest known freefall pit in the western hemisphere (1,220 feet to the floor). That journey included Haven Holsapple, Jim Ratz, George Hunker, and Allen Robinson, supported by Beverly Holsapple, Linda Miller, and Martha Wakefield. In 1989, George Van Sickle sailed solo for six weeks up the coast of Labrador in a 14-foot dinghy. In 1997, Van Sickle and Steph White did an extensive exploration through the jigsaw puzzle of islands along the Chonos Archipelago in Chile in a 21-foot open sailboat named *Sea Pearl*.

Some especially notable climbs in the annals of NOLS involved K2 and Everest. In 1990, instructors Doug Dahlquist, Rob Hess, Dan Heilig, Phil Powers, and Greg Collins returned to K2's Abruzzi Ridge, where Paul Petzoldt had set a world altitude record of 26,000 feet during his 1938 expedition. Petzoldt would have no doubt smiled to see Powers's conclusion about the trip as reported in *The Leader*

A STORM ON DENALI

By Molly Absolon, instructor

This is excerpted from an account of a storm that hit a NOLS course high on Denali in 1984.

"We have to abandon the tent," Glenn yelled over the roar of the wind.

His words whipped away from him as he struggled to remain upright. In the swirl of blowing snow, he could barely make out the bundled forms of his companions, who were shoveling by the nylon shelter that protected their colleagues inside. In addition to people, the tent contained cameras, clothing, boots, journals, pads, and sleeping bags. Abandoning it meant abandoning the gear, but for each shovelful of snow thrown into the air, two more drifted in. It was like being in the bottom of an hourglass with sand pouring in around them.

The storm occurred while Glenn Goodrich was camped with three other instructors—Dan Heilig, Rob Hess, and Katie Smith—and 14 students at 16,300 feet on Denali on a National Outdoor Leadership School expedition. It was July 5, 1984—day two of a storm that felt like it could blow the entire course off the mountain.

The group's summit day had started well. The skies were clear and the wind calm when they rose at 1:00 a.m. to cook breakfast in the gray twilight that is night in Alaska. By 2:30 a.m. they'd begun moving up the Harper Glacier toward the summit. Roped together in teams of three or four, the course formed a snaking line trudging upward; their eyes transfixed on the footprints in front of them. Altitude made every step laborious, and everyone fell into a slow, painful, private rhythm—step, breath, breath, step.

As they approached the summit, the weather began to worsen. Glenn weighed his options, trying to decide whether to continue or turn around. In his opinion, conditions were marginal but not clearly dictating retreat. He could see landmarks drifting in and out of the clouds; the students seemed to be comfortable and warm; and the summit was only 300 feet or so above them. Part of him thought they could make it to the top; part of him was plagued by nagging worry about the wisdom of being out at 20,000 feet in deteriorating weather.

Denali is a goal-oriented climb. The main reason people climb it is to stand on top of the highest mountain in North America. NOLS had a reputation for success on the peak. Since its first attempt in 1971, NOLS courses had successfully summited every year prior to the 1984 expedition. People at the school said the route could be "climbed by the numbers." If you used the same progression people followed in the past—camp here, then here, move up to Karsten's Ridge, traverse to Browne's Tower, move to the crevasse camp at 16,300 feet, summit—you were supposed to have it in the bag. Glenn, the one in charge in 1984, felt pressure to live up to past successes.

The burden of his position weighed Glenn down. He doubted there would be a second chance for this expedition to go for the top. If they turned around, they turned their backs on the mountain for good. Glenn knew that the students and NOLS would understand that decision, but he was torn by a sense of disappointment. He wanted to give the weather a little while to prove itself. He didn't want to give up.

But Dan and Rob were insistent that it was time to retreat. Glenn could hear their shouts, telling him they needed to turn around. He stared into the clouds ahead, and with resignation conceded that it was unwise to continue.

Within 20 minutes, any doubts about the decision disappeared. Visibility deteriorated rapidly as the clouds lowered, leaving the group enveloped in a cloak of whiteness. Being in a whiteout is like being deprived of your sight, but instead of blackness, everything is white. It creates a disconcerting, floating feeling, like being trapped inside a Ping-Pong ball.

In this claustrophobic fog, descent was slow. Dan was alone out front, connected to the others by a rope, but isolated by distance and the incessant howl of the wind. He led by intuition and feel, searching for signs of their passing: wands, tracks, even urine stains in the snow. Behind his stoic exterior and his methodical movement, his fear of what could happen if they failed to find camp drove him forward.

Eighteen hours after leaving for the summit, the team dragged itself back into camp. In their absence, fresh snow had buried two tents, destroying one. The students crowded into the remaining structures and fired up stoves to make drinks before collapsing into their sleeping bags to rest. But the relentless noise of the wind made sleep impossible. Tents flexed, snapped, and flapped; the wind roared and groaned like an angry animal; and drifting snow built up, pressing in on the nylon walls.

For hours, the group rotated in and out of the tents, shoveling away the snow to keep from getting buried. The wind continually increased until it gusted at 60 to 100 miles per hour. To support the tents, the occupants leaned back against the walls, using their bodyweight to try to counteract the flapping. Outside, people's eyelashes froze together and their beards caked with ice. Teams could only shovel for 10 minutes or so before the cold drove them to take shelter. To walk, they had to crouch, hands extended for balance or to catch themselves if the wind blew them over. Everyone stuck close together when they ventured outside or risked disappearing into the whiteout.

By the end of the first day of the storm, all of the student tents had collapsed. A snow cave the group built during a previous rest day provided a temporary sanctuary until its occupants could no longer keep the door free from the drifting snow and were forced to abandon it as well, leaving all 18 crowded into two tents: nine people in each three-person shelter. They sat wrapped around each other, huddled tightly together. Any movement sent a ripple through the group as everyone adjusted.

Hours and days blurred together. Glenn struggled to write in the course log. He stopped keeping track of the date and time, marking each new entry with a simple, "Later."

Finally, after days of relentless pounding, the storm began to abate. It was unclear how long it had lasted or when it actually ended. The wind's furor just became less constant, and people no longer had to shout to converse. Gradually they were able to stop shoveling and could relax and sleep.

When they ventured out after some rest, they found that their camp had disappeared. In its place was a flat white expanse. Almost all of the group's gear lay buried underneath.

For the next few hours while Dan and Rob, linked by 45

feet of webbing, descended to a spot where they could call NOLS Alaska for assistance, the course dug in search of the equipment. One tent was 12 feet beneath the surface. They cut a hole in its top and salvaged what they could through a narrow tube in the snow.

Eventually Glenn and Katie decided they had enough to move with what they had, but it took creativity to outfit the team. One person had lost his boots, so he shared with another; they wore a boot on one foot and a down bootie on the other. People without backpacks slung duffel bags over their shoulders. A couple of people used a single crampon, and some carried a metal avalanche probe in lieu of an ice axe. The instructors chopped steps through the steep, icy terrain down to Browne's Tower to provide footing for students without crampons. Below that the snowpack got deeper and less icy, so travel was easier for people walking in pillow-like booties. Slowly and steadily they moved down, fueled by a driving desire to get off the mountain.

Dan and Rob were able to place a call through to the branch from Browne's Tower. The call came in during the staff's midseason celebration. As Dan rattled off the list of gear the course needed to get to the road safely, the severity of their predicament sobered the festivities. They needed everything —tents, boots, food, fuel, clothing, and climbing gear. People immediately dropped what they were doing and began pulling equipment off the issue room shelves. In 20 minutes they had duffel bags packed and ready to be airlifted into the course on the Muldrow Glacier.

The airdrop exploded when it hit the glacier, sending equipment and food across the ice. When the course reached it, they descended upon the scattered treasure in a rush,

The Muldrow Glacier, northeast of Denali. *Drew Leemon*

savoring the instant gratification of candy bars and firing up stoves for hot drinks. That night they each slept in their own dry sleeping bag for the first time in nearly a week. Suddenly the storm was over and they were on their way home.

(November 1990). After three months in Pakistan, and 22 days of storms that descended just as all the high camps were established, he wrote:

> ... when I ponder the reasons that we were unable to make the summit, I find several—not the least of which is that we were very safe and did not take risks. I'm proud of that and of the fact we suffered no injuries and returned as five close friends.

In August 1992, 54 years after Petzoldt's K2 attempt, instructor Scott Fischer, age 36, stood on the 28,251-foot summit. He and Ed Viesturs were the first Americans to climb the notoriously challenging mountain free of supplemental oxygen. Eighteen months later, in May 1994, Fischer and fellow instructor Rob Hess stood on top of Mount Everest, again without using supplemental oxygen. They were the third and fourth Americans to climb the world's highest peak in that manner. Another instructor on that expedition, Steve Goryl, lingered for five days solo at the South Col (25,938 feet) waiting for favorable weather; he reached the summit Friday, May 13, the day before his 40th birthday.

Steve Gipe, medical leader on the 1994 Everest expedition, said that the feat by Fischer and Hess hearkened back to the day he arrived at NOLS in July 1967 for issue day at

Scott Fischer atop K2. *Ed Viesturs*

Sinks Canyon. "That afternoon, Paul came out onto the walkway from the dungeon [the old pumphouse] back up to the cabin. It was uphill, and he was giving us our first class on trail technique and rhythmic breathing and how to place your feet. He talked about how 'if you use these techniques, someday somebody will climb Mount Everest without oxygen'—an inconceivable feat at the time."

So much climbing inevitably led to incidents, both on courses and on personal expeditions. Over the years, the school had to mount evacuations off Denali, Aconcagua, and the Garhwal Himalaya, among others, mostly for frostbite and altitude-related illnesses. In April 1991, instructor Gershom Ebole Wayodi, 33, died of high-altitude pulmonary edema on Mount Kenya during a personal trip. In June 1992, instructors Colby Coombs and Tom Walter, along with a third climbing partner, were hit by an avalanche just 200 feet from the summit of Alaska's Mount Foraker; when he regained consciousness, Coombs saw he was the only survivor. Hampered by a broken scapula, broken ankle, and two displaced and fractured cervical vertebrae, he took 10 days to reach help. Phil Powers summited K2 in 1993, but one of his climbing partners died on the descent. In June 1994, instructors Patti Saurman, 32, and Chris Walburgh, 28, were killed in a fall on Mount Hunter, Alaska. A third expedition member was badly injured, and the fourth rope team member, fellow instructor Don Sharaf, made an epic walk for help with a fractured leg. Fischer, too, died, in a storm on Mount Everest in 1996 while assisting clients of his guiding business, Mountain Madness. That episode became the basis for John Krakauer's bestseller *Into Thin Air*.

No instructors died while working for the school during the 1990s, but three students perished on their courses: Richard Sarnoff in 1992, Katy Brain in 1996, and Thomas Nazzaro in 1999. All three died in the mountains, and all three incidents caused much soul-searching throughout the school. In many ways, the 1990s were the school's most serious decade. NOLS attempted to turn its losses into learning for the whole outdoor industry, while at the same time codify its leadership curriculum, stake its position as a world leader in minimum impact camping techniques, solidify its finances, and manage a difficult leadership transition. The school spent much of the decade "storming," as it completed a metamorphosis from its cash-strapped, freewheeling youth to a more mature educational organization with a professional image and global impact.

Teaching LNT curriculum in the field.
Marco Johnson

Core Programs and Initiatives

Petzoldt started NOLS with care of the environment on his mind, a care he practiced in his own life. Jim Allen—longtime instructor and Wyoming state representative for Fremont County in 2015—remembered the early 1960s when he was a boy of 12 riding in the backseat of his father's pickup truck. They were showing Paul, who was new to the area, around the southern Winds. On one trip, they were easing along a one-lane, boulder-strewn road to Shoshone Reservoir when Paul abruptly shouted, "Stop the truck!" Jim couldn't imagine what was wrong. Petzoldt got out, picked up a can that was lying in the road, threw it in the bed of the truck, and they went on their way. Although the Allens were already mindful of not leaving their own litter, Jim said, it was the first time it occurred to the Wyoming native to pick up someone else's.

NOLS Conservation and Leave No Trace

Paul's concern for the environment is evident in his very first board report: "In 1965 we found that the teaching of use, with conservation, of our recreational lands to be one of the most necessary parts of our program. In the end it will be one of the most beneficial parts of our program. We recommend a stronger emphasis on the above . . ." It is a constant theme. A PPWE catalog from the early 1970s devotes half a page to recommended conservation practices along with a discourse on conservation, saying, "NOLS feels that the wilderness should be used and enjoyed. We also feel that if it isn't used properly it will soon be destroyed." The 1972 annual report was printed on relatively novel recycled paper.

Inside the front cover of the December 1975 *NOLS Alumnus* is a drawing of a tree and this: "Conservation practices are the most important part of a NOLS expedition. Our ideas are spreading far and wide, combining with the thinking of others and evolving to fit various environmental requirements. They are not meant to be fixed rules, but tools of consciousness, expressions of our sense of responsibility to our mother earth." In that same issue, Petzoldt described specific methods of conservation, concluding with these prescient words: "We feel that using these practices, we can go into the mountains and leave no trace of our passing . . ."

Others were also tuning into the wisdom of promoting conservation-minded use of public lands. Multiple federal agencies, including the US Forest Service, National Park Service, and the Bureau of Land Management (BLM) understood that a purely regulatory approach would probably just antagonize people, and that the problems being encountered were more the result of a lack of education. They tried publishing various pamphlets and brochures on the topic, but it was evident that without centralized or cross-agency coordination, a unified message would not happen.

With the 1988 publication of *Soft Paths: How To Enjoy the Wilderness Without Harming It*, by Bruce Hampton and David Cole, NOLS solidified its emerging position as a leader in the area of wilderness conservation. "The important part of this book was that David, as a researcher, corroborated, using scientific literature, that our practices, which had really been developed by trial and error over time on courses, were actually legit," said Drew Leemon. With NOLS's growing stature in the field, land managers approached the school for instruction and help. The same year, the school ran a training course for the BLM called Low Impact Use of Arid Lands, which went on to run annually through 1991. In 1990 and 1991, NOLS provided low-impact instruction to Forest Service personnel at an annual training event for their leadership.

In May 1991 the Forest Service approached NOLS to develop the Leave No Trace educational curriculum. That resulted in a trip in June for Leemon and Molly Hampton to Washington, DC, to garner support from other agencies and sign a memorandum of understanding including the Forest Service, the BLM, US Fish and Wildlife Service, and the National Park Service. The ultimate result was a broad public education message and a unified, national training program.

"There are three components to Leave No Trace: 1) Public Awareness, 2) Education, and 3) Research," wrote Leemon in the school's instructor newsletter that August. NOLS would be taking on the educational component. He, Rich Brame, and Susan Brame taught the pilot LNT program called Master of Leave No Trace that September to prepare graduates to train others. LNT's "train the trainer" model initially targeted land managers such as backcountry rangers, law enforcement officers, line officers, and interpreters.

Marco Johnson and Rich Brame help a student weigh her pack in 1986. *NOLS Archives*

Beyond the Master Educator course, other early educational formats were the Trainer course (an abbreviated version of the Master course), workshops, and informal LNT presentations at visitor centers, in the backcountry and elsewhere.

It was an alluring opportunity for the school, both to create and distribute a national conservation educational program based on NOLS's practices and ethos, and to generate some welcome visibility for NOLS. It was also a huge

and costly task, and the bulk of the effort to wrangle disparate concepts and partners into a coherent program fell to Leemon, in his then-role of Wyoming branch planning manager. When he left to become director of NOLS Southwest in 1991, Del Smith and Rich and Susan Brame took charge. NOLS took the lead in developing field training, curriculum models and outcomes, and also writing and distributing a series of over a dozen LNT "Outdoor Skills & Ethics" booklets and environment-specific instruction guides and videos. These integrated information spanning multiple geographic regions and specific recreation activities from horsepacking and caving to sea kayaking and more.

NOLS paid for the design of the Leave No Trace logo, spearheaded curriculum development, and wrote an LNT Mission Statement ("to protect the outdoors by teaching and inspiring people to enjoy it responsibly"), as well as defined strategic goals and the principles underlying the Leave No Trace concept. It also supported a national toll-free LNT information number that rang at NOLS. For eight years, LNT work was the predominant focus of Rich Brame's job at NOLS.

"Doing the 'LNT dance'"—courting sometimes conflicting agency partners, youth groups, and the outdoor industry—" was incredibly time-consuming," he said. "Ultimately, it was very exciting because it was packaging NOLS's conservation curriculum for the world." The program that emerged was science-based and designed to be experiential. It built a wilderness ethic that was easy to practice, teach, and adapt to different audiences, environments, and situations.

As the program mushroomed in popularity, other groups got involved, including the National Park Service, US Fish and Wildlife Service, and the Appalachian Mountain Club. While the federal agencies provided overall steering and direction for the program, NOLS and other outdoor-oriented organizations took on the training, as well as development and distribution of the information.

But for NOLS, the commitment became increasingly onerous both in terms of cost and time. It was a lot for a school that was just regaining its footing after many years of shaky finances. Various factors began increasingly to limit the school's interest and ability to continue working so deeply with and for the LNT concept. NOLS began to encounter resistance and even some organizational jealousies from others for its dominant position among the numerous partners. And funding was tight, particularly federal funding.

A summit meeting was called between several outdoor recreation and outdoor manufacturing representatives, and the decision was made to spin off LNT as a nonprofit organization in its own right. Leave No Trace, Inc. (later renamed the Leave No Trace Center for Outdoor Ethics) would be based in Boulder, Colorado, with seed money from NOLS, the Sporting Goods Manufacturers Association, and the Outdoor Recreation Coalition of America. By the year 2000, the organization had 239 corporate sponsors and four active federal agency partners. The Boy Scouts had even developed an LNT merit badge. LNT training was available both domestically and in more than 10 international settings.

NOLS ROCKY MOUNTAIN

Over the years, the NOLS branch in Lander has been called several things. In 1965 it wasn't even a branch—it was *the* National Outdoor Leadership School. In 1970, field operations moved in at the Lumberyard, still under the direction of the executive director, who was at the time Paul Petzoldt. Within a few years, as branches opened in Baja, Alaska, and Africa, it became known as the Wyoming branch—still under the direction of the executive directors until Jim Ratz handed off daily operations and the title of branch director to Dave Neary in 1984.

The facility, from its bare-bones, decrepit, abandoned former lumberyard, has seen several facelifts through the years as well, although a student from 1973 remarked at the 50th reunion that the original portion of the issue room still smells the same. The Gourmet Gulch has retained its unique atmosphere remarkably well through the years, too.

It was renamed NOLS Rocky Mountain in 1989, in recognition that its operations by then extended to nine areas of the American West. It was the largest branch (by far) throughout the first 50 years of the school's history. In 2015, 1,818 students took a course under its umbrella, according to branch director Gary Cukjati.

In addition to mounting courses in its own region, the work of the Rocky Mountain branch in 2015 included supporting other areas and facilities at NOLS East Africa, NOLS Northeast, the river base at Vernal, Three Peaks Ranch, and the Noble Hotel. Many people have stewarded the heart of the school over the years:

Brad Christensen

1965-1975: Paul Petzoldt
1975: Jon Hamren
1975-1983: Peter Simer
1983-1985: Jim Ratz
1985-1989: Dave Neary
1989: Drew Leemon
1989-1995: Michael Lindsey
1996-2002: Tod Schimelpfenig
2002-2007: Dave Glenn
2007: Pete Absolon
2007-2015: Gary Cukjati

As of 2015, the school continued to provide administrative support and logistics for LNT training courses, as well as retaining partial ownership of the copyright of the LNT written materials. The LNT Master Educator certification was still included in the curriculum of many longer NOLS courses, particularly semesters. On a broader level, environmental studies and LNT concepts and terminology continued to permeate NOLS classes and activities. "The LNT lessons haven't changed much since 1965," said Liz Tuohy, director of education for the school, in 2015. "LNT ethics (even before there was an LNT program) are a key reason we've reduced course sizes over the years, and why today we split those small courses up into even smaller hiking groups: In addition to creating more leadership opportunities, it minimizes the impact on the environment and other visitors."

———————————

There were other NOLS conservation efforts as well. In 1987, instructor Liz Nichol was part of the North American Everest North Face expedition. She recalled that the volume of rubbish at the base camp on the Tibet side was appalling. The mess motivated Nichol, her then-husband, Bob McConnell, Steve Goryl, and other NOLS folks to mount three environmental trips to the region to clean things up, in 1990, 1992, and 1994. Borrowing a concept from the 1987 trip, they got financial support for the expeditions, in part, from including outdoor enthusiasts who would pay for the chance to hike to base camp on what came to be called "support treks."

Members of the 1990 Everest Environmental Expedition, dubbed "E3," worked for six weeks to remove more than a ton of trash left by previous climbers and trekkers at base camp and advanced base camp (18,000 feet) on the north side of the mountain. Trash was removed by backpack, then transferred to yak, tractor, and truck to be hauled 110 kilometers to a specially dug landfill in the town of Xegar (now Shelkar), Tibet.

Paul Petzoldt himself was able to join one of the several E3 support treks on the approach to Everest's north side. At age 82, he and his wife, Ginny, arrived at base camp near the 16,000-foot terminus of the Rongbuk Glacier via Pang La (a 17,060-foot pass). Although they rode much of the way in a truck, remembered McConnell, Petzoldt was able at last to catch his first glimpse of the world's highest peak. He spoke about the importance of saving the environment, saying, among other things, "It's high time climbers began working together to keep the pigs off the peaks."

The May 1994 Sagarmatha Environmental Expedition (SEE-94) used the Nepalese name for Mount Everest and

Paul in clothes a bit fancier than his usual mountaineering attire. *NOLS Archives*

was notable for more than putting two Americans on top without supplemental oxygen. As with the 1990 effort, there were several support treks, this time to the base camp on the Nepali side, that were dedicated to environmental cleanup. The expedition collected more than 5,000 pounds of trash, including discarded oxygen bottles ferried down from the higher camps by Sherpas. They were paid about $5 per bottle,

an incentive devised by team member Brent Bishop. Dubbed the "1994 American Clean Group" by the Nepalis, expedition members also gathered the GPS coordinates of major trash sites for future reference. The group was awarded that year's David Brower Award for Environmental Action by the American Alpine Club.

At a slide show in Maine about his SEE-94 experience,

Goryl presented Petzoldt with one of the retrieved oxygen bottles, signed by all the members of the expedition. It was a memento Petzoldt treasured.

Wilderness Medicine and Risk Management

Herb Ogden came to NOLS as a student in 1975, at age 22. He returned to NOLS in 1978 for the instructor course and spent several summers working for the school while teaching dyslexic boys in the off-season.

It was while teaching mountaineering, he said, that he realized the most difficult decisions and the things that mattered most were medical problems, particularly injuries. "I found myself reading a lot of *Medicine for Mountaineering*, and thought, 'I really should have been a doctor.' I decided to stop talking about it and go do it," he said.

In 1981 he worked the Denali expedition. His friend, Jim Ratz (who was an instructor on Ogden's climbing section during his 1975 semester), was by then the branch director in Alaska. "It was the summer we became best friends," Ogden said. "We got ourselves in all sorts of trouble, drinking and setting off firecrackers." The friendship endured, yielding big dividends to the school as the men grew into their careers. When the board increased its focus on safety in 1990, Ratz was executive director and Ogden was an emergency department physician.

For some time, conversations about the unique nature of wilderness medicine had been brewing, largely stirred at NOLS by Tod Schimelpfenig. In the school's early years, organizational attention to first aid was relatively limited; it wasn't until 1978 that instructors were required to have a first-aid certificate. A first-aid course relevant to the backcountry came when NOLS got a contract to teach survival and field risk management to ARCO geologists in Alaska, according to Schimelpfenig. The three-day medical course he devised with Len Paglario for ARCO became the basis in 1979 for what they dubbed Backcountry Emergency Care (BEC—the NOLS precursor to today's Wilderness First Responder, or WFR). The 56-hour program built upon the basic first-aid courses then available by focusing on backcountry-specific medical issues and care options.

With so much interest in the topic, Ratz asked Ogden, after he completed his emergency residency in 1991, if he would consider being the medical advisor to the school to oversee medical screening of prospective students, develop medical protocols, and improve the drug kit for field use.

"It was new territory," said Ogden. "There was no model for that." His malpractice carrier in Colorado confirmed that they'd never heard of anything like that, but that didn't dissuade Ogden from signing on, saying, "The stuff I do as medical advisor is because I believe NOLS instructors are the best."

Together, Schimelpfenig and Ogden wrote the first edition of the NOLS Medical Protocols in 1991. Schimelpfenig had attempted an earlier version in the late 1980s, working with some Lander-based doctors, but with Ogden fully on board, the concept blossomed. The protocols enjoyed immediate acceptance by most instructors, according to Schimelpfenig, and in coming years they continued to evolve in content and efficacy.

The protocols established first-aid treatment specific to wilderness practice, including such things as dislocation reduction, spine injury management, and wound care in the field. They provided guidance for making evacuation decisions, and formalized the indications for and use of the medications issued in NOLS first-aid kits. That same year, the first edition of *NOLS Wilderness First Aid,* co-authored by Schimelpfenig and longtime field instructor, Linda Lindsey, RN, was published. Designed to accompany NOLS's wilderness medicine courses and to support field course curriculum, it was eventually renamed *NOLS Wilderness Medicine,* and its sixth edition was slated for release in 2016.

Creating defined, written medical protocols were part of a more general push to examine risk management more systematically. Developing the protocols was a relatively

Drew Leemon, NOLS director of risk management beginning in 1996. *NOLS Archives*

Splinting practice on a WMI course in Nepal.
Evan Horn

easy process compared to the effort in coming years to build a more intentional conversation about incidents that occurred on courses for the purpose of learning from them.

Key to the effort was Drew Leemon, who succeeded Schimelpfenig as director of risk management in 1996. According to many people, Leemon's manner of approaching both evacuations and "near misses"—incidents in the field that didn't result in injury or evacuation—in a nonjudgmental manner was instrumental in developing a culture of open discussion.

"Instructors were concerned that if they had an incident on a course it made them look bad and their competency as an instructor would be questioned," said Leemon in 2015. "I set out to build off Tod's efforts to show that reporting near misses was important for the lessons we can learn from them. In addition, I wanted to be clear that I—and 'we,' as an administration—have a responsibility to respond to these incidents in an appropriate way, basically not to overreact and create policy or threaten someone's career."

Near-miss data, in particular, was tougher to gather; because no one got hurt, many instructors didn't report those incidents reliably. In the decade prior to 1996, the school averaged 53 near-miss reports annually. In the following 20 years, the annual average was 112. "This isn't because we had more, it is because we had more reported," said Leemon. "Our goal was to develop trust between instructors and the administration so we could get accurate information, and be able to use that to manage risk better and have better outcomes."

Board members Jed Williamson and Reb Gregg supported the increased focus on risk management. In particular Gregg, a Houston attorney who served as the school's legal counsel for 35 years, helped change the way NOLS thought about and communicated about risk. He was a primary voice in the change from "safety" to "risk management" in the school's vernacular, and helped craft the school's student agreement in a way that made clearer the risks inherent in the NOLS classroom. He also helped the school in its darkest hours during communications with the families of students who had died.

"He was a proponent of being honest and forthcoming with the families of fatality victims," said Leemon. "He believed, and counseled us to believe, that the families want answers [to what happened] and if we don't provide them . . . it can increase their anger and a lawsuit might be the only recourse to get the answers. He helped us convince our insurance carrier that this was the right thing to do." Although open communication like this was already a longstanding practice at NOLS, it was after the death of Katy Brain in 1996 that Gregg and Molly Hampton dug in to effect a change within the insurance industry from the prevailing standard of secrecy to being more open and telling the truth from the outset of an incident. It was a positive outcome in the wake of that tragedy.

John Kanengieter teaching a leadership seminar.
Brad Christensen

Talking more openly about risk management was itself part of a larger effort in the late 1980s and early 1990s to encourage better communication between instructors and program supervisors. "It was a fledgling aspect of NOLS, and in the 1980s we were trying to figure out how to do it. We'd never had any kind of training in this type of facilitation," said Leemon.

John Kanengieter, a P-Sup (program supervisor) at the Rocky Mountain branch at the time, was among those that began to place an increased focus on open communication during course debriefings. It was difficult at first for instructors to admit mistakes. "I wouldn't call it an ingrained habit, but there was a belief that was instilled in instructors that they were all-knowing, and experts in everything, and we bought into our [own] ego or hubris," said one instructor who began working in the 1980s. "When people like Kanengieter questioned us, we didn't have a good culture for talking about it without being defensive on both sides."

It required steady persistence to transition culturally from there to an understanding that such information was valuable for learning how to do things better. It required building trust, especially among field personnel, that reported incidents could (and would) be used productively. Over time, said Kanengieter, his focus during briefings and debriefings shifted from being "all about teaching technical skills [to] being more and more interested in the human dynamics and the leadership aspect."

At the time, Schimelpfenig was doing research on communication and decision-making among airline pilots, and noticing how that information could apply at NOLS. One tool he found that was especially effective in tough debriefings was to focus on the decisions that had been made, rather than on the people who had made them. As Leemon said in 2015, "We wanted to discuss and evaluate in an objective manner the decisions instructors made, but respect them as people and as professionals, and that approach helped set the tone."

Another tactic to foster a positive cultural approach to risk management was the publication of three special editions of the *Staff Newsletter*, in 1993, 1996, and 1999, titled "Highlighting Risk Management." The newsletters mimicked other publications, such as *Accidents in North American Mountaineering*, which was edited by Jed Williamson and published annually by the American Alpine Club. Each contained nearly 50 pages of accounts of injuries, illnesses, and near-miss situations, identifying the contributing factors of the environment (objective) and decisions that were made (subjective), and looking for what could be learned from each situation. The ultimate goal was to create a culture among instructors to share the lessons learned about near-miss moments (and worse) collectively, with an aim to preventing similar incidents from happening again.

Steady implementation of this new dynamic required time—a lot of it—but the result was better information that led to broader thinking as well as increased support for and emphasis on building resources for instructors and instructor development. "I think as a result, because NOLS has been doing all this debriefing stuff more honestly," said Kanengieter, "that it's become a model for organizational learning."

Tucked in for the night in Patagonia.
Ben Fox

A Growing School

THE GENERAL EFFORT to build intentionality and better transparency certainly seemed plodding sometimes, but it filtered into the overall culture of the school at a crucial junction. NOLS was not only growing up, it was simply growing: Between 1986 and 1996, "program days" more than doubled, from 65,000 to 131,000. From 181 field instructors in 1986, the numbers rose to 375 in 1996. (By 2015, there would be more than 600 field instructors and 250 WMI instructors, with more than a few teaching for both.)

In addition to sheer numbers of students, the school also finally had the financial steadiness to expand into new locations, both domestically and abroad. Realizing that "NOLS Wyoming" was actually operating in nine western states, it received the new name of NOLS Rocky Mountain in 1989, along with a facelift for the old Lumberyard facility at 5th and Lincoln. Likewise, the branch that started out as NOLS Washington and then became NOLS Cascades was renamed

NOLS Pacific Northwest in 1990, when its first semester programs led students farther afield regionally and out onto the water for sailing.

In January 1990, the school announced the formation of the Patagonia branch, the first new course location since the 1974 founding of the Kenya branch. Proposed and initially researched by instructor Tim Rawson, the area was scouted in 1989 by Molly Doran and John Hauf, who also ran the first courses there. Doran wrote in a letter during that scouting trip:

> Sitting there in the chill of the early dawn,
> watching ducks and geese take flight off of gravel
> banks as our boat navigated the river to avoid
> *remolinas* (whirlpools), straining our necks
> not to miss one of the immense glacial valleys
> we passed—landscape doesn't get much more

impressive. Or so we thought. We'd come to an emerald *campo* (small ranch) nestled against a mountain and I'd turn to John and say, "This is perfection," but each place was like that. . . .

At the time, the programs in the Southwest were also brand new; their second semester program in January 1990 was staged out of a hotel as a "road show" for lack of a base of operations. Farther afield, in the summer of 1991, the first mountaineering courses got under way in India with the goal (not realized, according to CL Tony Jewell) of summiting 19,421-foot Bauljuri at the head of the Pindari River.

Some locations, such as Tucson, Driggs, and Vernal, operated under the umbrella of the NOLS Rocky Mountain branch at the time; as such, they were referred to informally as "twigs." As of 2015, Vernal remained within the operational umbrella of Rocky Mountain, but the Arizona operation was named NOLS Southwest in July 1991, and the Driggs location was named NOLS Teton Valley in 1999.

PIC, ROPE, and Other Alternative Pathways into NOLS

Arguably, the best fun at NOLS accrues—has always accrued—to those who go into the field. The green valleys, sharp ridgelines, endless skies, and roiling waters of

the school's classrooms were as far from a desk as anyone could wish. Even the classroom courses at WMI were based around medical scenarios that, when possible, got students outdoors to practice skills in the sun and snow and freezing waters of a handy creek. To be a NOLS instructor was to find oneself at the emotional heart of the school, to be that person who could and did lead students to wondrous, transformative places. What a relief to set off at the trailhead and move farther away from civilization, with its briefings and emails and administrative demands; with each step, the instructor could be free again, to offer along with the hard skills that intangible essence of NOLS. The cachet of the instructor was—is—irrefutable.

Understandably, others in the outdoor education community began to ask about joining NOLS. In 1991, Jim Ratz, at the suggestion of Mark Cole in staffing, devised a way in for people whose skill-based credentials were unassailable. That May, the school conducted its first Summer Instructor Seminar (later renamed Professional Instructor Course, or PIC) in the Wind Rivers. It was a shorter course than the traditional instructor courses—just two weeks, but its curriculum and format were rigorous, and its acceptance criteria even more so. It was also highly subsidized, for pragmatic as well as altruistic reasons, since the school at the time was growing and needed more course leader-level instructors

Another day at the office for instructors Matt McArdle and Ryan Williams. *Matt McArdle*

than the regular IC track was creating.

"These people are competent outdoors people . . . and educators in general," said Marco Johnson, in 2015 the director of field staffing. "The goal was to show them how we do things at NOLS, because it's different from Outward Bound, or another program."

"Initially, the bar was very high," he said, but PIC eligibility requirements shifted over time. "You had to have 100 weeks of experience. Then as years passed, it dropped down to 60 weeks." That requirement dropped to as low as 30 weeks at times, but in 2015 the cutoff was at 50 weeks.

One person who entered NOLS via the PIC was Pip Coe, who was on the inaugural course in 1991. She was already an experienced commercial river guide and canoe/kayaking instructor. Early on, Pip helped develop the water-based programs in Vernal, Utah, scouted the meandering Owyhee River, and worked in Kenya before starting her tenure in the alumni and development office (where she was director in 2015).

Another innovation related to the PIC was the ROPE ("recognition of professional experience") program. It was a way, said Johnson, "to recognize and honor somebody who is coming in with 5 or 10 years of experience from another organization." This allowed qualified newcomers to start at a higher pay level than the basic entry level—something that generated resentment, according to Johnson. "The idea of someone starting to work for NOLS who didn't go through the five-week instructor course was change in a big way," he said. It got easier over time to appreciate the benefits of cross-pollination of ideas and approaches to outdoor education that arrived with many PIC instructors, but coming in from outside as an instructor was nevertheless a sometimes rocky road.

The same was true for those hired for positions elsewhere in the school. By tradition and precedent, administrative positions had typically been filled with field personnel ready to come in from the backcountry, usually (though not always)

PATAGONIA:
A RAW LANDSCAPE

By Drew Seitz, instructor

It all starts with the wind. In Chilean Patagonia, it is like a living thing, a presence that never fully leaves your consciousness. Its strength and consistency can be staggering; some of the locals refer to it as *"Escoba de Dios"* or "The Broom of God" for its ability to sweep the earth clean of everything in its path. As the only large landmass that pierces so deeply into the Southern Ocean, Chilean Patagonia is the first impediment for winds that have blown unobstructed around the entire globe. The landscape itself is shaped by wind: stunted trees with limbs growing only on one side, *pobladores'* houses huddled among protective poplars, the shorelines battered by wind-driven waves that make kayak landings difficult or impossible.

With the wind (and sometimes without it) comes the rain. Sometimes it is no more than a heavy cloud or mist. Sometimes it calls the story of Noah to mind. The rain and snow feed this lush land and fuel its wild rivers and massive ice fields. The Andes to the east force the prevailing westerlies to dump their moisture, meaning that in some places average yearly precipitation can top 70 inches. The wetness can seem omnipresent and overwhelming. Not seeing the sun for weeks at a time makes the sunny days even more special.

The mountains and coastline of southern Chile are some of the most remote places on earth. NOLS courses here feel different. The sense of exploration, of remoteness, of wilderness, is heightened. Only 100,000 people live in an area the size of Portugal, served by only one highway—the *Carretera Austral*—running unpaved for nearly 1,000 kilometers. Many semesters spend a week or so at the start of the course at the *campo* and don't return to hot showers and indoor spaces for 90 days.

From coastal rain forest to dry *pampas*, rock-strewn beaches to alpine peaks, the landscapes all share a rugged beauty but entail their own challenges. Nearly every course returns to the branch with a story that makes you shake your head and say "Only in Patagonia." Kayak courses trapped on a remote beach due to high wind and waves, running out of food and being rescued by the Chilean *armada*. Mountain courses underestimating the terrain on an exploratory route and missing a re-ration or pickup by three days or more. A volcano

Bushwhacking in Patagonia. *Ignacio Grez*

erupting, a region-wide strike that shuts down all the roads and prevents fuel from being delivered or courses from being picked up: "the Patagonia factor."

Coigüe form seemingly impenetrable coastal forests lining the *fiordos*, broken only by countless waterfalls. The vast landscape is made somehow smaller by bringing sea kayaking and mountaineering close to one another in a rugged country that averages only 100 miles in width.

Many of the students who choose Patagonia do so *because* of the challenging nature of the classrooms. They come to test themselves, and say things like, "I wanted the hardest course" or "I wanted to see if I could do it." This challenging location rewards those who enter it.

In addition to the rewards of natural beauty and wilderness, all students who test themselves "against" Patagonia come out of the experience with a sense of place that is unique at NOLS. The culture of the *pobladores* on their remote *campos* make us rethink our idea of wilderness as a place with no people. They are part of a unique but vanishing culture, living hours or days by horseback from the nearest road, with a deep love for the land and a connection to it. It is amazing meeting these modern-day pioneers who sometimes see only a dozen people a year outside of the NOLS courses that they welcome to their land: playing *truco* with them, listening to accordion and guitar music as a lamb cooks beside them, and seeing the landscape through their eyes. Beyond mountains or ocean, river or glacier, the people and the culture will endure.

Don Julio Romero drinks *maté* while visiting with members of a NOLS course.
Fredrik Norrsell

Jim Ratz and Wilford Welch. *NOLS Archives*

ple who help define and articulate a NOLS education, do so with no NOLS background?"

In 1989, Michael Lindsey arrived to fill the branch director position at NOLS Rocky Mountain from a 10-year stint at Colorado Outward Bound. Bruce Palmer had not been on a course or to Lander when he saw an ad in the *Chronicle of Higher Education* seeking an admissions manager for NOLS in 1990. His several years of experience working in admissions departments at three colleges made him an excellent candidate, and Ratz hired him, along with a cadre of five other administrative outside hires to help in admissions, public policy, marketing, finance, and development. According to Palmer, those people were needed because internal promotions couldn't keep pace with the fast growth occurring in that era—"hence the reach to the outside, but it wasn't necessarily well received," he said. Most of those hired from outside soon left, but their arrival had added fuel to some undercurrents of resentment that were brewing, including the growing perception that the school was getting too big and that it was losing its personality.

Business Practices for Growth

The board, too, got some new faces. One was Wilford Welch, a prominent business consultant from Boston. His introduction to NOLS was in 1979 after an unplanned first raft

with satisfactory results. LT Chu was the first top-level outside hire when she arrived as director of finance in 1985, but others followed as the 1980s gave way to the 1990s. As more people began to "jump ahead in the line," it didn't always sit well. That response, as one observer put it, "was driven by two factors. First, in a small organization, they were just unknown people. Who are these people when everyone else you see and work with has been around the block with you, in bad weather, in tough times? And second, how can people, particularly peo-

descent over a waterfall in Taiwan prompted him to seek better wilderness skills.

"My two instructors were Paul Calver, who had an eighth-grade education, and Lucy Smith," he said when recalling his "39ers" course for non-traditionally aged students. "They blew my mind, because they were so skilled and so full of integrity. I saw this little band of dedicated people, competent, pure as driven snow, who had no clue how important or good they were." At first, Welch quietly offered strategic advice to Calver, who became the school's marketing director (and "knew not squat about it," said Welch), and to Ratz. Then he joined the board in 1989 and was elected chair in 1992.

Welch soon recruited his friend and tennis buddy, Harvard MBA and finance professional Gene Tremblay, who had asked how he could help the school after both his children came back transformed by their NOLS courses. Tremblay joined the board in 1992 and began helping Mark Cole, an instructor with an engineering and astronomy background who had just been named finance director.

"Mark Cole was a delightful, smart guy, a good student, with a great temperament," said Tremblay, but as with so many others with in-town jobs, Tremblay noticed generally weak professional business skills. "[Business skills] were not given any value," he said. "And a widespread perception

Molly Hampton and Gene Tremblay. *NOLS Archives*

that as a nonprofit NOLS was not meant to make money, and that being a school, it was not a business was also unhelpful."

Tremblay began trying to instill the understanding that the school could not sustain itself if it was not operated more like a business—and that meant profits. "Call it whatever you want, if there's no contribution to reserves or the bottom line, you don't exist," he explained. "You have to make excess money to carry forward in order to be able to expand and grow. That was radical thinking at that point."

Above the clouds in
the North Cascades.
Ben Lester

NOLS PACIFIC NORTHWEST

Middle Fork Lake, Wyoming, summer 1970: Dave Polito gazed at the dozens of people on the NOLS course before him, and was wistful. Group sizes on courses had ballooned in the wake of *Thirty Days to Survival.* Polito wondered what had happened to the "old" days, when NOLS groups were small and everybody knew one another. He had done some climbing and backpacking in the Northwest, and went to Paul to see about doing some scouting in the Cascades. Petzoldt said "go check it out," and gave him $150 to fuel his 1958 Dodge pickup. Polito was back by late fall, and Petzoldt gave the thumbs up on NOLS Washington (later, NOLS Cascades, then NOLS Pacific Northwest).

Early the next spring, Polito rented a suburban ranchette in Redmond for $500 a month, with some acreage and outbuildings on a dead-end dirt road close enough to Seattle and its airport to be practical. Before they were totally set up, they heard they were already booking courses. "The reason it was great," recalled Polito, "was because it was a throwback to what Lander was when the groups were small and everybody knew one another. A small family. The pre-*Life* magazine NOLS."

The place was fondly dubbed the Sloth Farm. "It was that between-course aura it had," said Polito, "where everyone could be slothful." As one person said, "It was just a bunch of hippies living in a house. This was the first part of the 1970s. Everyone had long hair."

But on courses, it was all business. NOLS Washington was in terrain a far cry from the Wind Rivers. "Forbidden and Formidable, Fury and Terror, Triumph and Storm King,

NOLS Cascades in Sedro-Woolley, probably in the late 1970s. *NOLS Archives*

Inspiration and Despair—the names of North Cascades summits reflect their nature: challenging and unpredictable, yet beautiful," wrote Polito in the *NOLS Alumnus* in 1971. The close-knit Sloth Farm crew developed equipment and gear suited to the snowfields and glaciers of Glacier Peak Wilderness and the North Cascades National Park, and led three 30-day North Cascades mountaineering courses every summer. Groups consisted of 10 students with two instructors in three patrols, for a total of 36 people, crossing very steep, very glaciated mountains.

Unlike Wyoming, they learned quickly that they couldn't get far traveling off-trail in the steep Cascade valley bottoms, which were choked by Devil's club and slide alder. Instead, the easiest way to get around was up on the snowy ridges, even though snow was also the biggest risk. "We went up and down passes and couloirs with hard-pack snow with full packs," said Polito. "We taught self-arresting as the highest priority, because you couldn't stay roped up forever. You had, at some point, to trust in your ability to walk on the snow and get through these mountains."

The operation wasn't sophisticated at the start: "I spent money, got receipts, and threw them in a shoebox." said Polito. "I remember doing the finances and getting a lecture [about it from] Mrs. Johnson. She didn't have any idea what a funky operation we were running with a short staff."

In 1978, the branch moved to Sedro-Woolley, and the old Sloth Farm ultimately became part of the campus of the Microsoft Corporation. The new location was dubbed the "Rat Ranch" because of an infestation of huge Norwegian rats that even an exterminator couldn't budge. In 1983, Peter Simer asked George and Mary Jo Newbury to direct the branch and try to "tighten things up," said George. It was not a popular move initially, and the Newburys were briefly fired by interim executive director Charley Fiala before being reinstated by Ratz.

Under the Newburys, NOLS PNW expanded to new areas. The branch inaugurated expeditions into British Columbia's vast, remote Waddington Range in 1987 and supported NOLS India's mountaineering expeditions in the Garhwal Himalaya

Hiking the coast of the Olympic Peninsula. *Alexis Alloway*

enough land for 50 houses, but did not want it developed. The NOLS crew cleaned out years of farm debris, George mowed a pattern in the long grass to show the proposed branch buildings, and they welcomed the board there for a November meeting. Although the purchase was over budget, Conway became home in 1991 and hosted the first Wilderness Risk Management Conference in 1994.

The first Semester in the Northwest began in 1990, with mountaineering, rock climbing, hiking on the Olympic coast, and sailing. On 36-foot keelboats, the semester explored the Strait of Georgia and Desolation Sound. Students learned boat handling under sail and power, coastal navigation, and seamanship in a unique environment for developing leadership.

The PNW began hosting the school's sea kayak instructor course in 1992. That course followed the British Columbia coast from Bella Bella to Port Hardy. "It's a very challenging route, with high exposure to wind, waves, tides, and currents," said Craig Lenske, in 2015 the PNW director. Sea kayaking courses for students began in 2005 with the advent of the Semester on the Borders, a collaboration with NOLS Southwest.

The Newburys retired in 2007. "In the quarter century they ran NOLS PNW, they . . . mentored countless young instructors. George and Mary Jo's encouragement and welcoming nature are a big part of why I am at NOLS today," said Pat Mettenbrink, who started his career at NOLS in the PNW issue room working for Mary Jo in the late 1990s. "Mary Jo was your biggest fan and supported you adventuring in the outdoors and becoming

starting in 1991. Several other NOLS international programs, including Australia and New Zealand, were incubated under the PNW's aegis as well.

In about 1990, Newbury began looking for a new home for the branch. After searching endlessly, a man told him of three sisters living in Conway, 30 minutes south of Sedro-Woolley and an hour north of Seattle. They had a family farm with

Abundant moisture makes the
North Cascades a lush environment.
Ben Fox

a NOLS instructor if that is what you wanted. She gave you real responsibilities and never doubted that you could handle it."

Dan Harter took over as director when the Newburys left, followed by Chris Agnew in 2010, and Lenske in 2015. The branch had an uptick in courses through both NOLS Pro and WMI. An experiment in 2010 and 2011 brought WMI's wilderness medicine expedition (WME) to the PNW. Designed for medical professionals to earn continuing education while on a wilderness expedition, WMEs were normally largely land-based, but the PNW version also took medical professionals out on the school's keelboats.

NOLS Pacific Northwest, built from the ground up for NOLS.
Michel Raab

Part of the challenge was to build the business side of the organization in ways that could be stomached by people who had, many of them, come to NOLS to escape the conventional world. The school was already a leader in outdoor education, risk management, public policy, research, outdoor product development, environment, and more, but, as Welch pointed out, "you had to build an organization with the capacity to do that financially . . . People began to see the necessity of having a structured organization that could deliver on that promise. And the challenge was 'how do we remain pure while also developing some of the trappings of the corporate world that we cannot stand?'"

With the school finally out of the red, there was some optimism that allowed reinvigoration of a few back-burner dreams. Facilities upgrades, purchases, and renovations were urgently needed at each of the NOLS branches. But those dreams would cost money, and funding them meant fundraising. The concept of fundraising had been unwelcome since Petzoldt's days, for fear of becoming beholden to donors or losing sight of the mission in the search for dollars, as had happened at other outdoor programs. The concept of marketing was also viewed with disdain. The intense cultural resistance to fundraising and marketing, both long regarded as dirty words at the school, had to be overcome.

Before the 1990s, fundraising efforts had indeed been timid, according to Trina Peterson, whose 1982 Wind River Wilderness course had been the "classic transformative experience," she said. She received an "ask" postcard around 1992 from Steff Kessler, who had managed the Annual Fund since 1988. "They were so sheepish about it, it was the first thing I'd ever gotten. It was very low-key, asking, like, 'can you give $5?' I felt so strongly about NOLS, it was a pleasure to get involved in that way," said Peterson.

In 1992, Welch decided to put his money where his mouth was, kicking off the school's second-ever capital campaign, the "Next Step Expedition," with a $25,000 donation. Co-chaired by board members Duncan Dayton and Homer Luther, the goal of the campaign was to raise $1.5 million to be matched with operational funds for a total of $3 million for improvements. Despite the general trepidation about fundraising within NOLS itself, it turned out that alumni clearly agreed with Peterson: 202 of them helped the Next Step Expedition reach its target by 1994. In fact, for many, NOLS had become a family affair: A challenge for families with multiple alumni to send photos in the 1992 *NOLS Leader* led to more than a dozen responses, including the Armbrecht family showing 10 in a photo that included

PAUL PETZOLDT: MASTER PITCHMAN

Paul Petzoldt promoted NOLS at every opportunity, and often spent many weeks on the road speaking to college and school groups and doing whatever he could to get the NOLS name out there. Two of his promotional projects were especially interesting. On November 21, 1972, he was in New York City to tape show #1413 of the popular TV game show, *To Tell The Truth* at NBC studio 6A. The weekly show pitted a guest against a panel of questioners to see if they could discern whether he was telling the truth about his occupation. The show aired in March 1974. Petzoldt outfoxed the panel, one of whom pegged him as a gourmet cook in Florida because of his tan, and another who doubted if he'd ever seen snow.

In 1974, Quaker Oats was developing Quaker Oats Super-Plus, a cereal brimming with healthy ingredients. The company thought Petzoldt would be the perfect spokesman for it and sent a Chicago film crew with no outdoor camping experience for a five-day filming shoot on the summertime flanks of Denali. Another photo shoot occurred later in Sinks Canyon, according to Janet Jahn. Instructor Ken Clanton ended up with the prototype cereal box used in the filming, which shows ingredients, including whey, coconut, sunflower seeds, and more, that wouldn't become widely popular for decades. At the last minute, the company withdrew the product release, and the commercials were never aired.

staffers Molly (nee Armbrecht) and Peter Absolon.

The capital campaign funds brought about many badly needed facility improvements to the school's branches. Among the most notable was the purchase of the former Mystic Plains horse farm in Tucson to house NOLS Southwest, where they converted the horse barn into a rations room and constructed a 2,900-square-foot open-sided staging area plus a 1,000-square-foot equipment room. In Washington, a 30-acre parcel in Conway was purchased and became home to NOLS Pacific Northwest; the branch was the first location built from the ground up for NOLS, and the main building featured a striking roofline designed to mimic the jagged North Cascades. In Patagonia, property that had been purchased a few kilometers south of Coyhaique was upgraded with a new staff bunkhouse and a common building named "La Casa Comun."

Whether they continued to work for NOLS or stayed in Lander doing something else, the NOLS community began to have a more widespread presence in the communities surrounding each of the school's locations. "George and Mary Jo

NOLS Patagonia. *Alex Chang—Cornell Leadership Expedition*

Newbury raised two boys at the PNW branch and the Fords raised two boys in Palmer," said Leemon. "Two of my kids were born in Tucson and the third in Lander, the Brame girls spent their younger years in Whitehorse, and the Davidsons raised kids at Three Peaks Ranch." Although to a certain degree, the nature of NOLS would always remain transient, NOLS people were more and more among those cheering their kids from the sidelines at team sports events, coaching various sports, joining baseball leagues, and otherwise becoming more locally involved. Around that time, the school also saw the first of its second-generation students, including the children of Martha and Rob Hellyer: Jim (Alaska mountaineering, 1988), Jessica (Spring Semester in the Rockies, 1993), and George (Waddington mountaineering, 1996).

But within the wider Fremont County community, there was one lingering schism in community relations stemming back to the 1960s that needed repair. The same way he had reached out to Petzoldt and others since becoming executive director, Ratz wanted to try mending torn relations with the tribal communities. A new generation of leadership was arising on the reservation, and in an effort to mend the rift, Ratz initiated two cooperative ventures with the Shoshone and Arapahoe tribes. He obtained the board's approval to create a public affairs department that would "portray NOLS accurately and consistently to the diverse populations with which the school interacts in order to enhance their relationship to the school and its mission," according to The Leader, February 1991.

The true explanation for the rift still eludes reliable confirmation and corroboration, but the results of it caused an end to access to that part of the Winds that lies on the Wind River Indian Reservation. Toward the end of the 1960s, Hellyer remembered that perhaps permit fees rose astronomically. Others, including Skip Shoutis, recalled that there was a forest fire wrongfully attributed to NOLS

that burned in the Dry Creek area. Yet another explanation was that Petzoldt lost his temper in a meeting and offended tribal elders. Whatever the long-ago cause, Ratz hoped that by 1992 the time to reconcile had come.

One program would offer scholarships for Native Americans interested in participating on NOLS courses. The other idea, reported in the Spring 1992 issue of The Leader, was to invite tribal elders to present historical talks as a cultural component for some semester programs.

Enthusiasm for the overture was sufficient enough to lead to a gathering of NOLS and tribal members, and a sizable crowd came together on the lawn at the Rocky Mountain branch for drumming, dancing, speeches, and more. The following year, four NOLS instructors planned a personal Denali climb they dubbed "Climb for the Hoop" as a fundraiser for the Shoshone Tribal Cultural Center on the Wind River Reservation. Although the original goal of climbing a new route up Denali's 6,000-foot Father and Son face was scrapped after a series of setbacks, two members of the party reached the summit via the more common West Buttress.

For Gene Tremblay that spring day at the Rocky Mountain branch, festivities with guests from the Shoshone and Arapahoe tribes presaged challenging times ahead for the school. New to the board, he remembers standing on the sidelines, enjoying the scene alongside a NOLS instructor. He commented to her how wonderful it was to see the event going well. "Aren't we doing great?" he said.

No, she said, not really. Basically, he recalled, she said, "If you only knew how bad things really are." She was referring not to relations with the Native American community, but to the general mood in the NOLS trenches. From her, he discovered an ominous undercurrent of dissatisfaction among the school's instructors. Morale in the early to mid-1990s was headed for the dumps.

For many, the luster of the job was dimming. As it had always been, the work was hard and the paychecks skimpy. Now, for many instructors the hard work for little pay was increasingly in conflict with heightened demands for professionalism and the loss of freedom that came with it. Instructor performance expectations and the evaluation process were being revised. The administration was expecting higher standards for written evaluations, and, before Leemon began his campaign to gain instructors' trust, the increased focus on risk management made instructors wary that they might be fired for errors in judgment. Resistance still remained regarding the restrictions on romance in the field, and a few instructors continued to pine for the now-distant days when part of heading to a rock camp meant picking up a couple of cases of beer.

All these initiatives had the best of intentions, and the school needed to modernize. As one former instructor put it, "Some folks just were not going to make the change and needed to leave." However, as many who lived through that era reflected later, the struggle to meet mandates for change was compounded by the manner in which Ratz handled the message. "The school was growing, changing, and embracing new initiatives, but not doing the hard internal work to bring the whole team along," said another. An emerging sense of disconnection from the administration was developing among the instructor corps, many of whom were feeling marginalized and unappreciated. All these things were underlying what Gene Tremblay unearthed in his casual conversation with the instructor.

"It hit me like a sledgehammer," he said. When he mentioned it to others on the board, some agreed that they, too, had been picking up similar vibes but hadn't wanted to say anything. Over the next two years, the problem grew. Ratz was so busy focusing on the innovations and development of administrative systems and external initiatives launched during his first five years as executive director that he lost sight of an important piece of his job: his people. In the view of the instructors, he became increasingly distant and unavailable. Perhaps it started with an important dynamic shift in 1990; LT, who had married Ratz in 1988, left her

position as director of finance upon the birth of the first of their two children. "When LT left the school, the usually introverted, sometimes surly nature of Jim showed up a lot more," said one person who worked in the administration then. "LT softened Jim, and gave him an approachable contact in the school. When she was gone, staff felt they had no avenue to approach Jim."

By 1994, things were coming to a head. Even before attending her first meeting as a member of the NOLS Board, Trina Peterson was asked to join fellow board members Wilford Welch and Herbie Ogden in Lander to meet with staff and instructors about what was going on. Both she and Ogden had credibility as former instructors, and Welch had been on three courses, including Denali.

After a three-hour meeting with Ratz and the management team in a side office at the Noble Hotel, they walked into the dining room where a group of about 80 instructors was waiting. "We three were trusted by the instructors," recalled Welch. "It was our job to listen deeply to their concerns."

"There was this roiling unhappiness, and stress, and tension," said Peterson. "Everybody was so upset." The constellation of concerns ran the gamut: Wrapped up with the rise of policies and other signs of "professionalization" to address course tone and culture, there was the perception that instructor discretion was being lost. Blended with

that were accusations of lack of administrative transparency, and having little to no chance to participate in certain decisions. There was confusion about the role of the board and how a nonprofit works. The group overall distrusted the NOLS administration. And it didn't help, they said, that the pay sucked.

But the greatest frustrations were leveled at Ratz. Not a big "people person" at the best of times, the widespread opinion was that he had fallen out of touch and become disconnected from the instructors. He was distant and unapproachable, they said—in essence, ineffective as the school's leader. One of the most hurtful grievances, they repeated again and again, was that Ratz did not even know their names.

It fell to Peterson to report their findings during the February 19, 1995, board meeting at NOLS Southwest in Tucson. The youngest and newest member of the board, she had the unenviable job of explaining that the executive director had lost the support of much of the school. Also present at the meeting, charged with carrying the message that the instructors agreed it was time to replace Ratz, were NIA representatives Lynn Morrison and Abby Warner.

As LT recollected in 2015, the 24-hour nature of the position had finally taken its toll on Ratz after 10 years. "It was painful, painful," she said, referring to the events that contributed to his gradual isolation. "In the middle of the night, the phone would ring. We wouldn't get the call unless it was really bad, the evac coordinator couldn't deal with it, or whatever. So it was hugely stressful." And in his defense, she said, though he was never as welcoming and warm as Petzoldt, who was also notorious for not knowing names, the instructor group had more than doubled during Ratz's tenure.

But the writing was on the wall. In the best interests of NOLS, the time had come for a transition. With support and guidance from his best friend and board member, Herbie Ogden, and others, Ratz delivered his resignation notice in March 1995, agreeing to serve until his successor was chosen. However, by June, the school was effectively being run by a broad group of staff and board called the Communications and Visioning Committee. Led by John Gans with key support from Molly Hampton, it delved into rebuilding relationships, acting as a resource to the executive director search committee, and aiding with a transition to a new executive director.

Instructors scouting the route on the
Matanuska Glacier in Alaska.
Brooks Eaton

A New Executive Director

A BROAD SEARCH for the next executive director was launched with the assistance of a national search firm. The job announcement described three elements to the position, reading in part that "the executive director is an educational leader, the CEO of a nonprofit organization, and the chief staff officer of the board. As an educational leader, the executive director is expected to have personal experience in wilderness education, is looked to for inspirational and visionary leadership to lead the program staff, and, with that staff, provide creativity, excitement, and innovative zest to the school's core curriculum . . . As the CEO, the executive director manages and directs a $12 million enterprise [with] . . . strong skills in team-building, budgeting, and collaborative efforts in marketing, fundraising, strategic planning, and communications to nurture and sustain the school's mission . . ."

The board debated seeking a fresh perspective and new approach for the top job from outside the NOLS ranks, but, out of a nationwide field of about 50 applicants, ended up choosing two familiar faces as the top contenders: Samuel Ellison Belk IV (aka "Q") and John Gans. Belk, a student at age 15 in 1971, worked as an instructor and in the NOLS offices until 1984. He had been a prominent figure during the 1975 upset when Petzoldt was removed from office, and CL of the first post-strike course that departed from Lander that December. After earning his MBA at Stanford Business School, he had become a successful investment trader.

In September 1995, board chair Joanne Hurley announced John Gans, 38, as the school's fifth executive director. An Eagle Scout, he was the son of a Minnesota dairy farmer and a mother whose education had ended at sixth grade; Gans knew firsthand about hard work and the importance of education. His easy manner and popular leadership style served him well wherever he went.

Gans came to NOLS by way of the Africa branch in January 1979. After hearing about the school from an instructor on an Outward Bound winter course, he discovered that he could get college credit at NOLS, and blended the Kenya semester program with a study-abroad opportunity in Germany. After college, he and some friends started Baker River School, an alternative high school based in New Hampshire; the 20 students and 10 staff spent much of the year traveling America's back roads in a "rolling classroom." Gans taught physics, math, and chemistry, and managed the outdoor programs plus the business side of running the nonprofit school.

He took a 1980 NOLS instructor course, then returned in 1981 for the summer season. By 1984 he found himself in various administrative roles: Alaska director (1984-1988), director of marketing and admissions (1989-1990), and in 1990, in the newly created role of operations director. As was written in *The Leader* when he was hired as executive director, "This is the guy you want steering the ship."

Gans had a knack for making others feel heard when conversing with him. He learned names, and used them. He seemed well aware of what mattered at the school. He trusted instructors, knowing they were the foundation of what made the school great. At the same time, "he took us a little bit more into the rest of the world. We weren't just this island anymore," reflected John Kanengieter in 2015. "We're a global organization, and I think he really put some good structure to the school that has helped it grow in a stabilized way, instead of just an ideology. I think he really helped people understand that without a positive bottom line, your ideology is only going to last so long."

As with other executive directors before him, Gans's first priority was building his team.

In particular, his old job of operations director had gained enormous importance since its 1990 inception, and involved managing enrollment and staff support, facility upkeep, equipment, and rations for the different school

John Gans sea kayaking in Alaska. *NOLS Archives*

Molly Doran. *NOLS Archives*

Michael Lindsey. *NOLS Archives*

locations, as well as negotiating and mediating finances, course mix, and hiring. Michael Lindsey, Rocky Mountain branch director since 1989, moved into the position. It was soon evident that his plate was overly full, so Molly Doran became associate operations director. She had been an active field instructor since 1978, and had administrative and director experience at branches including Kenya, Alaska, Patagonia, and western Canada. While Lindsey attended to the branch locations in Kenya, Patagonia, Canada, and India for part of his workload, Doran took on overseeing Rocky Mountain, Teton Valley, Southwest, and Pacific Northwest, plus Mexico. It was a notably complementary partnership, with high marks to Doran for her

savvy internal communication and field credibility.

It was an exciting time in the branch locations. During Ratz's administration, outreach to make NOLS accessible to the local communities where the school operated outside the United States became a school-wide initiative. In January 1991, James Kagambi (KG) and Peter Blessing taught the first NOLS Outdoor Educator Program (NOEP) in Kenya with secondary school teachers from Nyeri who were leaders for wildlife clubs. That same year, Dave Kallgren and Rachael Price piloted the school's first course in Spanish for Mexicans. In Chile, John Hauf awarded semester scholarships to park rangers. Realizing that targeted training could have a broad impact, Price designed a two-week customized

Tod Schimelpfenig teaching an early wilderness medicine course to Kenyan park rangers in 1994. *James Kagambi*

program that included wilderness first aid, Leave No Trace, and wilderness travel skills. Price observed that, "with this training, park rangers "could patrol the areas under their charge safely, get farther away from the roadheads to see what's going on, and then also have tools to educate visitors."

In 1994, the Kenya branch ran eight NOEP courses, and Spanish language courses were on the rise in Mexico and Patagonia. By 1996, of $354,586 in scholarships awarded, 12 percent went to Kenyans and 13 percent to Chileans. The

following year, Price said, "through operating dollars and fundraising, we were investing almost half a million dollars a year in national programs in Patagonia and in Mexico."

———————————

It had not escaped anyone's attention that NOLS itself was hardly diverse with regard to gender and race. NOLS was largely male, even though Petzoldt himself had been clear that NOLS was also a place for women. In 1991, an anonymous NOLS alumnus donated $5,000 to research and analyze who was using the wilderness, and why. It was the school's first hard look at particular demographic trends regarding minority involvement in outdoor education and recreation. That year, at NOLS, 70 percent of instructors were male, and an overwhelming percentage of both students and instructors were white. Although some argued about how much of a priority, or even possibility, it was to change this fact, a position for a NOLS diversity manager was created in the mid- to late 1990s to address demographic considerations. Molly Doran initially held the position, but it didn't apparently last, and the job lay dormant after her early efforts.

The position was reinvigorated in 2006. Price, who became the school's diversity and inclusion manager in 2015, said, "Being female [in those early days] was a mixed experience. Egalitarianism was a strength of the school, and at the same time women often needed to assimilate in order to succeed within male-dominated paradigms of success, strength, and leadership."

—————————

Even before taking the top job in September 1995, Gans knew the school needed to heal from the divisiveness that had crept in, and he initiated a project intended to reunite disparate NOLS constituencies. He contacted former NOLS instructor Steve Harper, a psychologist adept at facilitating groups. Harper, with the assistance of Molly Hampton and Wilford Welch, embarked on a five-month process to revisit the school's mission and values. It started with a school-wide questionnaire and interviews, asking employees, "What are the primary challenges that NOLS is facing?"

Using that information, Harper convened focus groups. Discussion centered around the challenges that were identified, and how to meet and overcome them. From each group, two were chosen to speak on group members' behalf at the next level of focus groups.

The ostensible goals were renewed vision and mission statements, supported by a list of NOLS values. The process, however, served an additional, important purpose. When asked about the lengthy proceedings, Harper answered that, while good documents would result, "this is really about a healing process, about getting administrators talking to board members again, and board members talking to instructors, and . . . seeing they are human."

He maintained momentum by sending feedback via focus group participants to every corner of the school, plus delivering a presentation at the Wilderness Educator's Conference. Then Harper convened instructors (and writers) Dave Kallgren and Molly Absolon to develop a document detailing the mission and values that the process had made apparent. Because the resulting document was a viable reflection of the school's values at the time—a living document—Harper suggested it needed to remain close at hand and not merely filed away. Taking to heart the suggestion that it be used regularly, Don Ford, as the Alaska branch director, read it out loud when he opened his meetings. And in 2015, the mission statement and values remained prominently posted in the entryway foyer at the international headquarters.

Keeping the school's mission and values in mind often proved helpful as touchstones in times of crisis. One such challenge arose at 3:00 p.m. on June 26, 1996, on the 24th day of a 30-day Absaroka Wilderness course. Student Katy Brain, 16, was on a student-led hike in anticipation of the next day's start of "small group expedition" (as "survival" had come to be termed). While crossing the South Buffalo Fork River, she and another student lost their footing in the swift current. The other student was carried a couple hundred feet

NOLS MISSION AND VALUES

OUR MISSION
The mission of the National Outdoor Leadership School is to be the leading source and teacher of wilderness skills and leadership that serve people and the environment.

NOLS VALUES
The NOLS community—its staff, students, trustees, and alumni—shares a commitment to wilderness, education, leadership, safety, community, and excellence. These values define and direct who we are, what we do, and how we do it.

Wilderness
We define wilderness as a place where nature is dominant and situations and their consequences are real. Living in these conditions, away from the distractions of modern civilization, fosters self-reliance, judgment, respect, and a sense of responsibility for our actions. It can also be a profoundly moving experience that leads to inspiration, joy, and commitment to an environmental ethic.

Education
We believe that education should be exciting, fun, and challenging. With this in mind, our courses are designed to help people develop and practice the skills they need to live, travel, and play safely in the outdoors. On our expeditions, people learn by accepting and meeting real challenges. Our instructors are educators, not guides. They are committed to inspiring students to explore and develop their understanding of wilderness ethics, leadership, teamwork, natural history, and technical skills.

Leadership
We believe that leadership is a skill that can be learned and practiced. With students and staff, we encourage the evolution of judgment, personal responsibility, and awareness of group needs—key leadership traits—through practical experience and timely feedback. We value integrity, experience, accountability, and humility in our leaders.

---

downstream and escaped injury, but Katy was swept around a bend in the river and sustained a fatal head injury.

It had been nearly four years since a death had occurred at the school: In December 1992, student Richard Sarnoff, 36, had been buried and killed by an avalanche near Holmes Cave in the Togwotee Pass area during a mountain ski course. And the school was rocked yet again on July 11, 1999, when word came that a student on an Alaska Mountaineering course, Thomas Nazarro, 17, had disappeared. After a long hike on a rainy, cool day, his small group expedition had camped on a moraine of the Matanuska Glacier. Nazarro left camp with two pots to fill for drinking water but never returned. After

Safety

We accept risk as an integral part of the learning process and of the environments through which we travel. The recognition and management of risk is critical to both the development of leadership and to the safety and health of our students and staff. We believe successful risk management stems from good judgment based on experience, training, and knowledge.

Community

NOLS is an international community composed of talented individuals who care deeply about what they do. We value diversity, integrity, and personal responsibility, while recognizing that our strength lies in teamwork and commitment to our mission and each other. We appreciate creativity, individuality, and passion among our staff and as an institution. We take our jobs seriously and pursue our mission with enthusiasm, and we cherish our sense of humor and our ability to laugh at ourselves.

Excellence

We seek excellence in all we do. We recognize that maintaining excellence requires that we question decisions, learn from failures, and celebrate success. We are committed to high quality experiences where every moment and every relationship counts. We evolve and adapt with new technology, changing techniques, and differing circumstances.

days of searching, it was deduced that he probably fell into a large moulin (a vertical shaft in the glacier formed by meltwater) just 200 feet away. His body was never found.

The impact of any fatality at the school is always profound. "Each death rocked NOLS deeply," according to Liz Tuohy, who was the CL of Katy Brain's course. "The emotional impact of every such loss to the NOLS community was—is—lasting and can never be overstated, for those in town, or those present at the scene: on a wintertime slope, an icy glacier, a river. To sustain four deaths in just over a decade was especially hard."

While the personal responses to loss cannot be ignored

or minimized, each fatality was also thoroughly scrutinized. Grieving was funneled into a commitment to improve education and risk management measures. This analytical review process included both internal and external investigations that resulted in detailed, thoughtful, and insightful reports. The Nazarro disappearance was documented in a 12-page report; the ultimate conclusion was that it was an unforeseeable accident.

Similar reports are written for every significant risk management event, and are often the genesis of measurable changes at the school. For example, an outcome of the Sarnoff investigation was a wholesale shift in how winter instructors are trained and supervised, plus improved avalanche training, an effort spearheaded by instructor Don Sharaf, who two years later would himself narrowly escape death in an avalanche in Alaska.

Development of the NAFPs

In the case of Katy Brain, both the internal and external reviews identified several areas for improvement. "The biggest learning that came out of the review of Katy's death was that because of our tradition of instructor judgment, combined with our growth as a school, we had lost the ability to communicate among each other about what practices are preferred and which ones aren't," said Leemon. "There was

too much variability about how we were teaching things that had a strong threat to life and limb [such as river crossings]." Instructors found different advantages and disadvantages in certain practices, he said, "and we didn't have a mechanism to share this information and wisdom." With the intention of providing just such a mechanism, Leemon spearheaded development of what became known as the NOLS Accepted Field Practices (NAFPs).

Where once NOLS could defend an oral tradition for methods of handling potentially hazardous situations, that was no longer true. As Schimelpfenig put it, "We're too wide. There are too many of us." With the historical resistance to written policies, the school's high value on judgment and leadership, and the unpredictable nature of the wilderness classroom in mind, Leemon and a group of program supervisors and instructors avoided creating prescriptive policies to try to cover all situations. "I was not going to try to tell instructors what they should do and which practices to follow. I wanted it to come from them. There was resistance, but eventually they learned to understand that I was relying on them as experts to define NOLS's practices," said Leemon. The goal was to be able to easily update the document as practices evolved and changed, and give instructors latitude to use the (accepted) methods of their choice. "The idea was to try to honor and embrace the judgment culture and the decentralized culture of decision-making," said Leemon, "while providing more framework for it. It's not 'policy' *per se*; it's collective wisdom."

The NAFP project eventually earned buy-in from the instructor community because of Leemon's efforts. "Drew very slowly and tactfully and patiently started going, 'You know, these are our standard practices,'" said Schimelpfenig. Over time, the NAFPs became the modern version of Petzoldt's "must-knows"—aspects of competence in the essential skills of outdoor leadership. "It was a way to cut through everything we *could* know and identifying what we *must* know," wrote Leemon and Schimelpfenig in a later paper.

By 2015 the NAFPs had become a fundamental part of NOLS. Newer generations of instructors embraced them. "Today, they're shocked if they weren't around the school [before the NAFPs came out]," said Gans in 2015, "because today there's a growing interest (driven largely by faculty and the P-Sups) to refine and record more of our curriculum." They also serve to answer questions from outside sources as to why things were done a certain way. They have, in essence, become policies. As curriculum and research manager John Gookin pointed out in 2015, "If we're on a stand in a courtroom, people are going to be calling the NAFPs 'policy.' That's where we'll be held accountable by our peers."

Another lesson to take to heart stemmed from the fact that both Brain and Nazarro died while apart from their instructors. Although independence is a key part of the NOLS experience, stemming from the first hungry survival walkouts of the earliest courses, some began to call that aspect of the curriculum into question in the wake of the two fatalities. Were these leadership opportunities, with the risks that were clearly present, something that NOLS was still committed to offering?

The answer was a resounding "yes." But at the same time, NOLS used the lessons learned to refine the policies and information surrounding independent student travel. It was suspended on glaciers for the remainder of the summer of 1999. By 2000, the practices were rewritten to provide clear expectations for instructors on how to organize their courses. "If the instructors wanted to climb peaks, then independent travel likely wouldn't be a curriculum focus, and so wouldn't occur. One the other hand, if student independence was the ultimate goal, the climbing would have to take a back seat," said Leemon.

In addition, the wording of catalog course descriptions was reworked in an effort to provide the best possible communication about the various risks at NOLS (such as glacier and independent travel) for the benefit of prospective students and their parents. The term "small group expedition" was changed to "student expedition" to make it clear that instructors would not be present. "Independent student expeditions were never close to being on the chopping block," said Gans. "But we needed to be much clearer in the catalog and other places that students were at times on their own and why we did that."

The Positive Learning Environment

Another emerging development at NOLS in the mid-1990s was a hard look at certain interpersonal behaviors and methods of instruction. In society at large, there was a new sensitivity to and awareness of tolerance and respect for differences among people. Expedition behavior had always been a core curriculum element at the school, and it was time to add some modern insights to its framework. An effort to develop clearer tools for outlining group values from the outset of an expedition would help each evolving NOLS community identify boundaries of acceptable behavior and ways to respond effectively to poor behavior. For example, certain student behaviors, often toward one another, were being increasingly questioned. Anecdotally, behaviors including sexual harassment and generalized intimidation and discrimination (inadvertent and otherwise) by both instructors and students had occurred at NOLS—as elsewhere—for years. It was a situation, one instructor said, that "students simply endured and instructors largely ignored."

During his tenure as director at the Rocky Mountain branch, Michael Lindsey, who had a degree in therapy, noticed the situation and initiated improvements to remedy it. He starting having a staff person meet with semester students after every section, "to talk about everything from identification of sexual harassment to what non-discriminatory behavior looks like," he said. He introduced more training and guidelines on behavioral issues that could impact a course, and tried to show instructors how a change in course culture could "make courses better and their jobs easier." The overall concept came to be known as the "positive learning environment," or PLE.

But it was still a problem when Tod Schimelpfenig took over as Rocky Mountain director in 1995. "We were getting phone calls from parents upset at hearing about what had happened on their children's courses," he said. Beyond just making folks unhappy, many people around the school were becoming concerned that such incidents negatively affected the course's educational outcomes.

As a field instructor in the mid- to late 1990s, Jim Culver was present for the shift to a more positive learning experience for students. "We needed to be more proactive [in being sure] that students understood where we stood as a school, and what we needed to talk about to have an environment in the field where people felt safe learning," he said.

Living in small groups makes teamwork a necessity. *Adam Swisher*

As older instructors began to hear consistently from program supervisors that implementation of these new ideas was expected, and newer instructors came in and never knew differently, the change took hold. Over time, said Culver, it has "evolved more into a discussion with students as to what culture we want to have in the field, where everyone feels supported within this opportunity they have—but still with clear statements where we stand regarding things like harassment issues. That is still very directive." The benefit of creating a supportive and respectful climate, he said, is that in instances where issues arise on a course, the instructors can effectively refer back to the framework agreed upon at the outset by the group.

Climbing above the Pared Norte Glacier
in Chilean Patagonia.

NOLS PATAGONIA

John Hauf and Molly Doran found a different world as they explored Patagonia for NOLS in January 1989. Their maps showed many blank spaces. Stunning green archipelagos and blue ocean met the dark jutting peaks of the Andes and their bright white snowfields. The region was largely roadless, the weather often fearsome. A general election to end a harsh 16-year military regime headed by the dictator Augusto Pinochet was 11 months away. The place was, wrote Andy Cline in *The Leader*, "a kaleidoscope of beauty and uncertainty."

The astonishing contrasts and grandeur of Patagonia were perfect for NOLS, they agreed, and the Patagonia branch opened in 1990 in the town of Coyhaique. It was the first new branch formed since the 1974 founding of NOLS Kenya. On January 12, the first 15 students arrived and were housed in two local hostels. Operations were at a small rented house where gear was piled to the ceiling in one room, and food rationing was done along the dark hallways. Boot fitting was in the bathroom, with the student sitting on the porcelain, picking out his or her boots from the bathtub.

The semester—Patagonia ran only semesters for a long time—from January to April was a success, led by Doran and Hauf with three assistants. The group passed through just one town and over two dirt roads in 80 days. Six of the students were Chilean, two of them from the Chilean equivalent of the national parks system. By the 1993-94 season, the branch would be up to three full semesters in both spring and fall.

Watching icebergs stranded after a strong onshore wind.
Fredrik Norrsell

In November 1991 the school purchased 437 acres of land 11 kilometers south of Coyhaique. Known as "Las Vertientes" ("The Springs"), the *campo*, or farm, rested on the flanks of the Divisadero Range overlooking the Simpson and Claro valleys. In 1992, Sergio and Veronica Vasquez arrived while Veronica was pregnant with their first son, Humberto. They became the facility's caretakers, and the family was still there in 2015, working the farm as it became fully functioning with produce gardens and many animals.

Hauf was director at the Patagonia branch until 2003, when Judd Rogers took over. Rachael Price replaced Rogers in 2010, and Raúl Castro took over in 2014. Over time, they added various courses to the Patagonia season, which ran from September to April. An extension office 650 miles to the south in Puerto Natales opened in 1996 and served the Magallanes region for nine years. The branch started mountaineering courses (1994), many Spanish language courses, educator courses in English and Spanish, sea kayaking (2002), integration of WMI into courses in both English and Spanish (2003), and Prime sea kayaking courses. The Year in Patagonia, inaugurated in 2006, was the first year-long program in outdoor education. At 135 days, the expedition included comprehensive backcountry immersion to build skills in mountain and subalpine glacier travel, rock climbing, and sea kayaking. The students also earned Wilderness First Responder and Leave No Trace Master certifications, and lived and worked for several weeks with local *poblador* families. The culmination was an eight- or nine-day independent student expedition.

After an enrollment downturn in 2010, the branch began to rebound, leading to one of its best years in 2014, with 20,967 student days and three Patagonia Year courses. In addition, the operating calendar and fabulous landscape made Patagonia an increasingly attractive option for NOLS Pro business school clients. In January 2015, Columbia, the University of Texas, Cornell, and Northwestern all offered 7- to 10-day leadership expeditions for their MBA students at NOLS Patagonia. It was a popular place—in fact, that same year, the humans at the Patagonia branch were joined by 2 new calves, 60 new lambs, 2 cows, 4 bovine yearlings, a bull, 110 sheep, 6 dogs, 5 cats, 10 chickens, 2 roosters, and 5 horses.

And Orion hung, as it always had, upside down in the night sky.

Maté and a traditional *asado* are part of the Patagonia experience. *Alex Chang—Cornell Leadership Expedition*

NOLS Pro courses offer MBA students the opportunity to learn leadership and teamwork in challenging environments.
Brian Hensien

Can Leadership Be Taught?

AFTER 30 YEARS with the words "leadership" and "school" side by side in the name, the question was raised: Does NOLS teach leadership? Historically, "during the era of Paul, a lot of staff tried to teach leadership or be a leader like Paul," said John Gans. "And there was no clear curriculum, so they kind of did what he did. That wasn't always effective for them, and it certainly wasn't consistent in style or content." So early in his tenure as executive director, Gans asked the question and discovered that "many people (including our curriculum manager) said we teach outdoor leadership, but we don't teach leadership. Others struggled with what that meant or how it was defined." At the time, the subject of leadership wasn't even on student evaluations.

In 1996, Gans convened a committee to examine the topic. He could see that, without a clear objective or definition of how NOLS taught leadership, justifying many of the mainstays of the program, particularly independent student group travel, was difficult. "I strongly believe in those, but if you didn't have a goal of teaching leadership, one would argue what is the point and why take the risk?" he said.

The Leadership Project, funded by a $200,000 grant from the Richard King Mellon Foundation in Pittsburgh, was led by Molly Doran, and the development group consisted of John Kanengieter, Rachel Green, Molly Absolon, John Gookin, and board member Alan Macomber. A survey that was circulated through NOLS yielded an impressive 90 percent response rate, and the answers revealed that although everyone intuitively knew NOLS did leadership development, no one knew quite how to explain it. It was also apparent that people were eager for tools to do so.

Originally slated to take about nine months, the project took two years. "It was very intense," said Doran, who was concurrently earning her master's degree from the Leadership Institute of Seattle. Some of the research models she was learning about came in handy at NOLS as the group defined NOLS leadership philosophy and clarified the audience and its expectations.

The process wasn't without the same predictable bumps that always arise with the specter of change. "There's always pushback," said Gans. When the model was initially introduced, Doran agreed, "people didn't like it. They accused us of doing group therapy, and said, 'This isn't our mission, this is Outward Bound,'" she remembered. In seeking the best model, she remembered, "We weren't right all the time. We had to find our way to the right way to articulate leadership at NOLS." The process included studying different realms of leadership: psychology, military, business, religion; an attempt to produce a book containing leadership "teachable moments" was eventually abandoned.

The outcome was the 4-7-1 leadership model, a framework intended to define the skills necessary for good leadership. With an effective model in hand, the ultimate goal of an intentional, accessible leadership education curriculum for students began to gel. "People really came on board when they realized, yes, curriculum can be defined and sometimes even prescribed, and still they were given a lot of latitude in terms of how it's delivered and taught," said Gans. "The

A key goal of the Leadership Project was to provide instructors with better language to talk about leadership with their students. *Alex Chang—Cornell Leadership Expedition*

LEADERSHIP AT NOLS

At NOLS, leadership is situationally appropriate action that directs or guides your group to set and achieve goals. Great leaders create an environment that inspires individuals and groups to achieve their full potential.

NOLS developed the 4-7-1 model to describe the elements of leadership.

FOUR ROLES

Self Leadership
Peer Leadership
Designated Leadership
Active Followership

SEVEN SKILLS

Expedition Behavior
Communication
Competence
Judgment and Decision-making
Tolerance for Adversity and Uncertainty
Self Awareness
Vision and Action

ONE SIGNATURE STYLE

The one signature style is the leadership style that works best for each individual. This style is based on tapping into the leader's personality, learning preferences, passions, strengths, and experiences.

---

goal wasn't to write something new. The goal was to identify what we were doing at its best when it worked."

Ever since the project ended in 1998, the phrase "4-7-1 leadership model," along with the *Leadership Educator Notebook* and other support materials, have provided instructors improved methods for leadership conversations with students, including more specific feedback. It was a huge leap forward for the "leadership" school.

Financial Stability ... at Last?

When Gans took the helm of the school in 1995, the fiscal situation was no longer dire, but the school wasn't quite out of the woods yet. In four of the previous five years, there had been negative cash flow even as net assets were beginning to rise, largely due to property acquisition. (For example, the school had purchased the Kennedy Building, behind the Noble Hotel on 3rd Street, to alleviate an office space

THE STRAIT OF GEORGIA: A DIFFERENT KIND OF LEADERSHIP CHALLENGE

By Ben Lester, instructor

Semester courses in the Northwest always begin with either mountain or sea kayaking sections. In those contexts, leading always entails doing the same things as your followers; everyone hikes. Everyone paddles. Group decisions involve much discussion.

Then students start sailing, and the goalposts move. To make a sailboat slip through the water takes specialization, and that includes specialization in leadership. A person calling the shots who focuses too much on a specific task loses the ability to orchestrate the whole scene, especially when students are just learning. "It's a complex enough task just to grind a winch properly, trim a sail properly," said Alan Neilson, who had worked more than 30 sailing courses in the Pacific Northwest by 2015.

NOLS teaches that there are different leadership roles in a group. In a highly functional team, people understand their roles and lead from them. That *must* happen on a sailboat. Someone needs to give direction. Someone else needs to trim the sheet. Both are leadership roles in a dynamic environment where changes can be big and fast and abrupt.

Being on a keelboat thus teaches communication skills in a way unique at NOLS. "It's a different leadership style," remembered Emily Rich, who was a student in 2012. "You have to learn to give really clear, concise directions to the crew. That's really tough when you yourself have no idea what you are doing."

Added to the challenge is the physical closeness and lack of activity. The confined nature of the boats robs students of the catharsis and solitude of long hiking or paddling days. "You can't get away from each other," she said. "You have to navigate people's emotions as well as the map—trying to read their perceptions, trying to deal with that and wind, weather, your crew—every detail, all at once."

A sailboat is a physical manifestation of the harmony of its crew. With poor teamwork comes the dismal sound of sails luffing, and the deck underfoot feels dead. But when everything clicks, the boat comes alive. The lines vibrate with tension. The crew laughs and hollers with excitement. The wheel in your hands pulls and presses, like the leash of a dog on the scent of a squirrel.

The Strait of Georgia and surrounding areas of the Salish Sea are challenging places to sail, and not just because of the strong winds that rip along the strait, fueled by massive storm systems born over the northern Pacific and funneled by the high mountains to the east and west. The bed of the sea is still young and sharp, and granite outcroppings are scattered around in profusion. The area's mammoth tides mean that sometimes the waters are safely deep, and sometimes danger lurks just below the surface. Ferries and container ships ply between Vancouver, Seattle, Nanaimo, and north through the Inside Passage. And the steep, glacier-carved inlets can be many meters deep within a stone's throw of the shore, making anchoring a challenge.

In a dynamic environment, leadership in every task becomes important. *Ben Lester*

On the other hand, the area's complex geography makes it possible to find shelter relatively easily, which means NOLS boats can venture out in "big" conditions. "I love the fact you can get spanked so much by Mother Nature," said Neilson. "In the right circumstances, we can poke our noses out and get beaten up, knowing we've got a really good port to go into. In a little boat, you realize nature is way more powerful than you are."

situation that was "bursting at the seams," according to Gans. By then, offices for the school's many different departments were situated in various buildings around downtown Lander. Communication often meant walking outside and down the block for face-to-face time, or making phone calls in the days of busy signals and no voice mail.

Although tuition dollars could mostly support operations, the school had grown and spread in the past 10 years while Ratz and then Gans developed various administrative initiatives, creating new budget demands for departments such as alumni and development, outreach (including LNT), marketing, research, and more. The Annual Fund, which had been reinvigorated in 1988 with the intention of providing funding for these programs as well as scholarships, brought in an average of $248,000 from 1992 to 1996. But with 40,000 alumni by 1997, there was much more that could be done.

Gans thrived on meeting people and understood the benefit of reaching out. Once an ambivalent board gave the okay, the push for donations began in earnest—except for one thing: The key to reaching school alumni to solicit donations was on handwritten sheets in decades worth of student files mouldering in the basement of the Noble Hotel.

The solution was computers, on a much larger scale than the few placed in service in 1986 by Bruce Hampton. The board approved establishment of a stand alone Inforsystems (IS) Department in 1996, and former mountaineering and sea kayaking instructor Patrick Clark was named its first director. Described variously as a visionary, conspirator, adventurer, and major consumer of Dr. Pepper, Clark championed the school's entry into the technological age, staying in the position until his death from esophageal cancer in May 2005.

The age of computers unleashed the same torrent of information on NOLS as it did for everyone else worldwide, starting with development of the school's first sophisticated database. Clark and others who gravitated to the new technologies, including Don Webber (who was still in IS in 2015), developed the database software, mining those index cards and manila folders in the Noble Hotel basement for years. And Clark introduced the mystery of email to a skeptical crowd; as John Kanengieter said, "Why would I write Claudia [Pearson, rations manager] an email, when I can just walk over there and talk to her?" The IS department named the software developed for the admissions department "Flamingo," in honor of the NIA mascot.

Whether or not intended as a wry joke, Clark chose April Fool's Day 1995 to launch www.nols.edu. "I distinctly remember when he brought us all over to the front office in the Noble, and he turned on the computer," said Rich Brame. "He showed us this thing called the World Wide Web. None of us had ever seen it—it was incredible." The NOLS website was among the first 6,000 created in the United States, although few people at NOLS really understood the significance of it at the time. But Clark got it: He could foresee that the Internet would enable the school to stay in touch with graduates worldwide, help broadcast its educational message, and allow far-flung NOLS locations to communicate in real time.

As it became easier for the school to reach out to alumni and other potential donors, fundraising took off. In 1997, the Annual Fund jumped past $400,000 for the first time. In addition, the board created several capital campaigns to fund specific projects, starting with the Campaign for Leadership in 1996; it was designed to raise $8 million for the school's endowment fund, which would also become a means, in addition to the Annual Fund, for offering scholarships and supporting certain school departments such as research, wilderness advocacy, and outreach.

At the same time, the alumni and development office started to ramp up its outreach efforts. Dave Glenn, who was working there at the time, remembered being shocked

WELCOME TO THE

NATIONAL OUTDOOR LEADERSHIP SCHOOL

~NOLS is a wilderness-based, non-profit school focusing on leadership and skills~

↗ Web Site Index (School Guide)
↗ How to Contact Us
↗ Explore our Courses (Course Guide)
↗ NOLS FAQ's (frequently asked questions)
↗ Alumni Information (for our 40,000 graduates)
↗ Leave No Trace Program (land stewardship, minimum-impact skills, and wilderness ethics)
↗ Publications
↗ Información en español
↗ Mail Order
↗ What's Old (Last updated May 24, 1996)

[Give us a Holler I Help]

NOLS, 288 Main Street, Lander, WY 82520-3140, USA (307) 332-6973

admissions@nols.edu For questions about NOLS
webmaster@nols.edu For questions or comments about this server.
Copyright © 1996 National Outdoor Leadership School

The original NOLS homepage. *NOLS Archives*

at the success of reunions. "In the big cities—Boston, New York, Chicago—we'd have events with 200 people. And all they wanted to do was talk about their instructors and their experiences, what they learned and how they've used it in their lives. It was pretty much the best marketing tool NOLS could have: a businessman or businesswoman 30 years later, saying [NOLS] made him or her who he or she is."

WHITE ENVELOPE THEORY

By Jared Spaulding, instructor

Longtime instructor Marco Johnson refers to it as the white envelope theory. I think of it more as a cardboard box. Several times a year I take my life and shove it into the box. I shove everything I can into it. Unwritten letters, family members, college loans, bills, telephone calls, conversations, dreams, desires, nightmares, disasters, death, heartbreak, love, wants, needs, friends, projects, plans, current events, things left unsaid—they all get shoved in there.

When I go into the field, the baggage associated with my frontcountry life needs to be left behind. We ask our students to be fully present on courses, and we need to be as well. That is hard to do if I am preoccupied elsewhere.

Back-to-back courses are easier. I imagine it is the same for students on a semester. If the transitions are tight, there may be no chance to unpack the box: drop a letter into the US Mail, quickly check the email. Maybe I'll turn on the phone, but probably not.

The repeated packing and unpacking of this box is one of the reasons that instructors often move on from the school, or move to in-town jobs; unlike packing a physical bag, packing the box often becomes harder the more we do it.

As for our students, packing the box well and unpacking it smoothly are life skills. Knowing they are capable of packing such a box is one thing they can walk away with from their time at NOLS.

The innovation of alumni trips was also popular. Some were brief, many educational. Sea kayaking was an instant hit, with trips in the Everglades and Baja announced in *The Leader*. Skill-building kayaking clinics were held in Chicago. Others trips were more difficult—for example, climbing Gannett Peak in the Winds. In time, itineraries expanded to Europe, the UK, and elsewhere. Many allowed and even encouraged grads to bring non-alumni guests and family members to share the NOLS experience.

A Challenging Decade Ends

When the 1990s began, NOLS was growing fast and attempting to transform itself into a more professional organization. Jim Ratz had a vision of where he wanted the school to head, but if his first five years (1985-1990) were marked by many creative innovations and initiatives, his second five years were marked by his growing isolation from the instructor group and ultimate departure once his skills were no longer the best fit for the school's growing needs.

The values and mission definition process that followed his departure healed much of the divisiveness that had fractured the school, but it did not bring back the school's pioneering early days. John Gans's leadership helped rebuild the school's sense of community, while moving the maturing school toward the future by increasing financial stability, expanding marketing, and codifying the leadership curriculum.

Yet in some ways, the latter years of the 1990s were as tumultuous for the school as had been the early part of the decade. While many in the NOLS community could celebrate the school's evolution during that time, for some, its transformation yielded the same regret for the irretrievable past that hits every organization moving away from its impulsive, wondrous, and sometimes misdirected youth.

Certainly the changes in the 1990s were not the first seismic shifts the school had experienced. Several times, the school community had been hit by evolutionary waves of change, forcing people to decide whether to move, adapt, or leave. The first organizational tsunami hit NOLS when Petzoldt was fired in 1975: Some staff adapted and stayed, but others reacted by leaving either Lander or the school altogether. Other waves of change came with each new executive director, with upheavals in board composition, with professionalization, and with growth. New faces arrived and others departed. There were some who stayed aboard through all the big transitions and were still working at the school at its 50th anniversary in 2015. (The honor of being a field instructor in each of the school's first five decades accrued to just one man: Doug Dahlquist.)

Because of the unusual intensity of the NOLS experience, it typically engendered fierce loyalty; because of the nature of adventure and risk, it drew in strong, committed people. NOLS culture included—demanded—participation and thus discussion over the big issues that came up. This often resulted—will probably always result—in healthy debate, and vocal resistance to things that didn't sit well. Over time, the willingness of the NOLS community to speak out added value, because it yielded deeper and more thoughtful work; it helped the school hew to its mission.

The two most visible elements of NOLS culture, instruction and administration, represented a foundational aspect of the school. The purpose of the first was to teach. The purpose of the second was corporate management of a multimillion-dollar enterprise. Neither could exist without the other, but the separate lenses by which those groups tended to view NOLS sometimes proved contentious. As a unified voice, instructors sometimes shifted the course of events, such as when the NIA formed in 1975 and battled the board when Petzoldt was ousted, and again in 1994 when they expressed to Welch, Ogden, and Peterson their loss of faith in Ratz.

"When you start at NOLS, you're so excited. It's the best thing ever," said Molly Absolon in trying to explain the evolution of discontentment. "Then after awhile, you see through the cracks. It's great but not perfect." In the 1990s, "there was a group of us who had been around for 10 years, and felt we brought value by longevity and commitment and the building sense of recognition," she said. It was this cohort of experienced instructors that was particularly frustrated when the sense of disconnection with the administration took root. "I'm not sure it was all Jim's fault," she said, "but he was the head guy, and a stony guy who didn't make us feel as if we were being heard. It was a building thing, where a fair number of us had reached that point. So Jim happened to be around when that wave crested."

By 1998, yet another swell of discontentment began to rise among a segment of the instructor community. This time, there was a sense that NOLS was selling out to corporate America: make money, build assets, develop a product line. They felt that fundraising and marketing were eroding the long-standing NOLS culture of egalitarianism and simplicity. They felt words such as "resource" and "industry" and "accountability" were supplanting their much-loved sense of tribalism and trust. For some instructors watching from out-side the halls of NOLS power, the changes emanating from headquarters were consuming the soul of the school.

Perhaps the most outspoken of those who felt this way was instructor and writer Morgan Hite, who wrote in his 1997 essay, "An Industry in the Wilderness: An inspired outdoor community wrecks on the reef of a corporate model," about his perception that the school had drifted away from "its irreverent style, its integrity, dedication and awesome community."

Hite's views were not shared by all. From the day the first boys hefted backpacks and walked into the Winds behind the school's founder, NOLS had existed in a changing and increasingly complex world. By necessity, it had to change as well. To most in the community, negotiating differences—an essential aspect of expedition behavior—remained, as with all organizations, an ongoing challenge. As the century waned, NOLS had weathered many storms and gained powerful insights about how to move into its coming years. But understanding that is not the same as accepting it. Over time, many NOLS instructors have stayed on, wanting to teach, even in the wake of heartbreaking moments and after examining which course in life to navigate. "Leadership is not always clean, and learning is full of mistakes, and embarrassment, and improvement," said Liz Tuohy, reflecting back on the 1990s. "It was tricky for both administration and faculty to navigate these changes. A long, wet, cold, and hard day in the field often brings people together in the end."

Like her, many instructors found ongoing joy at NOLS. Others found the coming millennium a natural time to depart a school they still loved. Hite, along with others frustrated by the evolving state of the school, moved on, typical of the ebb and flow of all maturing organizations. But Hite left a gift to the school—an enduring tribute written early in his career called "Briefing for Entry into a More Harsh Environment." In it, he defined 11 skills NOLS teaches, a reminder of its core messages, of what students really bring back from their experience. "They will serve you in good stead in any environment in the world," he wrote. "They are habits to live by."

If anyone asks what your course was like, you can tell them. "We were organized, thorough, and prepared. We took care of ourselves in basic ways. We entrusted people with our lives, learned to do without, and persevered at difficult things. We learned to use new tools and we took care of what we had with us. We lived simply.

For most in the NOLS community, those lessons remained as true in the year 2000 as they had for the 35 years that came before.

End of an Era

After he left NOLS, Paul Petzoldt forged ahead in his commitment to the conservation of wilderness through education of its users. In 1977, he was among the founders of a new outdoor organization called the Wilderness Education Association. Envisioned as a network of decentralized affiliates teaching from a standard program, the WEA consisted primarily of a standardization and certification program for university outdoor education programs.

He married the former Virginia Stroud Pyle (Ginny) in 1987 and took up residence in Raymond, Maine, with summertime stays in Idaho, on the west side of the Tetons. He had met Ginny in the 1960s; Ginny's son Wilton (Will) was a student in 1968, and her daughter Sherry in 1970. When Wilton was killed in the Vietnam War in 1969, the Pyleses sent NOLS its first substantial scholarship in his memory. The following year, when Petzoldt was in New York for the premiere of *Thirty Days*, they met and then kept in touch over the years. Seventeen years later, shortly after Ginny's first husband died, they were married in her adopted state of Maine.

In 1985, Petzoldt realized his lifelong dream of a college degree. Although he attended both the University of Idaho and the University of Wyoming as a young man, he always ended up dropping out for lack of funds. Finally, at age 77, he

Tap Tapley and Paul Petzoldt. *Snowbound*

was awarded an honorary PhD from the University of Idaho for his contribution to the American outdoors. In 1999, Unity College in Maine awarded him another honorary PhD, this time in environmental stewardship.

Petzoldt was given the title of founder and president emeritus of NOLS at the school's 25th anniversary in 1990. He and Ginny stayed in close contact with many NOLS people and the school itself for the duration of his life.

The mountains remained Petzoldt's greatest love, and his eyes—despite advancing glaucoma—never stopped looking up. He continued to climb the Grand Teton, reaching the summit on the 60th anniversary of his first climb in July 1984, at age 76, with Andy and Nancy Carson close at hand. "He was bound and determined," said Andy, "and I guess so were we. It was terrible weather."

In July 1994, Petzoldt returned to visit his old friend, the Grand Teton, for the 70th anniversary climb. At a banquet in his honor the evening before, he was on a foot-high podium and quipped, "Is there a rappel off here?" The 86-year-old's climb the next day was hampered by more than 120 other hikers who stopped to greet him and get autographs. He reached the Lower Saddle at 11,200 feet, but rain and fog forced the group to turn back. "Since situations in the outdoors are seldom alike, the problem of knowing when to turn back must be based on known ability and a realistic assessment of the circumstances. False confidence based on questionable attitudes and unrealistic hopes is dangerous in the wild outdoors," quoted instructor Tom Reed from Petzoldt's *The New Wilderness Handbook* later, commenting that indeed they were "wise words from an old mountaineer with nothing to prove."

In 1998, more than 200 old friends held a three-day tribute in honor of Petzoldt's 90th birthday at Grand Targhee resort in Idaho. Mike Williams, who was a 15-year-old student on the second NOLS course in June 1966, asked who amoung the crowd had been fired by Paul while working for NOLS. Most of the room stood up, he recalled. Then he asked, "How many have been fired more than once?" Most of the people in the room stayed standing.

On October 6, 1999, Paul Petzoldt died in Maine at the age of 91. Thelma Young, NOLS's equipment seamstress and at the time the longest tenured NOLS employee, died the following month at age 69. As Diane Shoutis said at Petzoldt's memorial service in Jackson, "Paul always said he had no children of his own but that he had a very large family. He considered us all his family."

Teaching first-aid
curriculum in the field.
Adam Swisher

Threats To Life ABCs

A < Alertness (AVPU)
    Airway (Remove Obstructions)
          Chin Lift / Jaw thrust

B reathing (Look, listen, feel)
   12-20 breaths @ inhal +1/5 sec.
   per min

C irculation (Pulse + Blood)
            Sweeps
   Lg Direct Pressure, Elevation,
                    Pressure point

D isability
   Lg spinal?

E nvironment

"Stop and Fix"

2000-2005

BROADENING THE SCOPE

There is this magical niche right next to rivers. That is true both ecologically, and, I believe, almost spiritually for a group. There is a magic in being near water. Sleeping near it. Floating on it. Traveling on it.

–Laura Hudecek, instructor

As the twentieth century waned and the rest of the world fussed over the dire predictions surrounding "Y2K," Petzoldt made one final journey to the Grand Teton—this time by air. It was a few weeks before New Year's 1999, and, recalled one longtime NOLSie who was onboard, "I'm sure it was totally illegal, but four of us put his ashes on the top of the Grand Teton out a plane door."

A new era for the school was dawning. The April prior to Petzoldt's death, the school had announced acquisition of the Wilderness Medicine Institute (WMI). When Tod Schimelpfenig and Len Pagliaro had developed and begun teaching NOLS's Backcountry Emergency Care course in 1979, they weren't the only ones aware of the need for wilderness-specific medical knowledge. There were many forgotten pioneers who made contributions to the evolving world of wilderness medicine, as defined by Otto Trout, MD, in 1979: "The expression 'mountain medicine' applies not to the medicine itself but . . . to the circumstances and specialized surroundings of the victims. It is the prolonged exposure, weather, and distance from medical help, plus the quality of the care, which make [wilderness] medicine different."

Schimelpfenig first met WMI founders Melissa Gray and Buck Tilton around 1988 when he visited the wilderness medical training center called SOLO in New Hampshire's White Mountains. They were working with SOLO founders Lee Frizzell and Frank Hubbell, who had founded the center in 1976 and were among the first to use the Wilderness EMT (WEMT) and Wilderness First Aid (WFA) nomenclature. When Gray and Tilton joined SOLO in 1984 after instructing for Outward

Class time aboard a keelboat in New Zealand. *Cass Colman*

Bound, they were among a handful of full-time wilderness medicine educators in the United States. As a colleague with a strong common interest, Schimelpfenig kept in touch.

Gray and Tilton relocated to Pitkin, Colorado, in 1990, representing SOLO in the western United States on a handshake agreement. They named their operation the Wilderness Medicine Institute (WMI). Schimelpfenig, who had recently been named training and safety manager at NOLS, hired WMI to teach wilderness medicine courses for NOLS field instructors. "For a lot of years, myself or Buck, or myself and Buck, would come to NOLS for up to 10 or 12 weeks a year," said Gray. "NOLS was one of our first contracts."

Through the 1990s, Tilton taught and wrote the books and curriculum materials for WMI, while Gray taught and managed the business side. WMI grew fast. Gray credits the mid-1990s hiring of Shana Tarter and Judy Crawford with much of WMI's success. Someone dubbed the synergistic trio the "Warrior Women of WMI," and the name stuck. Together, they led WMI to 1,000 percent growth between 1995 and 2007. "We had different skill sets and attacked problems from very different directions, but we came to decisions easily," recalls Gray. "The combination was very effective."

In the mid-1990s, strategic planning for WMI led to a decision to sell. When an employee buy-out proved unfeasible, NOLS was the obvious next choice. "We were culturally very similar, with about 30 percent of our staff already working for NOLS in what was the off-season for wilderness medicine," said Gray. In 1995, Gray and Tilton were teaching a course in Lander when they attended the meeting where John Gans was announced as the new executive director.

"Buck comes up afterwards and he said, 'You know, we should be together someday,'" Gans remembered. "And

The Warrior Women of WMI—Judy Crawford, Melissa Gray, and Shana Tarter—in front of the WMI office in Pitkin, Colorado. Fiona Stringer, another long-time staff member, is second from left. *Melissa Gray*

The WMI logo. *NOLS Archives*

that planted the seed. There was already a great crossover between the organizational cultures, and the emphasis on quality teaching was very high."

There followed several years of quiet negotiations, spearheaded by Molly Hampton. There was concern at NOLS about the hazards of too much growth, and whether such an acquisition would cause the school to lose its focus on expedition-based programming. Those worries were

counterbalanced by significant financial considerations. Traditional catalog course enrollment was, in the words of board member Michael Schmertzler, "in a flat spin. It couldn't sustain itself. The trajectory was not going to work, and the sooner [the school] did something about it, the better." While no one wanted to lose sight of the school's mission, no one wanted it, either, to fall victim to the economic and demographic forces that were beginning to affect the

NOLS EAST

Bill Garrison, a teacher, met Paul Petzoldt in 1968 at Culver Military Academy in Culver, Indiana, during one of Petzoldt's recruiting tours. Intrigued, Garrison attended a NOLS course, along with his children, Janie and Matt, in 1969. When he subsequently became director of the Horace Mann School Outdoor Center in Washington, Connecticut, the entrepreneurial gears began to spin. NOLS East was born.

In the spring of 1970, he and Mary Jo Hudson, then a young instructor, loaded a stock truck in Lander with equipment and drove east. The smaller wilderness areas of the eastern United States demanded a different approach than the way expeditions unfolded in the Winds. Students spent their first few days in Connecticut, then headed out on a month-long caravan of adventure tapping into a variety of wilderness classrooms. Curriculum included the usual NOLS skills—and also use of firearms and chainsaws.

On the first of two courses that summer was a girl named Paula Lumme. "We did a lot of moving. We had so much fun—we were on the loose!" she said, as they migrated place to place. "We didn't have buses. We had green trucks. . . . They were all questionable. You could get a whole course in the old cattle trucks with the tall sides."

Each course was a little different. They backpacked in New Hampshire's White Mountains or in the Adirondacks, and hiked in the Mahosuc range in Maine. They summited Mount Marcy in New York and Mount Katahdin in Maine. Rock climbing sections often took place at the ancient ridge of bedrock in the Catskills known as the Shawangunks. They canoed on the Penobscot River in Maine, the Pemigewasett in New Hampshire, the Miramichi in New Brunswick (Canada), and on the whitewater of Webster Brook at Baxter State Park.

"There was an old guy there who did dam control," said Paula, "and he'd see us and think we knew what we were doing so he'd change the water level on us."

They rigged their 26-foot fiberglass canoes with Grumman canoe sails and tried to race the ferry across Lake Champlain, "and got dumped more than once, and had to be rescued by the Coast Guard," she remembered. Paula stayed to work the second course in 1970 and came back for both courses in 1971, then went to Lander in 1972, where she met and married George Hunker, also an early instructor.

"Mr. Garrison kept our finances in a shoebox," said Mary Jo, who hand-carried it on the plane to Lander to deliver to the school secretary, Mrs. Johnson, after the first season. The man who picked her up at the Riverton airport was George Newbury. The two hit it off, and would go on to serve NOLS for decades in various capacities as a married couple, including as longtime branch directors in both Kenya and the Pacific Northwest.

NOLS East ceased in 1972 after just two seasons, but reopened as NOLS Northeast in 2011. Operating in Adirondack Park in northern New York—at 6.1 million acres the largest park in the Lower 48—it is only hours from New York City, Toronto, and other major population centers. The new operation opened with two-week adventure courses for 14- and 15-year-old students, most from the eastern United States. By 2014, the branch also offered 21-day backpacking/canoeing courses, a nine-day

Portage in the Adirondacks. *Rob Kinzel*

"prime" course for students age 23 or older, and an increasing variety of custom expeditions for NOLS Professional Training.

The Adirondack Mountains provided a spectacular setting for adventurous mountain travel for NOLS's newest wilderness classroom. For Lindsay Yost, program manager from re-inception past the school's 50th anniversary, one of the most exciting elements of the reopening was that the majority of the students came from the eastern United States. Thus, the sparkling lakes, tannin-colored ponds, many rivers punctuating the landscape, and the many high peaks presiding over countless lesser peaks and valleys gave the students an opportunity to explore wilderness close to their own backyards.

outdoor industry. It was getting more difficult to find people interested in and able to venture far from the comforts of home for an entire month or semester. Somehow, the school needed to attract students. Gans and certain board members were struggling in their meetings against a historical logjam of resistance to establishing a more sustainable financial model. The opportunity to acquire WMI came at a perfect time; it would both diversify revenue streams and also broaden educational offerings.

WMI and NOLS officially joined forces on September 1, 1999. WMI offices would remain in Pitkin until the new NOLS headquarters building in Lander was ready for occupancy in 2002. At that time, the WMI management team made the move to Lander. In 2007 WMI, already a powerful presence throughout the western states, expanded operations into 13 southeastern states through a partnership with a private outdoor education enterprise, Landmark Learning, in Cullowhee, North Carolina. That initiative added 55 courses and 1,091 students to the NOLS bottom line in the following year alone. By 2015, WMI had more than quadrupled in size since 1999. It became a powerhouse for NOLS programming, and a major contributor toward development of a more enduring financial outlook. In fiscal year 2015, the institute educated a total of 19,401 students on 855 courses around the world.

The WMI curriculum is based around scenarios—learn the skills, and then get outside and practice them.
Marcio Paes-Barreto

Pundit predictions of mayhem surrounding Y2K were a bust, and the turn of the millennium likewise found NOLS moving forward unimpeded. The biggest change was a matter of scale; the school was growing. For each new field student taking the first tentative steps into the wilderness, it took a small army of people to make their NOLS experience possible. Admissions personnel sifted applications, checked medical records, arranged college credit, and answered questions; those in finance kept the books, and risk managers worked at keeping everyone safer. Branch staff arranged permits on nearly 40 individual land districts (plus private land access) in the Rocky Mountains alone, and dozens of others in the school's diaspora. Other staff purchased and repaired equipment, and bagged rations tailored to the needs of course types, terrain, weather, and elevation. Program supervisors briefed instructor teams. Re-rations were scheduled. Once a course entered the backcountry, the team in town remained poised to activate the evacuation system, if needed. Upon return, staff de-issued student gear, debriefed their experience, and introduced them to alumni services.

Likewise, WMI continued its own well-established process for course delivery, which kept staff numbers relatively small by relying on the organizations that sponsored courses—universities, companies, and the like—to provide the venue and handle student registration. "We're subcontractors, really," said Gray, who in 2015 remained director of WMI. "We're in major colleges and universities all over the country. We train most of our competitors in the outdoor industry, and governmental agencies including the Park Service, Forest Service, BLM, and Game and Fish."

One WMI process differed markedly. Unlike traditional field courses, which were sent out to the backcountry from branches and therefore provided opportunities for instructor teams to mingle and exchange ideas, sponsor-based programming meant that WMI instructors rarely saw more than one or two of their colleagues. In order to build consistency and a sense of identity, starting in September 1995, an annual staff meeting was instituted to bring instructors together for curriculum updates, team-building, professional development, and re-certifications. (For the first two years, the group was small enough to hold the meetings on a houseboat on Lake Powell.)

In October 2000, NOLS celebrated its 35th anniversary with a party in Lander for 400 staff, alumni, and friends. Although Petzoldt was gone, Tap Tapley was there, as were Rob and Martha Hellyer and many other "NOLS originals." With average instructor age at 31 years, Gans observed, "We are now in an era where the majority of NOLS employees were not even born when the school started."

Noting that "thousands of businesses and nonprofits have come and gone in the past 35 years," Gans reported that the school was thriving, with nearly every branch and department of the school meeting or exceeding expectations, and a new record set for field program days the previous year. There were some 50,000 alumni of NOLS expeditions scattered worldwide and more than 16,000 WMI alums. From a total of three courses in 1965, the school had run nearly 450 in 2000 alone, of which nearly 200 were WMI courses. In

ROCKFALL AND SYNERGY

By John Hovey, instructor

My student, Kaggie, had slipped while descending a steep snow slope. In her attempt to self-arrest with her ice axe, she dislocated her right shoulder—but eventually came to a stop on the slope. While laying on the snow in pain from her shoulder, she was then struck in the head by a rock knocked loose by another group descending the slope. The rock made her slide another 50 feet down the slope, where she came to rest on a flat rock near me. She couldn't move her arm and she was scraped and bruised, dirty from the gravel, crying. She was breathing and she could talk to me, which was good, but blood trickled from her head and legs.

This was my worst day working for NOLS. My students would live through this mess, but in the moment I knew it was totally up to me to make that happen. Resolving this situation would require all the skills, knowledge, and decision-making abilities I had gained as both a field and WMI instructor.

Once I was able to move my students out of immediate danger, my initial assessment of Kaggie's condition and the remoteness of the scene made me decide to notify NOLS Rocky Mountain about the emergency immediately. "Do you need a helicopter?" asked the evacuation coordinator over the satellite phone. I said yes, erring on the side of caution, knowing that it takes time to get special clearance to fly into a protected wilderness area.

Then I performed a complete patient assessment, exactly as I had taught so many students to do at WMI. Kaggie's chief complaint was a dislocated shoulder that was cutting off the circulation to her right hand—an injury that could jeopardize her whole arm if not resolved quickly. Anyone with a Wilderness First Responder (WFR) certification would know to employ the so-called "herringbone technique" for reducing (relocating) a dislocated shoulder: Pull the seated patient's shoulder back, bend their elbow, and bring the arm down to the patient's side, then slowly rotate the arm externally, and finally push the elbow forward and fold the forearm across the body. I knew this method well and tried it for more than an hour on Kaggie, with no success.

fact, the 4,500 new NOLS alumni who were WMI students more than doubled the school's student numbers that year. 2000 also marked the first time in history that some of the school's classrooms had four walls. It was a big transition for the school.

At the same time, although the methods of course delivery and pedagogies of WMI and traditional field expeditions were separate and different, in many ways, according to Schmertzler, "they were fantastically complementary." It was an apt union.

I phoned NOLS Rocky Mountain a second time to update them on Kaggie's status, and they confirmed that a helicopter would be heading our way. The flying conditions were marginal, and the extraction would be risky for both Kaggie and the rescuers. But if we couldn't reduce the dislocation, we had no other choice.

My co-instructor Jen then suggested we try another move taught on the WFR, called the Stimson method. We gently placed Kaggie face down on a large boulder with her right arm hanging over the side, and we suspended about 12 pounds of rock in a bag from her wrist. Voilà! In just one minute, Kaggie could feel that her shoulder was reduced. Circulation was restored to her arm, so her condition was no longer urgent. At the last moment, I was able to phone NOLS to wave off the helicopter. Kaggie still needed medical attention, but she was stable enough to walk out instead of flying.

Kaggie's rescue was a turning point not just for me, but also for the entire NOLS course. During the emergency, things had gotten pretty serious pretty quickly, and everyone played an essential role. The leadership and knowledge of the instructor team, the bravery and cooperation of the students—these ingredients combined to safely move Kaggie from the rockfall zone and down the mountain, reduce her shoulder, patch her wounds, and deliver her to the hospital. It was an extraordinary event that none of us will ever forget.

Drew Leemon, risk management director, and Tod Schimelpfenig, WMI curriculum director, debriefed the accident with me afterward. This incident validated teaching shoulder reduction in wilderness medicine and, on longer courses, teaching two methods to give the caregiver more options. Without that second technique, our choices would have been bleak. In the end, WMI training saves the day in a NOLS accident, and a NOLS accident supplies information that improves WMI training. A powerful synergy!

NOLS Professional Training Institute Begins

Since the very beginning of NOLS, queries came in from time to time asking about custom-made courses. Perhaps a company wanted a special team-building experience, but they could only spare a week. A family was looking for off-the-grid bonding. Or a youth organization wanted a standalone course for their kids to learn outdoor skills. In fact, the school dabbled in such alternatives now and then. For three summers in the 1960s, Petzoldt helped arrange a

Astronauts learning teamwork in the canyonlands. *NASA*

mini-NOLS course for diabetic boys who were part of a national study. According to Rob Hellyer, the program was run at the Audubon camp near Dubois by John Walker of the University of Wyoming—a big reason Walker, who spent years on the NOLS Board, became associated with the school in the first place. The initiative ended when funding ran out.

By the early 1990s, recalled Rick Rochelle, the admissions office frequently got phone calls from people seeking to buy an entire course, or to do certain activities on specific dates. At the time, there was only one answer, and it never sat right: "Sorry," they'd have to say. "We don't do that."

People around NOLS began to wonder why not, and the idea of finding a way to begin meeting such requests became reality in September 1999. At first, it was called the NOLS Professional Training Institute, shortened to NOLS Professional Training or NOLS Pro in 2002. Developed to provide custom services for specific groups, NOLS Pro was another shift away from the traditional "open-enrollment" model at NOLS.

Since they arrived at the school in the same year, there was some early consideration of placing both WMI and NOLS Pro under one administrative umbrella, but that idea was soon nixed. The two had little else in common, and their business models and operational strategies were very different. NOLS Pro provided its services in one of three basic ways. First, a client could design an expedition of varying length with a customized blend of the essentials of the NOLS curriculum—leadership, outdoor skills, environmental studies, the ethics of Leave No Trace, and risk management. Second, NOLS Pro consulted on risk management, administration, and curriculum with organizations striving to build outdoor programs. Finally, NOLS representatives could serve as experienced and knowledgeable speakers and panelists to gatherings such as wilderness and outdoors-oriented conferences. The department was also charged with managing both the Wilderness Risk Management Conference and the school's ongoing support for Leave No Trace. Over time, the department tweaked the design of its expedition offerings, and also added classroom-based courses lasting one to four days, largely for leadership navigation challenges and risk management trainings.

Initial program development and marketing for the new department was done solely by John Kanengieter and a half-time assistant. Kanengieter, who came to NOLS in 1985 and stayed for 29 years, led NOLS Pro from inception until 2007.

NOLS Pro departed from the "business to consumer" model represented by the method students enrolled for regular field expedition courses or semester programs. For those students, attending NOLS tended to be an individual decision. In contrast, NOLS Pro clients were typically businesses and other organizations, and the transactions fol-

US Naval Academy midshipmen sea kayaking in Prince William Sound. *Ashley Wise*

lowed a "business to business" model. To them, a NOLS experience was a dollar value decision; the question they tended to ask was, "Will this add value to our organization if we are associated with this program and offer this opportunity?'" said Rochelle, who was director from 2008 to 2015. The department had a highly entrepreneurial feel.

NOLS Pro's first client, in September 1999, was Riverton Valley Electrical. "This rural electrical company . . .

wanted us to help teach some of the linemen who went out in the winter to go check on power lines about cold weather and dressing for the cold," recalled Kanengieter. "Our next client, in November of 1999, was NASA. . . . It was a good second client." Instrumental in landing the NASA contract were Rich Brame and curriculum manager John Gookin. In March of that year, Gookin had learned that NASA was seeking training specifically in "expedition behavior" (EB)—a term he knew could only have come from NOLS, but which was being confused at the time with Outward Bound.

Gookin and Brame wrote a proposal, and NOLS representatives took it to Houston in July to meet with the primary decision-makers and present a NOLS slide show. One of the astronauts, Shannon Lucid, was present. A veteran of five space flights, including 188 days in 1996 on the Russian space station Mir (at the time, the US record for time in space and the world record for women in space), she advocated for NOLS. The effort led in November to four astronauts including Lucid, plus two astronaut trainers, embarking for the Utah canyonlands on the inaugural NOLS NASA leadership expedition.

For eight days, they learned about expedition behavior, leadership, communication, and group dynamics while camping in the desert and canyoneering. The big question at the debrief was whether the EB training had been worth-

while. Gookin, who designed and ran the pilot course, paraphrased one of the astronauts (a former fighter pilot): "The only other school I have been to like this was Top Gun: You guys told us exactly what you wanted us to do, you role modeled what you expected, then you coached us, coached us, coached us until we got it right. It was perfect . . . When people had feedback, good or bad, it was very mission-oriented, timely, and direct. This is exactly what we need."

From there, the NASA relationship grew. In 2001, Rick Hudson, commander of the *Columbia* space shuttle crew, saw what the space station crews were doing and decided he'd like his team to go to NOLS too. Another astronaut, John Grunsfeld, was a NOLS student in 1974 and 1986. He had three space journeys to his credit before being named payload commander for the Hubble Space Telescope's fourth servicing mission, STS-109. He also signed his crew onto a NOLS Pro course. They were facing a mission in March 2002 that would entail five space walks to upgrade the telescope. The team of seven would spend 10 days in space, but first, they followed instructors Jeffrey Post and John Abel into the canyonlands from Gravel Crossing into White Canyon and circumnavigated Jacob's Chair in southeastern Utah.

The two-week mini-expeditions were designed to exercise the teams' leadership and expedition skills, and by 2003,

A student rappels in the canyonlands. *Brian Hensien*

nearly 30 percent of astronauts had been on similar NOLS Pro courses. "This belief in life as an expedition applies directly to life in Earth's orbit aboard a space shuttle," wrote Grunsfeld in *The Leader* in 2003. By 2005, the figure had reached 70 percent of astronauts.

Among them had been the team of STS-107. In August 2001, the crew of seven spent 12 days with NOLS, traveling 50 miles across the Winds. "It's probably been one of the more profound experiences that I've had, just watching this team move from where they were—a good team—to where they became this great team," recalled Kanengieter, who worked the course. "I think it was due to their diversity, and in some ways their vulnerability with each other. That was a new thing I think we got to on our NOLS trip."

WAKING UP IN THE WILDERNESS

By Carolyn Highland, Semester in New Zealand, 2012

This essay originally appeared on the NOLS blog in October 2015.

I woke in the middle of the night to cold on my nose and a black strip of sky smattered with stars in my vision. It was all I could see, my sleeping bag cinched up around my face, laid out on the bare ground. I lay there unmoving, every cell of my body awake and aware of itself. It felt as though I'd been tapped on the shoulder, as though some massive universal force had tugged at me, whispering, "You need to see this."

I'd spent the few days prior hiking through tussock and scree and contemplating the uncertainty of my future. In less than a week my semester in New Zealand would be over, and I would find myself yet again a recent college graduate without a plan. The mountain air had been whirring with questions I didn't have answers to yet, like where I'd live and what I'd do and who I'd be with. Would I choose the easy, comfortable route and try to find a job in a city I didn't really want to live in because my friends were there? Would I choose a route that was unchallenging but safer? Or would I do something entirely different, something that I felt in my heart but would require me striking out alone?

Out here, I woke up every day with a purpose—with the pure and yet complex purpose of picking up my home and walking to where I would place it next. Back in the frontcountry, the questions and options tumbled and spun and made me dizzy.

When two of my expedition mates tried to convince me to sleep outside on the night of Thanksgiving, one of our last in the backcountry, I declined, citing my exhaustion and desire to get a good night's sleep. I liked the idea of sleeping outside better than the actuality of it, especially at high altitude in mid-spring. I would inevitably toss and turn in the cold and wake up to sandflies biting my face. I wanted the comfort of the inside of the only house we had out here. But before I even entered the tent I felt called back outside, felt called to sleep beside my two best friends underneath the sky.

Instead of feeling irritated when I woke, I was seized by the feeling that, more than ever, I was exactly where I needed to be in that moment and in my life. I was suddenly calm. It was all simple, it was all right before me. It was all embodied by what I was doing in that exact moment, by the choice I had made that night. The choice to forgo certain comfort and sleep outside was one that seemed so insignificant at the time, but that I realized then actually represented everything I was about to do, everything I wanted my life to be.

In the tent, I would have had a warm, pleasant, uninterrupted night's sleep. I would have been comfortable. It would have been easy. It was my initial reaction because it was the path of least resistance, it was the choice that felt like the best one because it was the easiest. But it wasn't. The best choice was to drag my sleeping bag out into the chilly night air and lay it beside two people who brought out in me what I wanted to be brought out. And so I knew it would have to be, and it would be for the rest of my life.

Being in New Zealand had awoken me to exactly the way I wanted to live my life. Not in a literal sense—I was not planning on spending the rest of my days in the backcountry—but rather in the sense of the way I felt when I was out there, in the way I acted, in the way I was. In the way I inhabited my real self so fully and completely. In the way that I spent time with people who made me better. Who made me more me.

And I knew in that moment as I gazed up at the stars, my nose frozen from the air but my arms warm from my friends on either side of me, that this is the path I would follow for the rest of my life. I would travel uphill and jump into cold water and be kind and supportive and goofy and real. I would do what felt right in the deepest and purest part of me even when it was difficult. I didn't know yet what it would look like, but I knew what it would feel like. It wasn't even a choice, it just was. This is the answer, it whispered. This is the way. It was right before me, as clear as the night sky above our heads.

Three years after I took my last steps out of the New Zealand backcountry, I find myself thousands of miles from home on the other side of the United States, having heeded the pull of the southern hemisphere stars. I find myself living the life I'd imagined. One that looks different than anything I ever could have dreamed up, but feels precisely the way I knew it needed to. It was a difficult and confusing and exhausting and long and windy trail to get here, but it was the right one. And I am a fuller and richer and happier version of myself for it.

How incredible it is, to be able to—through your presence in this grand, vast environment—connect with something that lies so deep within your own soul. And that is the proof, I think, that everything in this universe is connected to every other

The stars in New Zealand. *Fredrik Norrsell*

thing. That by placing my feet on the mountains and my hands in the speargrass and my ass onto the slushy snow and my head on the tussock, I was actually connecting, little by little, with myself. With something inside me long before I ever set foot in New Zealand, but that was called to the surface by its long lost relatives. By the sky and the stones and the streams and the snow and the stars. A message that could only be heard outside.

That is the gift that wilderness gives us. It reminds us of who we are and pushes us to be that. You were always there, it whispers, but it provides us with the clear reflecting glass to see it. This is who you are, it tells us. This is who we are.

On their 16-day science mission on the shuttle *Columbia*, the STS-109 crew carried the topographic map of Wind River Peak that they had used on their summit day, and a pair of NOLS windpants. On February 1, 2003, during re-entry to the Earth's atmosphere, the space shuttle *Columbia* broke up, and seven NOLS graduates died: Dave Brown, Rick Husband, Mike Anderson, Willie McCool, Ilan Ramon, Laurel Clark, and Kalpana Chawla.

"I had just gotten an email from Rick, from space, which was cool," said Kanengieter. "He talked about his team, and how the NOLS training had had so much impact on them. And then the accident happened. That summer, [we took] all of the families up to Columbia Point in Colorado, a 14,000-foot peak, to get them up to the same elevation that the crew was on top of the summit of Wind River Peak. That was a pretty powerful thing."

Beyond NASA, one of NOLS Pro's longest running programs is with US Naval Academy (USNA) midshipmen. Bob Schoultz, a former Navy SEAL (who also became a NOLS instructor in 2005), was director of character development with the Naval Academy when he heard about NOLS from a fellow SEAL in 2003. At the time, he was seeking new opportunities for midshipmen underclassmen during what were typically uninspiring summers off. "I'd never heard of NOLS," Schoultz said, but his colleague went on to say, "Well, NOLS was what inspired me to be a Navy SEAL."

With a recommendation like that, Schoultz mentioned the idea to his staff, "and the more they looked into it, the more they liked it," he said in 2015.

John Gookin, a former Marine, had collaborated with the USNA on leadership curriculum development from 1996 to 1998, and because of this there was significant overlap in the leadership education models of the two organizations. At the Naval Academy's invitation, in the fall of 2003, Gookin went to Annapolis and did a NOLS leadership presentation to interested midshipmen, using his knowledge of military terminology to express some NOLS concepts in language the military folks would understand. "For example, I switched 'expedition behavior' to 'mission-oriented behavior,'" said Gookin. "It's exactly the same idea, just expressed in a way familiar to the Navy folks." The presentation was very well received. "Bob and his boss interrupted me about half a dozen times to tell the students, 'See, that's what we've been trying to tell you guys. This is the stuff that matters,'" remembered Gookin.

It didn't take long for NOLS summer courses to become one of the most sought-after summer training blocks to augment months of theoretical classroom learning on leadership. Describing their experiences, midshipmen often sounded like other field students: "We had two days with about two hours of sleep in between with crazy storms and hours of shoveling—probably the hardest work I've done in

John Gookin, NOLS curriculum manager from 1989 through 2015. *NOLS Archives*

my life. . . . We had unbelievable winds—winds that were knocking down 200-pound guys with 80-pound packs. . . . We were really tight before that, but going through that together it was, like, wow . . . we've really done something," said one midshipman. More than that, though, they dis-

covered a direct connection to their chosen careers: "The theory behind leadership can only take you so far," said one. "You have to get out there in the field and make mistakes. I know we're not going to be mountaineering as naval officers, but you're still managing personalities, dividing group abilities, trying to keep the group as a well-oiled machine." Said another, "You get really focused on peer leadership and small group unit leadership, which is really important in the fleet. You need to know how to work with people in some intense situations, and this really tested it." In 2015, more than 220 midshipmen passed through a variety of Pro courses: WEMT, mountaineering, sea kayaking, backpacking anywhere from Alaska and Canada's Yukon to the Pacific Northwest, the Rockies, and even the East Coast.

The arrival of the space program brought undeniable cachet to NOLS. For instructor Anne Cannon, it hearkened back to the first day of her student course on July 20, 1969, and the first moon landing. "I can remember thinking this was a historic event," she recalled in 2015. "We were in Dickinson Park, and one of the students had a tiny transistor radio. We sat out in the meadow, looking up at the moon, listening to the coverage. It was cool. Whoever thought that one day astronauts would be [students] of NOLS?" With the advent of courses for the Naval Academy, Petzoldt's dream reached not only into outer space, but also to the ocean depths.

NOLS MEXICO

Imagine a land of stark contrasts: ocean and desert, cactus and pine, teeming seas and sparse shores. This is Baja California as Tap Tapley found it while sailing the waters of the Sea of Cortéz. After witnessing its unique wilderness, he began dreaming of starting a branch there. When the busy summer of 1970 ended, he urged Petzoldt to take a break and drive with him and their wives to see it.

They trailered the *Lady Esther*, Petzoldt's powerboat, and *La Tigresa*, Tapley's sailboat, there and scouted around for a few weeks. They did some diving and got shocked by the electric pulses of a torpedo ray. Petzoldt sustained a severe

Sunrise on the Sea of Cortez. *Julie Brown*

sunburn. And Tapley got his way. By March 1971, NOLS Baja (now NOLS Mexico) was in business.

The first course gathered at Bahía de Los Angeles on the east coast of the peninsula. Eight intrepid students were shuttled by air from El Centro in a tiny plane. They used the motorboat and the sailboat to explore the area during the two-week course, base camping in the same place for the whole time. The water was good, the fish plentiful, but the currents and tides were difficult and the weather unpredictable.

Tapley heard Coyote Bay, near Mulegé, might be easier. There, he found the Díaz family, who would become key to the success of the Baja operation. The patriarch was Bonifacio, but it was his son, Manuel, who showed Tapley the country, taught him about the weather, the hideouts from the wind, fishing, and how to gather and prepare shellfish. "He wouldn't take any pay. We got to be good friends, like brothers, and he wouldn't let me go out alone until he approved it," recalled Tap on a video from the NOLS archives.

The only structure on the beach then was the Díazes' small thatched sun shelter. Tapley sent a message by airplane to his contact in El Centro, asking him to get in touch with the school to tell them where he was, and that he was ready for another group of eight students.

The next year, they added Folbots to the program. "The folding kayaks would make the migration to Alaska for the summer to ply the waters of Prince William Sound, much like the gray whale and bird migrations that make the round-trip each year," said Don Ford, who ran the branch with his wife, Donna, from 1979 through 1986.

Dinner in the early years of NOLS Mexico. *NOLS Archives*

By 1974 the branch was able to support six courses, which stayed mostly within the Bay of Concepción. But when Petzoldt left NOLS in 1975, Tap Tapley left as well. "This could have ended the program, [but] a group of instructors kept the program going," said Ford. Bart Womack led the first course down the coast from Coyote Bay to near Loreto in 1976, beginning the transition from the base camp format that Tapley had developed to a true expedition.

Womack ran the branch from 1974 to 1976, and then Charlie Fiala and Abby Caul stepped in until 1978. The Fords' tenure ran seven years, from 1979 to 1986, followed by Leslie van Barselaar and Dave Kallgren as co-directors for fourteen years, until 2000. That year, Francisco Castellanos took over, then Jon Kempsey

and Jim Chisholm in 2003, and Dave Lee in 2006, when Liz Hammond arrived, staying until 2009. Carolina González Cortés took the director position and was still in place in 2015.

The Díaz family continued to be a vital part of the NOLS community there, helping build the branch in innumerable ways. One of the earliest buildings they constructed was the one-room, windowless brick structure that first housed the branch. Many family members have been part of the history: Concha Díaz started working at the branch in 1987, just after Ignacio "Nacho" Ávila became the first Mexican employed there. In 2015, Ávila, Concha, and her siblings, Trinidad and Clemente, were still there.

During their tenure, Kallgren and van Barselaar made sweeping improvements to NOLS Mexico's facilities, including composting toilets, solar electrical power, and solar-heated water for showers. Communication was also improved with single sideband radio communication to Lander (replaced with satellite Internet by 2015). But even with the improvements, the branch always felt remote.

Semester programs had begun in Baja by the early 1980s, with backpacking, sailing, sea kayaking, whale watching, and mule packing. Around the same time, the branch got a fleet of fiberglass kayaks, putting an end to the Baja-Alaska Folbot migration. Semester courses by 2015 included hiking, sailing, and sea kayaking, as well as a cultural component.

In 1989, open sailboats known as Drascombe longboats were introduced, and the branch hosted the first Instructor Sailing Seminar. The Drascombes were ideally suited to NOLS-style expedition travel, due to the capacity to stow multiple

Looking out over the Sierra San Pedro Mártirs.
Nicholas Hall

weeks of food stores. Today, NOLS Mexico has one of the world's largest fleets of the boats.

Sailors and sea kayakers discovered that the winter wind pattern called El Norte is a cornerstone of the Baja experience. "Nortes" occur when cold, dense air from the Four Corners region of the United States rushes along the Sea of Cortez, funneled by the mountains lining the sea on both shores. Nortes can bring 20- to 30-knot winds for days on end, pinning sea kayakers to the beach and, at the very least, increasing the challenge for sailors. Courses thus learned quickly to take advantage of the relative calm of early morning, sometimes setting off at 4:00 a.m. or before. Lucy Smith recalled from working there in 1975, "What I learned from Tap most of all was respect for the wind." But it was worth it, she said, to experience the intense beauty of a Baja sunrise while paddling through the magical colors of marine bioluminescence sparkling in the water.

Over the years, opportunities for local educators, students, and land managers, as well as financial aid and scholarships for NOLS courses in both Spanish and English, were implemented, as was a long-standing partnership with the Universidad Autónoma de Baja California Sur, collaborating with their departments of marine biology, geology, and alternative tourism.

By 2015, in addition to semesters, NOLS Mexico ran stand-alone sea kayaking and sailing courses, Spanish language programs (usually hiking and sea kayaking), as well as WMI courses in Spanish, both at the branch and in La Paz or Mexico City. Semesters included hiking, sailing, and sea kayaking. Students began by traversing the San Pedro Mártirs, the Gigantes, or the Lagunas. The spine of Baja soars to over 10,000 feet at its highest point, and the rugged mountains of the peninsula support aspen groves, pine forests, and crystalline brooks. An evening thunderstorm in the mountains was always a surprise for those whose mental picture of the peninsula was a flat desert.

"The landscape reflects the ocean environment, nestling up to the desert ecosystem, which runs up to the jagged wild mountain ranges," said Lynn Petzold, a field instructor for over 20 years, in 2015. "The stargazing is phenomenal, without city lights to brighten the sky and diminish the constellations. The sunrises and moonrises up out of the sea are not to be missed."

Melding

The process of integrating WMI and NOLS Pro to the existing programs at NOLS was an interesting time for the school. WMI arrived as a known entity from years of collaboration. According to Schmertzler, it was a real and timely asset: "WMI was so well run, a wonderful contained unit," he said. "They knew how to deliver what they were delivering. They knew what they were doing. NOLS provided the overhead nest where they could sit, but they didn't need a lot of help."

NOLS Pro was a different story. Built from the ground up, its integration was often more challenging. For example, NOLS Pro courses were disruptive to operations because they were shorter in duration and had customized start and end dates that sometimes conflicted with routine field courses. In addition, traditional course routes "didn't quite fit requests for awesome short routes with short, easy drives," according to one person who remembered those days; in 2004, NOLS Pro courses averaged just 6.4 days, with an average of nine students. "There were just more players and new details to navigate, and a totally different planning schedule that made it very hard for branches to predict and plan for business," she said.

Time, as always, was the answer, especially as solutions to operational challenges were found. WMI and NOLS Pro courses became increasingly understood and accepted within the broader NOLS community. From a business perspective, the acquisition of WMI and founding of NOLS Pro proved themselves to be worthy diversifications for the school.

Nonetheless, it was perhaps not surprising, given the advent of two such new initiatives so close together, that staff again began to ask questions, such as: What was happening to the school? Was it losing sight of its mission? Would it become another glorified guiding/adventure travel company? There was worry about mission creep, and the impact of straying from the traditional 30-day and semester course formats. Could the NOLS experience be truly conveyed in the short courses at NOLS Pro, or in the classroom-intensive experiences of WMI? Would people who already knew one another upon arrival at NOLS alter the character and impact of the experience? Who was a NOLS graduate, anyhow?

The debates were vigorous, and the answers didn't come easily. The result, as the 2000s yielded to the 2010s, was a good start—but in all honesty, even as of 2015 the school was still working to integrate its disparate parts, both organizationally and psychologically.

The Noble Hotel housed much of the school's administration until 2002. Lander traffic was sometimes interesting.
NOLS Archives

Bricks and Mortar:
The International HQ

SINCE THE SCHOOL'S FOUNDING, NOLS administrative offices had been situated helter-skelter, at first in Jack Nicholas's basement office, then out in Sinks Canyon, then in a variety of rented spaces around downtown Lander. By the late 1990s, most had been condensed piecemeal into a cluster of buildings just north of Main Street: the Noble Hotel, the old post office building, and the Kennedy Building. But the situation was becoming untenable. It was a far cry from the Simer years when, he said, "we used to run NOLS from one room at the Noble Hotel." In 2000, NOLS Rocky Mountain staff alone easily outnumbered his entire NOLS administration.

The school's administrative offices were hampered by years of facility neglect. Some workspaces were outright decrepit, observed Rich Brame, and "for many years, we were fragmented around town, so these departments were isolated. You couldn't just pop into somebody's office and shoot the breeze, or jump into a conference room and brainstorm stuff." In addition, with the advent of NOLS Pro and WMI, the school was growing fast: According to *The Leader* (Winter 2000), "In the next 12 years, NOLS is expected to have an annual growth of more than five percent, and will need to double headquarters staff."

"The school was desperate," recalled John Gans. "We had gone 15 years at least with no attention paid to HQ facilities. We were scattered all over town in rental facilities and falling-apart buildings. We needed to act before the money would be raised." Knowing the historic Noble Hotel would not serve the purpose, the board launched discussions to examine the options, which for some time included whether to move NOLS headquarters out of Lander. According to Gene Tremblay, who had served on the board since 1992 and was weary of the journey to Lander, "The thought was maybe we should go to a bigger city, maybe Seattle or even Denver. There were persuasive arguments in both directions."

Gans led the charge to stay in Lander, recalled Tremblay. Many families had settled down and taken root. Lander had become home. His efforts were supported by the results of a $16,000 feasibility study funded by a Wyoming Business Council grant. Through it, the school received important feedback from a citizen committee. "NOLS put us on the map," said Lander's community resource coordinator, Linda Hewitt, who was part of the committee. "It made Lander world-renowned." Even the Wyoming governor weighed in. At the time, the state was losing its young people to outward migration, and the governor pointed to NOLS as a shining example of ways to meet the challenge of getting young people into the state. The decision was finally made: NOLS would stay in Lander.

Additional factors tipped the decision, including the donation to the school of three city lots one block due north of the Noble Hotel at Lincoln and 3rd Streets by longtime NOLS supporters Harry Tipton, a physician and Wyoming state representative, and his wife, Alex. The school was then able to arrange a $6.3 million Industrial Revenue Bond issued through the City of Lander and purchased by First Interstate Bank in Riverton. The result was a low-interest, tax-free situation—appealing, since, said Tremblay, "we

NOLS International Headquarters.
Brad Christensen

[still] had not broken into a really financially secure position. . . . The thought of spending all that money at that time was a big thing."

After the June 2000 groundbreaking, the community watched as the khaki brick, three-story NOLS headquarters building began to rise, with longtime NOLS staffer Karl Weller serving as project manager alongside Jim Childress of Centerbrook (CT) Architects and Planners.

The 44,000-square-foot building was built at a total cost of $8.67 million. As the *Wyoming State Journal* reported (October 17, 2001), it was brown on the outside, but "green" everywhere else: "Tables made out of soy plants and corn stalks. Floors made from recycled tires and energy-sensitive lighting . . . What else did you expect from the world's leading outdoor leadership school that lives and dies on environmental awareness?" Initially covered out of operating funds and the bond issue, the balance was paid off by the capital campaign known as "The International Base Camp Initiative." For the 80 staff that moved in that fall, the efficiency and comfort was a whole new world after decades of making-do.

The building itself was fairly conservative in design: U-shaped and similar in shade to the catty-corner post office and the Noble Hotel. But topping off the building was a metal structure that was nothing if not unconventional: a sculptured metal wing hovering over the southwest corner of the roof. Informed sources report that it was a rain cover for the outdoor stairwell below it, intended to look like an aspen leaf. The widespread opinion was that it missed the mark. Some referred to it as the "flying nun"; others said it looked like a whale's tail, or an ugly monster. Whatever the case, the rusted steel structure became an enduring element in the Lander skyline.

On Friday, October 12, 2001, the NOLS International Headquarters at 284 Lincoln Street officially opened with a ribbon-cutting. Surely Dottie Petzoldt knew of it, since she was still living at a retirement community in Lander. In April 2002, just a few months after the building was completed, Dottie Petzoldt, Paul's second wife—the woman who brought him to Lander to begin with, helped start the school, watched him leave, yet remained an advocate of the school—died. She was 94.

———

As one building rose that year, on September 11 others crashed to the ground in New York City and outside Washington, DC. On that day, Gans wrote later, 232 NOLS students were on field expeditions around the world. Grounded aircraft stymied 38 people in their efforts to reach NOLS courses about to start in Mexico, Arizona, and the Pacific Northwest. More than 100 additional students were already packing for upcoming semester courses. At WMI headquarters in Pitkin, the Wilderness First Responder Instructor Training Course (WFR ITC) was scheduled to begin at 8:00 a.m. The instructors, who had gathered in the classroom early to finalize their preparations and meet arriving students learned just before 7:00 a.m. that a plane had crashed into the World Trade Towers.

Isolated at 9,200 feet at the end of a dirt road in the Colorado Rockies, with minimal communication technology, "we restructured the day to allow our students to reach out to their loved ones; everyone had ties to New York, Pennsylvania, or Washington, DC," recalled instructor Gates Richards. Schedules were shuffled, and by the afternoon they were able to refocus on the ITC. "We spent the next 10 days working on our skills as wilderness medicine educators with a strengthened sense of the importance of imparting these skills to our students," he said.

In Lander and at the branches, expedition course rosters were scrutinized for anyone who might have been impacted directly. News of the tragedies was delivered as soon as possible to those in the backcountry, but the usual means of using aircraft flyovers for emergency communication was not an option for the first several days while the aviation industry remained shut down. In some cases, horsepackers carried in the news with scheduled re-rations. In others, staffers hiked in early to find affected students directly. Some were able to carry faxes from home to the students and instructors. In India, two courses were cancelled, and the India mountaineering course ended early.

Janeen Hutchins was in the cafeteria at the Noble Hotel the morning of September 11 for the start of her second-ever instructing gig. The students on a Semester in the Rockies course had just arrived, and the instructor team was doing the hiking section orientation.

"I had stepped away to use the bathroom," she said, "and when I came back, people were running around, frantic. . . . We stopped the orientation and basically spent that morning watching [9/11] unfold." Some of the students and one of the instructors were from Connecticut or had family in New York, so the course waited an extra day to depart to where they would be beyond the reach of further news.

Hutchins's husband, Ryan Hutchins-Cabibi, was already in the field, also instructing a hiking section of a Semester in the Rockies course. "One of his students' dad was on one of the airplanes," she said, "so they made contact with his course, and Ryan had to hike this young man out to the roadhead so that he could go home and attend the funeral."

Asked about instructing in such an unusual circumstance, Hutchins reflected on how much the instructor role can create the lens through which students see their experience. "It was fascinating. . . . [T]here was so much uncertainty right after it happened, because they didn't know if we were under attack and it was going to be a total dismantling of the United States," she said. "Then there was this thought that, 'Well, we're probably in the safest place because we're in such a remote part of the country—and how amazing is it that we have everything that we need on our backs, and we're self-sufficient.' How empowering that was. And the concept of how, on NOLS courses, we create our own course culture, and there is a lot of power to decide what the norms in our

HEARING ABOUT 9/11

By Ellie Chikkaraju, instructor

Semester in the Northwest, Pasayten Wilderness

Journal entry, Day 10, September 2001

"When we arrived at the landing strip, we walked past a guard station where a husband & wife had just arrived and were unloading their horses. Keep in mind—these are the first signs of civilization we've encountered since September 6, about 9 days ago. Anyways, they had some news for us that I don't think any of us were ready to handle. It turns out that the US had been attacked by terrorists early Tuesday morning, September 11th. From what the man could tell us, he said about 10,000 are dead. Airlines just started back up today after being shut down since Tuesday. Tuesday was the day we were climbing the ridge and we all remember seeing an airplane that completely turned around in the sky. We think it was either patrolling the border or ordered to land. Crazy. I can't even take it all in right now. Especially since we have no contact to the outside world. I know a lot of us are having a hard time dealing with it. Many of us know people or have close family members that live there. Our instructors told us that NOLS would be sure to find us if anything has happened and hopefully we will be able to make a phone call before our mountain section. That would lift a big weight off of our shoulders that is already heavy enough.

Ravi pulled us together for a nice meeting to share how we were feeling and to take a few minutes of silence out of our busy day to pray for everyone. It's such a different feeling out here. I'm mourning for those people inside but, at the same time, it's so hard to grasp that it actually happened. Leah and I were just talking about how we don't even realize that life is still going on right now in the rest of the world. And today we found out that it most certainly is. There is a definite lull in our campsite. I can tell everyone is in their own world with millions of thoughts racing through their heads. I have a big lump in my throat that I just can't swallow. It will go away soon enough. Gosh, it feels like I'm in a parallel universe. How can it be so peaceful here when chaos is breaking out on the other side of the country?"

culture will be—you know, non-violent, and accepting, and open communication. In such an uncertain, violent world, here we were, in our little utopia."

A Peripatetic Community

As the ranks of both instructors and alumni swelled, people carried forward the lessons and messages of NOLS to hundreds of different communities in the outdoors and elsewhere. As Sebastian Junger, himself a graduate and the bestselling author of *The Perfect Storm*, once said, "I'm not sure if 'adventurous' people go to NOLS or if NOLS turns people into adventure lovers. Probably a little of both."

Many racked up impressive achievements. In May 2004, four NOLS graduates summited Everest in nine days, including two-time graduate Britton Keeshan, who climbed the Seven Summits while completing a double-major at Middlebury College. Also summiting that day was noted filmmaker David Breshears, who took an adventure course in 1973. He transmitted the first live footage from the summit of Mount Everest in 1983, and once hauled bulky IMAX camera gear up the mountain for his acclaimed film *Everest: The Death Zone*. In 1999, alumna Kit DesLauriers, of a 1991 semester in Alaska, was the first ever to successfully climb and ski the Seven Summits. That same year, two-time grad (and future board chair) Tori Murden-McClure was the first female American to row solo across the Atlantic; she was also the first female to ski to the South Pole. Others explored Antarctica, climbed Fitzroy in Patagonia, and traversed uncharted jungle territory along the Mesilau Pinnacles in Borneo during an expedition to summit Mount Kinabalu (at 13,455 feet, the highest point in southeast Asia).

In various realms, the NOLS community—both instructors and the alumni, which by then numbered 50,000—was likewise gaining prominence. People affiliated in various ways with NOLS were to be found among writers and broadcast journalists, public affairs advocates, high-level business circles, and policy-makers. Instructor Terri Watson went on to executive directorship of Light-Hawk, a nonprofit founded to help environmentalists view human impact from the air, and Louisa Willcox, an instructor for 10 years, became director of the Wild Bears Project at the Natural Resources Defense Council. Alex Matthiessen, a 1984 Wind River Wilderness graduate, was executive director for Hudson Riverkeeper. Ellen Stein, a 1996 grad, was executive director of the Mountain Studies Institute in Colorado. Journalist Wanda Njuguna-Githinji looked back at her 1994 Kenya course when she won the African Journalist of the Year competition in 1999 and said, "I realized it was the most difficult thing I had done in my entire 31 years."

James Kagambi (KG), who had taught for NOLS for 735 weeks by 2015. *Evan Watson*

Families, too, became infused by NOLS. Parents sent their children, and some children sent their parents. It wasn't difficult to indulge the urge to wander, with domestic locations in the Rocky Mountains, Idaho, Alaska, the Pacific Northwest, Utah, and the Southwest, and international branch locations in Mexico, Africa, Canada, Patagonia, India, and Australia, as of 2001. Opportunities to travel and still be held in the familiar context of NOLS led to seasonal migrations for many, such as Rachael Price, who made annual rotations from Alaska to Patagonia to Mexico for years, with stops in Wyoming along the way. KG Kagambi moved for many years between Africa,

Crossing the Hurunui River in New Zealand. *Rachael Curtis*

Patagonia (where in 2015 he was the longest-tenured instructor), and the United States each year. Their cases were hardly unique. A nomadic churn of instructors went from one branch to another, and WMI instructors likewise traveled from one sponsor location to the next. For everyone, the goal was, and is, to carry the core messages of NOLS to students regardless where the splints and bandages were laid out or where the cookstoves were lit.

Some instructors tired of the migration and settled in to work at a branch for a change of pace, or at headquarters for a job in administration. Headquarters staff, meanwhile, often moved to branches, and vice versa. Whether from headquarters or a branch, most staff who were also instructors found ways to rack up at least a couple of weeks of teaching every year.

Chris Agnew, whose student experience was on a semester course in Africa in 1998, had never been to Lander until he arrived for his instructor course in 2001. His perception of NOLS was formed by his experiences in the vicinity of Mount Kenya, where he'd remarked on the NOLS practice of hiking off trail—something few other outdoor programs do, and something his background in the thick, steep forests of the Cascades had largely precluded. "I think a lot of that comes from the organization starting in a place where traveling off-trail was so nice, such a positive environment for students to learn from. That's kind of what was baked into organizational values, which, if not necessarily stated, are sort of just implied in our culture," he said in 2015. "It was fun to be in Lander and later live in Lander and start to see core pieces of NOLS's DNA that I had noticed were parts of the experience in Kenya that I think grew out of the town where the organization started, in the landscape of the Winds."

For various reasons, the urge to find new classrooms, which had waxed and waned over the years, was rekindled in the early 2000s. The board felt it was a good time to consider again expanding the school's international course offerings. People were traveling internationally more, and interest in cross-cultural experiences was on the rise. Courses in new regions would create additional capacity for the school and provide more off-season employment for staff.

The question was, where to go? The process of scout-

The Waddington Range offers a mix of good rock and vast glaciers. *Tom Cunningham*

ing new course locations had evolved since the early days, when all a person needed to do was bounce an idea off Paul Petzoldt and get his ok. In 1983, Peter Simer sent a group to scout Canada's Northwest Territories on a 60-day expedition along the Thelon River. In the 1990s, Molly Doran was sent to scout various locations, including Scandinavia, central Africa, Suriname, and also the eastern United States.

Although some ideas (such as sailing in the East Indies, as proposed by George and Mary Jo Newbury) didn't work out for various reasons, others did. One was British Columbia's Waddington Range, a location that offered a new level of alpine adventure when the school began operating there around 1990. Even as late as the mid-2000s, NOLS courses were still putting up first ascents in that vast, remote wilderness.

A marketing study in 2004 polled alumni about places to consider for future branch locations, and Baffin Island and Brazil percolated up. Starting in 2006, both locations began hosting expeditions, but Baffin Island was a victim of the 2008 recession, and NOLS Amazon closed in 2014.

The school's long history in Kenya, which started in 1974, had its final chapter in June 2003, when the board voted unanimously to close the NOLS East Africa branch. Enrollment had been declining since the 9/11 attacks, and Kenya's porous border with Somalia and rising threats of local acts of terrorism were generating risk management concerns too great to ignore. In addition, changes in government were creating too much general unpredictability to warrant continuing to operate courses there. It was a thoughtful decision, not made without sadness and regret.

Another New Era Begins

In June 2002, Deborah Nunnink succeeded Michael Lindsey as the school's operations director. Like LT Chu 17 years earlier, Nunnink, an MBA, came directly from the business world. Nunnink had spent over a decade in marketing and operations at a Boston corporation that arranged educational international travel programs for 100,000 students every year.

Nunnink grounded herself in the NOLS experience by taking a Wind River Wilderness course within a week of arriving in Lander. But she could not have known how much her hiring represented a larger crux move for the school. Her arrival was, in some ways, the last major aftershock of the shift to a more business-focused administration that had been ongoing for several years. Gans had been implementing financial measures to ensure a more sustainable future for the school, cemented by the founding of NOLS Pro and the acquisition of WMI. Hiring a business professional to run the school's operations, including the branches, was a part of that strategy.

The changes, though, had also broadened the school well beyond the expedition roots of its early days. They were not always popular even at the board level, although Gans was encouraged and supported by Gene Tremblay, Michael Schmertzler, and Pete Colhoun. Many in the NOLS community, both on the board and within the staff and alumni communities, believed that the business focus in general was

Practicing rescue skills on the Wilderness Medicine and Rescue Semester. *Tim Doyle*

threatening the school's emotional heart, and even its ability to deliver on the mission.

Nunnink's closest competition for the job had been Molly Doran, a much-respected pillar at NOLS. After her IC in 1977, Doran had worked many years in the field and in various key capacities at multiple branches. Her administrative resume was solid, culminating in assistant operations director under Lindsey. For many at the school, Doran embodied the program focus and dedication to the student experience that some at the school feared were being subsumed. "Everyone loved Molly," remembered Judd Rogers, director of NOLS Southwest in 2002. "[When] she didn't get that job. . . . talk about [Deborah] walking into a landmine."

Lindsey and Doran had split responsibility for the branches, but Nunnink elected to work with the branches as a single group. One of her key roles became to create real teamwork among the branch directors—a complex task, given that they only saw each other at branch director meetings twice a year. Until the late 1990s, they had operated as more or less independent entities. Under Gans, there was less emphasis on branches competing and more emphasis on collaboration, both in terms of idea exchange and of sharing resources.

There was resistance against her efforts to foster collaboration, according to several sources. As their new manager,

Nunnink's interpersonal style was direct and hands-on, with great attention to detail, especially regarding budgets. She was a proven decision-maker who was not focused on making the most popular decision, which at times had haunted Doran. Gradually, the group began to build better systems, and the advantages of working collaboratively began to be more apparent. "For example," said Rogers, who left NOLS Southwest in 2002 to become Patagonia director until 2010, "We had bad apples going from one branch to the next. They were slipping through the cracks due to lack of communication. She systematically went in and tied up loose ends on things [like] that."

Another focus for Nunnink was regarding legal compliance, particularly internationally. When the school was small and struggling to survive, such things didn't seem to matter as much and were handled more casually. For example, there was not yet a visa program for international staff when Doran (a Canadian) became an instructor in 1978, so she worked her first course for free. Another longtime instructor from Canada was reportedly quietly married to an American instructor solely for the purpose of meeting work eligibility requirements, although the two never lived together and had separate life partners.

But after 35 years, NOLS had fully blossomed as a leader in the outdoor education world. Nunnink discovered certain international matters needed urgent attention. Faculty contracts, labor laws, visa rules in various nations, land-use permits, registering vehicles, and taxes—"We were doing a lot of 'under the radar' stuff," she said. It took a concerted effort to make sense of and then stay on top of the diverse rules and laws governing the various branch locations.

One particularly thorny challenge was at the Mexico branch, where three separate leases ranging from 30 to 50 years plus difficult land-ownership rules meant years of effort to safeguard the campus at Coyote Bay. The job was finally done in 2015 under a new legal entity called NOLS Mexico.

The school also wasn't properly trademarked in most international destinations. To be registered and acknowledged as a legal entity sometimes took years. In India, for instance, the government rejected the name "NOLS" because, they said, there was nothing "national" about it for them, so the legal NOLS India entity was registered as the "Nanda Devi Outdoor Leadership School."

Sadness and Joy

In the spring of 2005, the school was shocked to learn that Jim Ratz had died. By then a co-owner of Jackson Hole Mountain Guides with former NOLS colleagues Phil Powers and Rob and Katherine Hess, he had continued to live in Lander and pursue his passion for climbing. According to the sheriff's report, on May 5, he was rope-solo climbing on a familiar route along the first sandstone buttress at the mouth of Sinks Canyon, and planning to join two friends on a climbing route just around the corner. When he didn't show up, they went to check on him, and found him lying on his back at the bottom of the climb. Hundreds of people came to his funeral, and in the balm of time his positive contributions to the school were increasingly acknowledged and celebrated.

Later that year, the school celebrated two anniversaries at once when 400 members of the NOLS community gathered for three days in October: the 15th anniversary for WMI, and the 40th anniversary for NOLS. At the event, two former board members received recognition: Joan Chitiea was announced as "trustee emeritus," and Gene Tremblay was named "chairman emeritus," joining Homer Luther, who had received the same accolade in 1994.

Wyoming governor Dave Freudenthal was in attendance for the event. In his evening address, he spoke of the importance of teaching people to value each other and the wilderness—something those in the crowd already knew a lot about, as did the thousands of alumni spread across the world.

Jim Ratz in Sinks Canyon. *NOLS Archives*

WMI students practice litter carries.
Justin Alexandre

RISING RECOGNITION

On any NOLS course, you take away things that can be used the rest of your life. It's the community on a NOLS course that keeps us coming back and continues to drive us to go outside even more, seeking that adventure, that challenge, and that sense of elation with accomplishment. It's why we do what we do.

–Jake Wallace, instructor

What *is* this magic called NOLS? Carolyn Highland (Semester in New Zealand, 2012), said:

Being in New Zealand had awoken me to exactly the way I wanted to live my life. Not in a literal sense—I was not planning on spending the rest of my days in the backcountry—but rather in the sense of the way I felt when I was out there, in the way I acted, in the way I was. In the way I inhabited my real self so fully and completely. In the way that I spent time with people who made me better. Who made me more me ... That is the gift that wilderness gives us. It reminds us of who we are and pushes us to be that. You were always there, it whispers, but it provides us with the clear reflecting glass to see it. This is who you are, it tells us. This is who we are.

For 50 years, NOLS alumni have finished their courses in places across the world, and then, for most, life morphed into raising families and building careers. Their NOLS experiences became fond, if distant, memories—until the day it all flooded back. For Tobey Ritz, it all bubbled up again in 1996 when he read in the newspaper that Scott Fischer had died on Mount Everest. Ritz's NOLS instructor in 1976 had been a woman named Jeannie—Scott's wife. "NOLS is like an invisible thread that kept going until it resurfaced in my life, an undercurrent pulling me back to something that

Instructor Louisa Hunker teaching on a winter course.
Marco Johnson

front-line leaders who introduce students to such insights are the instructors. And they are not immune to the magic either, returning as they so often do to teach with dedication and loyalty—or, as in the case of Tobey Ritz, finally realizing that dream to become an instructor at age 48. It never goes away: Years after hanging up his boots, longtime instructor Tim Rawson said in 2012, "I miss having that feeling in my life. It was one of those delicious feelings that's hard to capture in any other way." Even his earlier transition in 1984 from field instructing to in-town work was wrenching. "Being picked up as an instructor, [you had] this feeling of 'thank god it's over, thank god everyone's ok, but think of what we've accomplished,'" he recalled. "It took me a year to get over that. I wasn't ready to be weaned from that."

WMI instructor Jake Wallace expressed similar sentiments: "After being on course with these students for 30 days, you develop into somewhat of a family, with the same trials and tribulations, highs and lows, bickering fits, and fits of joy. But at the end of the course, you have this overwhelming sense of genuine pride and happiness for your students. . . . On the WMI side of things, if my teaching drives students to be passionate about what they do and they help others in need, I'm happy with having a part in that. . . . It's a full-on experience where they grow as leaders, grow as care providers, and even more so, grow as human beings in their desire to help."

became a part of me and had a huge influence on my life," he wrote in 2006, when he finally acted on an urge to pursue an old dream of becoming a NOLS instructor.

The lessons that students take home—many of them intangible—are the power of NOLS. Testimonials point time and again to deep impacts, everything from confidence when facing adversity to courage when confronting fears.

If such robust lessons stem from a NOLS experience, the

NOLS Rocky Mountain transportation manager Steve Matson had been dropping off and picking up courses for 30 years when he said in 2015, "I have no idea how many courses I've dealt with, but there's this common thread that has remained constant, of taking courses out, where there's this certain pensiveness, and then picking them up and seeing them thinking, 'Wow! Look at what we've accomplished!' It's mostly unspoken, but you can sense it among these students. There's that incredible feeling."

As the new decade progressed, the generation known as the Millennials—those born between 1982 and 2004—began joining instructors from previous generations who were still placing their stamp on the school. Noted for the generally positive traits of being open-minded about controversial social topics and having a strong altruistic streak, the newcomers were also the first "digital natives," having grown up with computers. As they began to exert their demographic influences on the NOLS community, they were mentored and influenced by a deep well of experienced people. The master of the Wilderness First Aid course, Sascha Paris, taught 133 courses on weekends while continuing his full-time job. Daniel DeKay, who initiated the California WEMT program, taught for WMI year-round starting in 1993, and Gates Richards started full-time with WMI in 1998. As of 2015, Leslie Appling was still a field expedition instructor

Fall Semester in the Rockies students on a summit.
Pascale Gulick

after 32 years, and James Kagambi (KG) had racked up more than 735 weeks in the field.

Second-generation instructors began to join the ranks. Emily Shoutis-Frank, daughter of Skip and Diane Shoutis, was the first, in 2002, followed in 2003 by Dan Short and Dave Schimelpfenig, and in 2004, Louisa Hunker, daughter

AJ Linnell snowboarding off the summit of Denali.
Evan Horn

of George and Paula Hunker. Many others followed. In 2012, Dave Schimelpfenig headed into the Winds as CL for a 23-and-over backpacking course; his PL was his father, Tod, making them the school's first father-son instructor team.

The average age of instructors had continued to rise, reaching age 35 in 2007, in part because of other late arriv-als like Ritz, such as Suza Bedient (who arrived at age 36), Sam Talucci (who became an instructor at age 40 after a career in the hospitality industry), and former Navy SEAL Bob Shoultz (who was over 50 when he became an instructor in 2005).

The new generation of NOLS instructors was as adventurous as their parents' generation—and, in some cases, the parents themselves. Paddling the length of the Madre de Dios River in Peru in 2007 was just one of various multiweek expeditions for Nate Shoutis and Dave Schimelpfenig. In 2006, Louisa Hunker joined Rainbow Weinstock, Nick Cross, and Scott Christy caving in Mexico's San Luis Potosí region, 32 years after her father, George, plumbed the depths of El Sótano de las Golondrinas.

Other new instructors may have arrived without NOLS in their blood, but certainly with a sense for adventure. Alexander Martin completed a 4,300-mile canoe traverse from Portland, Oregon, to Portland, Maine, in 2010, plus a 2,500-mile traverse of Europe the following year. Several other instructors made the paddle between Juneau, Alaska, and Vancouver, BC, through the Inside Passage, and at least one pair—Tod Sutherland and Clair Bond—did the same transit in the open ocean.

In 2006, Nate Ostis was part of the first descent of the Yalong River in southwestern China. Eight kayakers paddled over 160 miles on the Class V river, with only Google Earth and some Russian maps from World War II to guide them.

Instructors continued accomplishing astonishing feats in the mountains, too. Dave Anderson, Jimmy Chin, and Brady Robinson were part of an expedition in 2000 that made the first ascent of Tahir Tower in Pakistan's Kondus Valley via a hard 3,200-foot face. Chin went on to success as a mountaineer, filmmaker, and photographer. In 2015, Robinson directed the climbing advocacy group Access Fund. Anderson began exploring remote unclimbed peaks on the Genyen Massif in Sichuan, China, in 2006. He was joined on a few trips by Szu-Ting Yi, and on one by Andy Tyson and Molly Loomis. A few years later, in 2013, Loomis and Tyson were part of an American-Burmese expedition that made the first ascent of Myanmar's Gamlang Razi (19,259 feet), one of the highest peaks in Southeast Asia. And in 2014, Roberto Morales put up a new 2,300-foot big wall route on the Uli Biaho Gallery in Pakistan's Trango Tower group.

As with every NOLS generation, Denali remained a favorite for private instructor climbs. In 2008, Evan Horn, Jaime Musnicki, AJ Linnell, and Alex Everett added a twist by climbing with their skis and snowboards and making a rapid descent down the steep and challenging Messner Couloir.

Trevor Deighton, Dave Anderson, Laura Schmonsees, and Andy Rich were the first to visit a remote area that they

Instructor Cody Paulson teaching students to recognize different birds from below. *Riley Hopeman*

named Greyskull Valley in the mountains of southeastern Alaska in 2004, but poor conditions hindered their climbing. In 2015, instructors Max Fisher and Erik Bonnett returned there, and completed the first ascent of a peak they named Kooshdakhaa Spire. They then returned to Haines, Alaska, on what was the first complete packraft descent of the Chilkat River.

Not every expedition met with success, of course. In 2012, Josh Beckner, Willy Oppenheim, Ben Venter, and Jake Tipton tried a new route on Nafee's Cap, a 3,000-foot golden granite buttress on the west side of Pakistan's K7 (22,749 feet). That same year, Pedro Binfa, Patty Soto, and Tre-C Dumais attempted Nepal's Manaslu (26,781 feet), but they ended their climb after a massive avalanche higher on the mountain killed 12 climbers. In 2015, Jared Spaulding, Anderson, Yi, and Matt Hartman attempted a first ascent of a 3,000-foot granite wall on South Avellano Tower in Patagonia; later that year, Fisher and a climbing partner attempted but did not summit the unclimbed Tangra Tower (17,913 feet) in Pakistan. Sadly, Linnell and Tyson were killed in a light airplane crash in 2015 in Idaho while scouting for a solar energy project.

Over time, earning a place as a NOLS instructor became more competitive than ever. Instructor course applicants tended to have impressive levels of outdoor experience and excellent skills, often in multiple course types. They might be fluent in multiple languages, or offer attractively diverse personal attributes. Many had notable education or leadership backgrounds.

"When I first came to NOLS in the early 1980s," said Marco Johnson, staffing director in 2015, "[working here] was still very much a counterculture type thing. You did this as your way station en route to a real job. And now, outdoor education *is* a real job. The expectations of good pay and benefits are out there. People come to NOLS now with much more of a personal and a professional background than they did [back then]. When I became more senior and was part of the review process for the instructor course applications, we would always remark that, 'nowadays, I wonder if I would even get on it!' And that's good."

Instructor courses did not change significantly over the years, either in length or in the goal of teaching people how to teach and manage students in the backcountry. They remained very demanding. "Regardless of what anybody comes in with, everybody has to meet the same bar," said Johnson. "That's an important thing, because we know that everybody coming off an instructor course has met a certain threshold, and that helps when you work with somebody you've never met before. You know you have this common experience."

As Johnson reflected, "We have to trust that the faculty are going to do their job in an excellent manner. I would say that 99.9 percent of the time, that is exactly what they do."

"It's one of the empowering aspects of working as a NOLS instructor," reflected Tod Schimelpfenig. "The trust given to you to take these students into the wilderness with an independence rarely found in outdoor education, deliver the curriculum, the experience and take care of everyone. I have never had a more empowering job than CL-ing a [Wind River Wilderness course] at age 21."

WMI, too, set high standards for instructors beginning

Being a NOLS instructor means managing risk in dynamic environments. Here, Nick Storm on the oars in the Gates of Lodore. *Brad Christensen*

at inception in 1990. "One of the first positions we had at WMI—before we could even afford it—[was] a curriculum director . . . we set ourselves up culturally from the beginning to put a high emphasis on education and educational quality," said Melissa Gray.

Over time, many instructors found themselves teach-ing both on field expeditions and in the WMI classrooms, and discovered interesting things from that crossover experience. "The didactics and pedagogy of WMI's classroom-based teach-ing brings tremendous balance to the field-based approach," noted Nate Ostis, who came to NOLS in 2000 and began teach-ing for WMI four years later. "Field-based classes have looser expectations in regards to time management, whereas on a WMI course you have only 30 minutes to solidify three salient take-home points or learning objectives. This challenges us to be more intentional with word choice, questioning techniques, progressions, and execution of practical sessions. The trickle-down effect I've seen is getting field instructors to be more in tune with intentional lesson planning versus winging it or just jotting down notes to regurgitate."

One lesson that field instructors often gave on courses was described on the CL's class list as "stages of group development." A common approach, described in the *Leadership Educator Notebook* (LEN), was to break down the maturation of a group into stages: forming, storming, norming and performing, and transforming (the Tuckman model). Within most groups, there is an initial phase when members are meeting each other, feeling out likes and dislikes, an setting a group culture (forming). Tensions inevitably result, and the group works them out, sometimes constructively, sometimes less so (storming). As the LEN puts it: "This is analogous to a group's adolescence. It is generally characterized by some turmoil and struggle over power and decision making." With the kinks worked out, the group finds its groove (norming)—often much more able than before to accomplish goals together (performing) until something changes. A group member gets sick and leaves. A re-ration brings in

Instructor Jim Chisholm caring for a student in the Amazon. Curriculum crossover has been useful to many instructors. *Dalio Zippin Neto*

unexpected news from the outside world. The course ends. Each such occurrence upsets the groove and causes the group to reset, starting the whole cycle again (transforming). Successful teams reach higher levels of understanding and function with each cycle.

As NOLS grew, as people came and went, and as the school responded to outside events, the organization as a whole was susceptible to the same ups and downs of group dynamics. According to curriculum and research manager John Gookin, the advantage NOLS had over other organizations was that most of the people at the school could recognize the dynamic nature of community. "Every time NOLS has a significant growth spurt or redefines the school, we need to go through a transformation that inherently spurs conflict between old and new systems," he observed in 2015. "I think this parallel from field to office helps people understand that conflict can be both natural and helpful."

When applied to the larger metaphorical journey that the school itself had taken for a half century, that familiar NOLS-grown concept of expedition behavior (EB) aligned elegantly with the Tuckman model. Whether in the conference rooms and hallways of HQ, or in the field or classroom with students, calling upon the precepts of expedition behavior brought to the table a familiar touchstone that could help ease tense situations. EB served as an apt means for working on any project, including impending changes, through deliberate, respectful examination and serious contemplation of current issues and opportunities.

New Courses and Fresh Processes

Between 2006 and 2011, new operating areas opened on Baffin Island and in the Amazon, Scandinavia, the Adirondacks of New York, and Tanzania. Combination ("combo") courses were catching on by then, so the Baffin Island itinerary included both hiking and canoeing in what was a unique sub-arctic environment. Jaret Slipp, who served as both

CL and P-Sup in the barebones venture, met the students in Ottawa, where they issued gear at a local outfitting store and bagged rations at the Bulk Barn—a commercial bulk grocery version of Lander's Gourmet Gulch—before flying to Iqaluit. After 10 days of hiking a treeless peninsula, a float plane resupply came, also bringing folding Ally Pak canoes. After paddling about 10 more days, they reached the Arctic Ocean village of Kimmirut. The local Inuit were welcoming, said Slipp. "We later turned it into a five-day Inuit cultural section with activities such as seal hunting, eating raw seal meat, checking out icebergs and whales, getting mussels from a 1,000-year-old family harvesting spot, and cooking them ocean side by burning heather plants." Groups carried bear fences and guns, but the only polar bear they saw was already dead, killed by an Inuit elder.

The program ran three years, with full enrollment and wait lists. Unfortunately, said Slipp, the 2008 economic downturn meant scaling back pilot programs and other small operations to weather the storm. "It was an amazing program," he said, but while waiting for the economy to recover, "the program lost momentum and ultimately never got back in the catalog."

The Amazon program, which also launched in 2006, brought its own unique hazards, including leaf-cutter ants with a penchant for tents, packs, boots, and more, according

Instructor Sarah Manwaring-Jones coaches students on their line on Baffin Island. *Moe Witschard*

to program director Jon Kempsey. "It was not an infrequent occurrence to have to relocate the whole camp in the night if leaf-cutter ants began an attack." The program was scouted in 2003 by four instructors—Kempsey, Brazilians Fabio Oliveira and Atila Regio-Montero, and Jim Chisholm—who were just the second group ever to descend the Amazon tributary called Rio Roosevelt; their primary guide on the 28-day journey was *Nas Selvas do Brasil*, Teddy Roosevelt's original book (in Portuguese) about the challenging territory.

Initially a semester program, NOLS Amazon included lengthy canoeing components and also hiking in the savannah uplands of northwestern Brazil or Venezuela, plus a strong cultural component; later, the branch added standalone canoe courses and short courses with the Brazilian equivalent of the National Park Service.

The tropical environment was a departure for NOLS. Canoeing in the Amazon wrought unique challenges, remembered Rachael Price. Below a certain waterfall, electric eels populated the river, making it risky to spend too much time in the water, so rolling and swimming drills were done further upstream. The worst incident, said Kempsey, happened in November 2012, when two separate student groups of a semester course on its very last day were hiking out of the mountains to rendezvous at a hotel when each encountered a nest of Africanized honeybees. Everyone sustained multiple stings, and one student was stung approximately 200 times (to no lasting ill effect, fortunately). But of all the challenges, from snakes to dengue fever, Kempsey said, the "really big learning curve was trying to help [students] protect themselves from insects and skin infections," which in the tropical environment could be lasting and severe.

The school purchased 10 acres of land for the Amazon program base in 2011, but by 2015 low enrollment resulted in closing the branch except for some ongoing WMI programming. Kempsey was proud to note that at least 10 Brazilians had become instructors for NOLS, and that during the school's brief tenure they created solid land-use models for and with the Brazilians for their national parks. "NOLS was greatly respected in Brazil as a center of expertise," he said. "We brought a level of professionalism to operating in the outdoors that was lacking in Brazil, and we were role models."

In 2008, another new location opened in Scandinavia, hosting backpacking and sea kayaking courses in the rugged

Brazilian park manager Cristiane Figueiriedo teaches a land management class, translated by instructor Atila Regio-Montero. *Dalio Zippin Neto*

lands north of the Arctic Circle. Operated technically by the Pacific Northwest branch, NOLS Scandinavia was based initially in Norway, but relocated to Katterjokk, in the far north of Sweden, in 2013, where it continued to thrive in 2015. The wilderness came almost to the door of the branch, and courses sometimes hiked out that very door, and weeks later hiked straight back in—no driving required.

In June 2011, NOLS returned after some 40 years to one of its earliest branch areas: NOLS Northeast resumed

NOLS Amazon offered lush beauty. *Mario Friedländer*

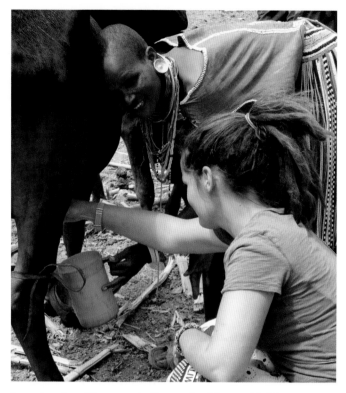

Learning to milk a cow in Tanzania. *Megan Binkley*

operations. There were multiple adventure courses for 14- and 15-year-old students, plus courses for older teens and adults, combining backpacking on the peaks and canoeing in the valleys of the 6.1-million-acre Adirondack Park. That same year, NOLS also resumed operations in Tanzania, south of the school's former location in Kenya. The East Africa branch offered 75-day semester courses that included a summit bid on Mount Kilimanjaro and backpacking off-trail among local tribes, plus two-week courses across diverse equatorial terrain for students age 23 and up.

In addition, new course designs filtered into the mix, including year-long programs in both Patagonia and the Sonoran Desert, and combo courses. More and more students wanted to do multiple activities, so backpacking/sea kayaking, rock climbing/whitewater, sailing/mountaineering, and other combination offerings began to fill that niche at most NOLS locations. New outdoor skills came along as well, notably snowboarding and split-boarding in winter, plus lightweight backpacking and packrafting in other seasons. Caving, which was suspended at NOLS Southwest in the fall of 2010 due to white nose syndrome in the bat population, resumed in August 2014.

The process for inaugurating new courses or new operating areas had changed since the early years, when all a visionary instructor needed was an idea and a "go try it!" from Petzoldt. The operations department spearheaded a highly deliberate approach toward the school's course mix. First, the idea—whatever its source—got a thorough vetting from the branch director where it would run. Then came a 31-question, three-page template examining the idea from every angle. Considerations included staffing and permitting constraints, financial impact, and the effect of a program that might compete with others. Any additions had to meet certain criteria, such as being consistent with mission and goals, meeting or exceeding student expectations, having a manageable level of risk, and being productive financially (or, for those courses vital to the mission or strategic goals, worthy of subsidy). Although the process added steps, it also helped the school function as a smooth machine, rather than a collection of colliding parts.

Course development at NOLS Pro leveraged that process. Each course was unique, blending the core NOLS curriculum to design a custom, client-driven experience. Courses ranged in length and emphasis; some were 7, 10,

Caving in the Southwest. *Rainbow Weinstock*

14, or even 30 days long. "We are usually riffing on a catalog course: shifting focus, maybe operating area, shifting length, emphasizing certain curriculum foci, etc." said Anne Magnan, who became NOLS Pro director at the end of 2015.

Rachael Price worked as a NOLS Pro account manager from 2007 until 2010, returning in 2014 after directing the

Patagonia branch for four years. The trick, she said, was to align the end result with what the client was promised the course would do.

"It was a wonderful opportunity because you have to learn about these other organizations, like the Naval Academy or NASA, and their needs and priorities. Then you map those onto the NOLS mission and expertise and say, 'Well, this is what we can do that aligns with your needs,'" she said. And, "I've also told people, 'You don't need a NOLS course. Have a barbeque. You don't really want to do this work.'"

In 2006, NOLS Pro and WMI created a partnership with the Harvard Affiliated Emergency Medicine Residency (HAEMR). The goal was to take medical students into a NOLS classroom at the start of their residency. After a six-day wilderness medicine course, they left on a 21-day expedition in the Gila Wilderness in New Mexico. The curriculum included peer leadership and teamwork, wilderness travel and living skills, medical education techniques, and how to influence environmental policies that impact human health.

A senior medical resident from HAEMR was a vital linking element as a member of the instructor team; once the WMI instructors addressed management of injuries and illnesses in the wilderness, the resident could continue the story and describe subsequent in-house clinical care. The resident could also facilitate transference of the NOLS leadership tenets for the soon-to-be medical residents: Cold, wet, tired, and hungry residents in the Gila Wilderness could look much like stressed, tired, and overwhelmed residents on the tail end of a 24-hour clinical shift. The coping skills they built would serve them well in the professional setting. In addition, they finished their course with an increased awareness of their role as educators in providing health care. Other medical schools, such as University of Wyoming, began to embrace similar concepts for their students.

Over time, WMI had established sponsorship relationships in far-flung places, including its work in 13 southeastern states with Landmark Learning in Cullowhee, North Carolina. In 2010, WMI established its largest partnership, with Recreation Equipment, Inc. (REI), bringing wilderness first-aid education (and the NOLS name) into REI locations nationwide. That initiative had consistently high growth every year, including 22 percent in 2015, when it ran 182 WFA courses through REI, educating over 4,600 students. By 2015, WMI courses had been taught in all but two of the 50 states and in 35 countries, and in English, Spanish, Portuguese, Swedish, and American Sign Language.

NOLS AUSTRALIA AND NEW ZEALAND

When instructors Alan Neilson, Pippa Gowen, and Chris Burke began scouting the Kimberley of Western Australia as a possible operating area in the early 1990s, they were drawn to the immensity and remoteness of the landscape. The meandering Drysdale River and the rich Aboriginal history were very far away from the daily life of most students.

The second group ever to descend the Drysdale River was the very first NOLS semester in Australia. "We flew into a cattle station (ranch), got into canoes, and then spent five weeks paddling from one end to the other, [with] no contact with anyone else," remembered Neilson, who was the program's first manager. "We didn't see a paved road for the entire 75 days of the semester."

The Kimberley is otherworldly. Aborigines have inhabited this part of Australia for at least 50,000 years, and as courses descend the river, students see handprints and other ancient art. Small freshwater crocodiles inhabit the upper part of the river, and big "salties" cruise in the estuarine waters near the ocean. Much of the land is blanketed by eight-foot cane grass, demanding that students gain strong compass skills before leaving the river for the hiking section.

Immersion in that landscape, said Neilson, was a good precursor to the final section of the semester: spending time in the Bardi community on Sunday Island. "The river and the hiking slowed the students down, made them more observant. By the time they got to the Aboriginal community, they were very receptive to learning."

Drysdale River in Australia. *Willy Hazelhurst*

For the first three years, the Australia program was based out of a rented house in Kunumurra, a small town on the border of Western Australia and Northern Territory. Students met and issued their gear at the Pacific Northwest branch in Washington, and flew to Australia as a group. In 2000, the branch moved to the coastal town of Derby for better access to sea kayaking, and the next year to its present location in Broome.

Aboriginal children try out the NOLS backpacking experience. *Brian Hensien*

The biggest change to operations in the region occurred when New Zealand joined the roster of NOLS options under David Summers, who took over from Neilson in 1997. "An instructor named Rob Maclean, a Kiwi, had been hounding NOLS to start a branch in New Zealand for years," remembered Summers. (In the late 1990s, Molly Doran had looked into the possibility as well.) In 2002, Summers and Maclean went to New Zealand and spent several months exploring the country.

"The main question we had was: Can we run a 30-day hiking course? If we can do that, we can do other stuff too," said Summers. The verdict: yes. In 2003, the first NOLS New Zealand course—a hiking course for people 25 and older—started from the garage of Maclean's rental house. "Students loved it, so the following year we started a semester."

Several others went to New Zealand to help scout areas for different course types. Summers and Maclean met up with

Jenny Riley and Travis Holmes and chartered a speedboat to look into sea kayaking, and Heather Hamilton joined that crew for a canoe scouting trip. Stephanie Van Den Hoek helped with sailing; Tony Jewell and others assessed the mountaineering options.

"There are so many different ecosystems in such short proximity, and it's so dynamic," said Summers of New Zealand. "Massive glacial peaks right next to the ocean. River crossings like Alaska. Beautiful rocky river valleys through beech forests up into the alpine bush."

The Australia program began under the auspices of George Newbury and the Pacific Northwest branch. When New Zealand opened, Rob Maclean became New Zealand manager under Summers, who was named Australasia manager, still under the PNW aegis. In 2004, Australasia came out from under the PNW, with Summers as director. Summers spent half the year in each location, with program directors in both. When Rob Maclean left in 2009, Allen O'Bannon took on the New Zealand role, followed by Mark Jordan in 2010. In Broome, Graham Neilson (Alan's brother) was Summers's assistant for more than a decade. Brooke Cunningham took over in 2007, followed by Suza Bedient in 2010 and Cass Colman in 2012. In 2013, under Mark Jordan, the Australasia operations HQ was moved more permanently to New Zealand, and Sharon Ferguson was hired as the Australia program manager.

In 2010, the school began to look for a more permanent home for the Australasia branch, and settled on a 40-acre plot in the Aniseed Valley outside Nelson, in the northeast corner of the South Island. The 2011 earthquake in Christchurch had made suitable property difficult to find, and the new branch was closer to the school's operating areas. As of 2015, NOLS

Bottlenose dolphins in Marlborough Sound on New Zealand's South Island. *Fredrik Norrsell*

New Zealand was offering semesters, sailing, and backpacking courses. NOLS Australia offered a spring semester, and sea kayaking, hiking, and combo courses.

Working through the crux
in the Rocky Mountains.
Ignacio Grez

NOLS in a Changing World

Despite word of mouth from generations of NOLS alumni and improved efforts at marketing, enrollment in the traditional, long expeditionary programs of the school had remained mostly flat since the late 1990s. Growth in student numbers—from 2,900 in 1998 to 23,700 just sixteen years later—was predominantly through WMI and NOLS Pro. Both departments incorporated the two elements—compelling instructors and the power of the wilderness classroom—that had put NOLS on the map in the first place. Yet discussion and soul searching surrounding the programmatic changes wrought by NOLS Pro and WMI remained ongoing—a test looking for answers to such questions as the role of remote wilderness in student learning, and whether the length of a course or expedition was a critical factor. Would—could—people have life-changing NOLS learning experiences in two days or a week? Passion and personal experience resulted in different answers to different people.

Said John Gans of the long-standing conundrum: "We are still talking about the integration of all elements of the organization, and find ourselves struggling with how to fully harness the natural synergies that brought us all together. This challenge is keeping NOLS from reaching its fullest potential. We are much larger, our product offerings are more diverse, and NOLS is an increasingly complex organization to present to our many audiences—students, parents, alumni, and the outdoor and educational communities."

Expedition 2013

In 2008, NOLS launched a strategic plan called Expedition 2013. Designed as "a commitment to the core experience that NOLS offers and the desire to keep making this experience better," said Gans, Expedition 2013 was formulated after a year of broadly canvassing the NOLS community in an attempt to figure out the best next steps for the school.

Fishing in the Northeast. *Rob Kinzel*

The plan, facilitated by John Kanengieter, who had transitioned out of NOLS Pro to become director of leadership, had five main themes: staff excellence, diversity, evidence-based curriculum development, environmental stewardship, and philanthropic support. Six areas for ongoing attention were also named: risk management, access to wilderness classrooms, technology, financial equilibrium and strength, student-focused concerns, and expanding brand awareness.

For some, it might have looked a lot like corporate-speak injected into a wilderness school, but as board member Pete Colhoun was often fond of saying, "What makes NOLS successful is that it operates like a school in the mountains and a business in the board room."

Diversity and Inclusion

Almost since the beginning, NOLS had women in its ranks, but for much of its history a male-centric flavor had predominated. Even at NOLS, which in the 1960s and '70s was very progressive for the times, there were mixed messages for women. Petzoldt himself often traveled in the backcountry with a tent companion, often a woman, who did all the cooking. In the 1980s, Linda Lindsey, five feet one inch and 118 pounds, worked with much heftier colleagues, and everyone carried 80 or 90 pounds. Not until the early 1990s would a guideline be developed for packs not to exceed 40 to 45 percent of a person's body weight. "We didn't get cut any slack," she said; the most successful women tended to be those who best fit the classic male style of leading and communicating.

When Leslie Appling grew up in the 1960s, it was with "the internalized sense of having limited opportunities because of my gender," she said. When she got to NOLS in 1983 at age 29, she said, "For the first time in my life, being a strong woman was not a problem . . . or something to hide. It wasn't an issue that could derail my career. It was an asset.

What a concept." Yet when Nancy Pallister became the first female course leader in the early 1970s, according to Anne Cannon, who was also an instructor, "there were hidden agendas. There were guys who had trouble with that. You just [had to] try to deal with things." When Cannon wanted to join the first NOLS McKinley (as it was known in 1971) climb, she first had to work to convince Rob Hellyer that women had a place on the mountain (she and Annski Williams finally got to go).

Trying to "deal" with being different is what happens to anyone outside the dominant culture, although it is worth noting that by 1997, 30 percent of instructors were female, and 37 percent by 2006. Instructor courses reached gender parity for the first time in 2015. But according to diversity and inclusion manager Rachael Price, dominant culture was still defined at NOLS, even in 2015, as the physically fit white male in his late 20s to mid-30s, from a middle or upper-middle class background.

After a stutter-start in the early 2000s, the real work on the concept of diversity at NOLS began in 2006 when board chair Fred Kleisner championed the project. The topic became a main theme in the Expedition 2013 strategic plan, and the board funded a dedicated "D&I" position. Lindsey hired Tania Tam-Park, who was succeeded by Aparna Rajagopal-Durbin in 2011, and Price in 2015.

Anne Cannon with dinner in Mexico sometime in the 1970s.
NOLS Archives

EXPEDITION DENALI

By Kim Freitas, staff writer

In 2013, an inspired team of nine African-American climbers ranging in age from 19 to 56 years made a bid for the summit of Denali (20,320 feet). None of them was a professional climber, but each was excited and motivated to inspire all Americans, especially minorities, to embrace the wonders of the outdoors.

Brought together and trained and sponsored by NOLS, theirs was the first expedition composed of all African Americans to attempt to climb the highest mountain in North America. Their common goal was to be role models for minority enjoyment of the outdoors. It's time, many believe, to rewrite the narrative of outdoor education to be more inclusive, and they knew their efforts could go far to inspire others.

The members of Expedition Denali climbed to within 600 feet of the summit before being turned back by a lightning storm. After a safe descent, they turned to the second half of their mission: grab every opportunity to speak—on tour or at home—especially with young people of color, at schools, churches, and community centers nationwide.

"The goal of the expedition was to engage a broad constituency in a public dialogue about diversity in the outdoors, specifically in the field of outdoor recreation and education, and to make a profound impact on the lives of today's underrepresented youth, who are tomorrow's adventurers," said Aparna Rajagopal-Durbin, who was the NOLS diversity and inclusion manager at the time. It is a crucial endeavor: By 2042, people of color will represent the majority of the population in the United States, and play a pivotal role in the protection of the nation's wilderness areas.

The Expedition Denali team at 17,000 feet on the mountain, with Mount Foraker in the background.
Hudson Henry

Additional expedition sponsors for Expedition Denali were REI, The North Face, the White House's Let's Move Outside! Campaign, the Foundation for Youth Investment, and the Sierra Club Foundation. The film *An American Ascent* and the book *The Adventure Gap* by James Edward Mills, chronicling Expedition Denali, were released after the climb.

Having someone working full-time to generate broader diversity and inclusion awareness at the school helped. "When you are coming from a background of poverty, or you are not white or you are female," said Price, "how do we have conversations about bringing in and leveraging the richness of those diverse backgrounds into our expeditions and communities?"

Opportunities to fulfill the school's mission relied on reaching out to as broad an audience as possible. "NOLS's purpose is to positively impact society and to serve wilderness by influencing all backcountry visitors with the NOLS curriculum," said Linda Lindsey, director of human resources. "The broader our constituency, the greater the impact." With about 80 percent of young people living in urban areas, that constituency needed more nudging than ever, if wilderness was going to stand any chance at all.

The initiative was not only an outgrowth of ethical concerns; paying attention to diversity was becoming good business at a time when the American social landscape and balance of demographics was evolving.

One way of reaching new audiences came with development of "Gateway Partner" relationships with various organizations and institutions nationwide. The initiative focused on building opportunities to provide NOLS experiences to young people from underserved and underrepresented com- munities. As of 2015 there were more than 50 such partnerships. NOLS Pro also used scholarship funds to assist specific clients with course tuition. One of the longest running such partnerships was with the Student Expedition Program (STEP), which brought 236 low-income students to 20 NOLS Alaska sea kayaking expeditions beginning in 2005. "Working with STEP students has been a highlight in my 22 years of working NOLS field courses. Being in a completely new environment, the students are pushed beyond their perceived limits and really shine in this transformational experience," said Lynn Petzold, also a NOLS Pro account manager.

The work of building diversity also included finding ways to bring people of color into the staff and instructor communities, with the goal of providing role models for a broader student base. Two avenues the school chose to effect this were through scholarships for the instructor-in-training program, and with a diversity fellowship program that began in 2011.

Twenty fellows had served in various roles by 2015, many as seasonal support staff; a few continued to be employed full-time. The next goal was to create a framework to help retain more of the fellows and help them become instructors. Price and John Hauf had created a similar initiative in Patagonia in the early 1990s, at a time when very few instructors were Chilean. "I remember John saying that

Instructor Nate Steele reviews the route with students on the STEP expedition. *Tracy Baynes/STEP*

in five or seven years he wanted 20 percent of our instructors to be Chilean. I thought, 'My god, how do we get there from here?'" she said.

But by 2015, "over half the instructors in NOLS Patagonia are from Latin America, not only from Chile but also from Brazil," she was proud to report. "We have a Chilean branch director and assistant director, and the vast majority of in-town staff is Chilean. We drove that with scholarship money, by getting Chileans on summer courses and on custom courses." At that time, the NOLS locations in India, Mexico, Canada, and East Africa were led by citizens of the host country as well.

For Price, more challenging than addressing diversity was the work to be done regarding inclusion, because it relied on finding ways to shift the habits and awareness of those in the dominant culture. As she said, "Part of what holding privilege and holding dominant culture means is that we just do the things the way we do because they work for us." That mindset has always required people who are not from the dominant norm in a society to assimilate, rather than having everyone doing the more conscious work of increasing the breadth of "who we are and what we do. . . . In the nitty gritty, I think that there are systems of oppression in our society and that when you are from a privileged group or a dominant class, you can inadvertently be perpetuating these systems of oppression without even knowing that you are doing it," she said.

The challenge was to guide people within the dominant culture to see the impact, and learn ways to be an ally for inclusiveness. "If you can't see it, it's not a choice," she said. For example, a female course leader—the only female on the course—as recently as 2015 reported feeling exhausted after dealing with and confronting sexism again and again. "Where was the ally-ship?" she wondered. Why didn't her male coworker, seeing what she was dealing with, step in?

Interrupting biases rather than perpetuating them involves facilitating conversations or decision-making without standing on a pile of assumptions. Regardless of the differences at hand—ethnic, racial, sexual, gender, language, national, whatever, "there are some really specific things to make ally-ship a role that people understand and fulfill," said Price. "By ally, I mean individuals who are part of a privileged group interrupting discrimination or oppression. But in order to do that, you have to be able to see that it is going on.

"I think the most important thing is to make that work actually positive work that invites people into a space where they learn more about themselves, not work that is the police function of inclusion where they are going to police and identify the naughty white male. I think it actually has to be a very open and warm and inviting space. Or people won't do the work."

Philanthropic Support

One of Petzoldt's biggest passions was ensuring access to NOLS, regardless of ability to pay. The earliest NOLS scholarships, the "Pay Back When Able" agreements, allowed many young people to come to NOLS and worry about the finances later. They often worked off their debt in the Lumberyard or by becoming instructors. Although the PBWA loans became a major contributing factor to the school's financial quagmire and near-bankruptcy in the mid-1970s, a large percentage of the PBWA loans were eventually paid—some later than others; in a June 1999 letter to NOLS, William Murdock said, ". . . Find attached a contribution for $400. Consider this payment

NOLS branch directors in 2015. Back row left to right: Mark Jordan (Australasia), Gary Cukjati (Rocky Mountain), Abby Warner (Teton Valley), Craig Lenske (Pacific Northwest). Front row: Raúl Castro (Patagonia), Lindsay Nohl (Southwest), Carolina González Cortés (Mexico), and Janeen Hutchins (Alaska). *Brad Christensen*

for my student course in 1970. I was one of those folks Paul said 'come on out—we'll get pay with work.'"

But while Petzoldt was always willing to extend credit to students, he and the school were resistant from the beginning to receiving the largess of others. Over the years, those fears necessarily receded as the benefits of fundraising—mostly

The Alaska "farm" in Palmer in the early years. *NOLS Archives*

for scholarships and facilities—were proven, first with the Annual Fund and also with several capital campaigns.

The first major fund-drive was not actually a formal capital campaign, but rather an effort championed by board member Joan Chitiea. She was determined that the Alaska branch should have a proper base, and almost single-handedly raised the $170,000 needed to purchase the Alaska branch property in Palmer in 1982.

The school's first named capital campaign was the Next Step Expedition (1992-1995). It raised $3 million for sorely needed real estate purchases and facility improvements, mostly at the school's branches. Two other capital campaigns were directed toward facilities development as well. The International Base Camp Initiative (2002-2006) brought in $10 million for building the international headquarters in Lander and refurbishing the Noble Hotel. Finally, the Wyss Wilderness Medicine Campus was funded with $4.5 million raised in 2011 and 2012.

The Annual Fund, which was always a separate enterprise from the intermittent capital campaigns, supported other things; for example, in 2015, 43 percent went to scholarships, 22 percent to outreach, 10 percent for curriculum, 10 percent for alumni services, and 7 percent for operations and administration.

The earliest reference to an annual fund was 1972, when the fund netted just $304 from a handful of donors. It was revitalized under Steff Kessler in 1988 after years of neglect, and any lingering cultural misgivings about asking alumni for support were quashed once it was realized that many of them *wanted* to give back to NOLS. Starting in 2005, the development office consistently exceeded the challenge it was handed of raising the goal 5 percent per year; in 2015, the Annual Fund appeal brought in a record $2,164,219.

Many people guided NOLS through the years with timely and valuable financial advice. In 1994, New York financier and NOLS parent Pete Colhoun joined Gene Tremblay and Wilford Welch and other board members on the support trek with the Sagamartha Environmental Expedition (SEE-94) in Nepal. A regular panelist on PBS's *Wall Street Week* from 1970 to 2002, Colhoun knew that his financial acumen could benefit NOLS. Before joining the board in 1999, he was already quietly talking to key people, and one of his most vocal messages was the need to grow an endowment. He believed it was time for the school to stop thinking in "break even" terms and build a sustainable future through better financial models.

Besides student courses, the Wyss Campus offers an excellent venue for staff gatherings. *Brad Christensen*

The push from Colhoun and others on the board led to the Campaign for Leadership, from 1996 to 2000. Some of the $7 million that was raised went directly to scholarships, but most of it was used to establish the endowment. Campaign NOLS (2011-2013) was launched when Expedition 2013 called for increasing the endowment; three-quarters of that $20 million fundraising effort (which ultimately totaled $21,187,500) was earmarked for the endowment, and the rest went directly for scholarships.

By its 50th year, the school's endowment had risen from zero to more than $30 million—a huge achievement that

The Wyss campus at night.
Miolsz Pierwola

WYSS WILDERNESS MEDICINE CAMPUS

The Wyss Wilderness Medicine Campus, just outside Lander in Red Canyon, was a remarkable addition to the NOLS list of locations. It created a dedicated home for WMI programming in a stunning setting of red rock hoodoos and sagebrush-covered hillsides, threaded by the Little Popo Agie River. Designed to support two courses simultaneously, the 20,000-square-foot main building contained classrooms, a commercial kitchen and dining hall, and common area. Separate cabins housed students and the caretaker.

A donation by longtime NOLS supporters and Lander locals, Charles and Mary Ann McMahon, made it possible to buy the 243-acre property, and $3 million in construction funds were donated by Hansjörg Wyss, a Swiss bioengineer whose twin passions were medicine and western land conservation. The school supplemented the gift with $1.8 million in fundraising.

Even before WMI had moved its headquarters from Colorado to Lander in 2002, some of its courses were being taught at Central Wyoming College's facility in Sinks Canyon. But by 2010, a number of factors made it necessary to look for a new home. WMI had dreamed of a facility of its own since inception; classes in the tiny town of Pitkin had been held at the local hotel, "which was, shall we say, rustic," remembered assistant director Shana Tarter. The Wyss Campus was a dream come true.

The campus opened in November 2012 with a simultaneous WEMT and instructor training course. The Wyss Campus's inaugural graduating WEMT class joined the more than 183,000 alumni WMI has counted since inception in 1990.

The Campus operated nearly year-round from the start, and each September it hosted the WMI community for its annual staff meeting. Built to be sustainable, the campus used a blend of energy-efficient strategies, including photovoltaic cells, geothermal wells, passive solar, rainwater collection, SIP panel construction, low-flow faucets and showers, composting toilets, and radiant floor heating and cooling. It was awarded a platinum certification (the highest level given) by the US Green Building Council's Leader in Energy and Environmental Design (LEED) program in December 2013.

The Wyss Campus was designed so that courses can easily head out of doors for skills scenarios. *Tim Doyle*

represented opportunities for sustaining the scholarship program and building a cushion against rocky market forces and other unanticipated financial demands.

Another more modest push to build enduring support for staff development also finally gained momentum. Discussed during the Campaign for Leadership in the late 1990s, the idea did not receive the attention it deserved for a long time, but it became a priority when 39 percent of those departing in 2009 said they were driven off primarily by inadequate compensation. The school established a million dollar endowment that was fully vested in 2012, and by 2015 its value had grown to $1.278 million. Staff development funding was also available through the Instructor Development Fund (IDF, established in the 1980s by Jim Ratz). Similar development funds, one for in-town staff and one for WMI, were established in 2015. The in-town staff fund had a $20,000 budget for such uses as attendance at seminars and conferences. The WMI Instructor Development Fund used its $7,000 budget that year for the professional development of wilderness medicine faculty.

Some staff support training was born out of tragedy. On August 12, 2007, Rocky Mountain branch director Peter Absolon, an instructor since 1990, was climbing in the Winds when he was hit by a rock hurled from a cliff above by an unsuspecting hiker. He was a respected colleague, good

Pete Absolon climbing in Sinks Canyon. *Dave Anderson*

friend, outstanding climber, and devoted father. In his memory, his wife, Molly, also a longtime instructor, founded the Pete Absolon Memorial Training Fund. It was designated for current instructors to "further their backcountry training by undertaking expeditions in 'Pete's spirit,'" according to *The Leader*.

Over the years, many memorial scholarships were funded—but the first has an interesting story. Enclosed in a letter dated July 7, 1969, from Rev. David Pyle and Mrs. Virginia Pyle were 165 shares of Travelers Corp stock valued at the time at about $5,000. It was a considerable sum, sent in memory of their son Wilton Pyle, a NOLS grad, who had recently been killed in the Vietnam War. The mists of time and administrative inattention during the school's hard-scrabble years obliterated the trail of the "Wilton Stroud Pyle Scholarship Fund." But the family's connection with NOLS endured: In 1987, after keeping in touch through the years, Paul Petzoldt married Virginia Stroud Pyle ("Ginny"), commencing what most describe as the happiest of his four marriages.

Funding from both the Annual Fund and the school's endowment served many scholarship students. Even when the school was still struggling financially, it had a scholarship budget of $30,000 (about 1 percent of school revenue) in 1985. By 2007, that figure had grown to $800,000 (5 percent of revenue), and in 2015, there were 38 endowed scholarships and 13 named annual scholarships, in addition to the unrestricted scholarship funds. Some had funded hundreds of students each over the years. Some were targeted at particular applicants—women, for example, or people living in particular geographic areas, or people bringing racial or socioeconomic diversity to the school. Several were named in honor of prominent NOLSies, such as Patrick Clark (the school's first computer guru), former executive director Peter Simer, and mountaineer Scott Fischer. Former board members Gretchen Long, Homer Luther, and Trina Peterson had named scholarships. In 1999, staff and students from the early years of NOLS created the Paul Petzoldt Legacy Scholarship and raised $65,000 in order to award a full scholarship to a deserving student each year.

For a school that started out with nothing but a dream and financial backing from people who believed in Petzoldt (primarily Judge Jack Nicholas and Dottie Petzoldt at the outset), it was a far cry from its unsteady days, and an impressive feat worthy of the respect and appreciation for the many people who made it happen.

Environmental Stewardship and Sustainability

Paul Petzoldt needed permission to access the Wind River classroom from the first day he led NOLS students into the wilderness. Back then, NOLS-style use of the backcountry, particularly hiking off-trail, was a new concept. Across the decades, that kind of use has allowed millions of student days in wilderness worldwide, each place with its own unique attributes both as a teaching tool and as a place to be treasured.

The realm of stewardship at NOLS has sometimes meant lobbying on behalf of the school's self-interest, but it has meant equally deep commitment to the fundamental ethos of the school to conserve and preserve the environment. "We found teaching people how to use our recreational

Taking a break to look down at Chitna Pass in the southern Talkeetna Range. *Zeno Wicks*

lands, while still conserving them, to be one of the most necessary parts of our program," said Paul Petzoldt in his 1965 year-end review and report to the board of trustees. "In the end, it might be the most beneficial part. We recommend a stronger emphasis on conservation, [and] cooperating with the agencies managing these lands."

Although securing permits was handled by each branch, NOLS formed a Department of Public Policy in 1991, and charged the director with developing an overarching, global view of access, federal policy issues, and anything to do with conservation. Much of the work entailed helping the school maintain reliable wilderness access via good interagency relationships.

When the department was formed, "it was a lot about protecting the integrity of our permits and protecting our access," said Aaron Bannon, in 2015 the director of what had become known in 2009 as the Department of Environmental Stewardship and Sustainability (ESS). "That evolved over time into more conservation campaigns to protect the integrity of our classroom." Some of the efforts over the school's history included being part of the clean-up efforts in Prince William Sound, Alaska, after the Exxon-Valdez oil spill in 1989, the founding of the Leave No Trace program in conjunction with the US Forest Service, and the fight to preserve the Wyoming Range from oil and gas development.

ESS in its various iterations has had a checkered career within the NOLS community. "Interestingly, there has always been some tension between those at NOLS who stress that we are not an advocacy organization, and those who feel that conservation advocacy is an important part of what we do," said Bannon. "John Gans on more than one occasion has pointed to some of the early films of Paul Petzoldt to reinforce his position that conservation work is part of what we do. He would say, 'We advocate for our interests.' And that means we defend our classrooms."

The four primary functions of the ESS department were spelled out in 2007. First was to track and monitor national legislative and policy issues that could potentially affect school operations, such as changes in parks or recreation/wilderness area management. Second was to provide local support to NOLS branches on permit and access issues, and third, to develop curriculum specific to public lands policy regarding timely issues and also provide materials for instructors about them. The fourth function was the Environmental Sustainability Initiative (see sidebar).

As a defender of NOLS classrooms, Bannon often found himself in the role of lobbyist. Asked if he had training for that, he said, "No. I'm an English major." He learned on the job in Washington, DC, with mentoring from other lobbyists from like-minded groups, such as Bart Koehler, co-founder of Earth First. Bannon said that his initial nerves over screwing up and somehow "throwing NOLS under the bus" yielded to the discovery that he could, in fact, do the work.

"It's all about connections and relationships," he said in 2015. "I've been successful in my work partly because of NOLS rapport. Everywhere I go, somebody has taken a course, or their kid has taken a course, and it opens up doors. I have this great entree with senators and even the Secretary of the Interior, Sally Jewell, who is a NOLS parent, as is [Secretary of State] John Kerry. It just happens all the time. They're out there and they're doing big things, making a difference, and they still have good connections with the school."

NOLS SUSTAINABILITY INITIATIVE

In 2007, NOLS got serious about walking the sustainability walk. A consulting firm was hired to do a school-wide assessment and establish a baseline for future improvements to build on. Not surprisingly, many good efforts were already being made, but they were uncoordinated. The goal of the initiative was to identify those piecemeal efforts and make the effort more widely deliberate.

Jen Lamb drove the effort, as director of the department of Environmental Stewardship and Sustainability. "The concept was to take the Leave No Trace ethic we use in the backcountry into the frontcountry," said Aaron Bannon.

The initial assessment evaluated every angle: energy use and emissions, water consumption, food and rations systems, solid waste and recycling, building design, toxic materials management, equipment purchasing, travel policies, mission, and values. With the results and recommendations in hand and funding from the Annual Fund, Karly Copeland came on board as the school's first sustainability coordinator in 2009. Her job was tracking the school's carbon footprint and reporting accurately carbon being used by the NOLS community. It was a big challenge.

Starting in 2009, Copeland posted regular updates in *The Leader*. Solar panels, low-flow water fixtures, energy-efficient lightbulbs, rainwater cisterns, and more put a considerable dent in the school's carbon footprint almost immediately. With 90 solar panels, the headquarters building in Lander had the largest array permitted by the state. In 2013, the Wyss Wilderness Medicine Campus earned platinum certification from the Green Building Council's LEED program—the fifth ever in Wyoming.

The branch with the longest-standing attention to matters of sustainability was NOLS Mexico. Off the grid, running entirely on solar energy systems, it also included composting toilets, wireless telecommunications (when hurricanes hit the peninsula, NOLS Mexico was possibly the only place that maintained communication, via satellite Internet), and more. It was a highly sustainable, self-sufficient (not to mention beautiful) place.

The school reached its first goal—reducing carbon emissions by 10 percent—a year early, in 2009. The next goal was loftier: reduce emissions by 30 percent by the year 2020.

The NOLS Southwest solar array. *Lindsay Nohl*

Research at NOLS

Almost from inception, the NOLS experience was ripe for research. The longest running project at the school is the incident database started by Tod Schimelpfenig in the late 1970s—now a gold mine of information. But smaller projects began as early as 1975. That year, seven instructors reportedly spent 20 days helping Lander District Ranger Doc Smith collect data to ascertain a carrying capacity for the wilderness surrounding the Popo Agie Primitive Area. In the summer of 1977, a two-year research project began with the goal of reviewing NOLS conservation techniques in Wyoming and Alaska. Unfortunately, as with many early research projects at the school, the results of both are lost to history.

In 1981, the board, reflecting on the school's mission to be the best source and teacher of leadership and wilderness skills, called for financing a "research and development department," but the idea took a backseat to more pressing needs. It was resurrected in 1983, when NOLS instructor and doctoral candidate Tim Easley submitted a research proposal to the Instructor Development Fund. His project received funding along with a matching award from the administrative budget. As he gathered his data in 1984, Easley met frequently with then-executive director Jim Ratz, which resulted in the chance for him to pitch development of research at NOLS.

In August 1986, those discussions led to the first Wilderness Research Colloquium, a three-day "meeting" in the Winds—actually a three-day backcountry trip—that included eight prominent wilderness researchers and NOLS instructors. The bilateral goals were for the instructors to learn about research methods from the researchers and to introduce the researchers to the NOLS experience. The colloquium was a success, with the result that a document outlining a strategy to implement research at NOLS was considered for implementation by the board. It took until 1990 before there was finally room in the school's budget to support the initiative, but a research committee was finally formed, and Abby Scott Caul was hired as NOLS's first research manager. Once again, a group retreated to the backcountry for five days that August to discuss goals, explore options, and begin their work as a team.

Chris Monz became the school's research manager in 1993. During his tenure, and with guidance from the school's research advisory group, NOLS looked into many elements of recreation ecology. From vegetation impacts, to human waste disposal, to Wind River water quality, to the social dimensions of wildland use, the goal was to become a source of legitimate knowledge for the land management agencies, academia, and the world. One area of research under Monz was to find out how many passes by humans it would take to hurt different kinds of vegetation. "What came out of that was teaching students to avoid as much as possible the grouse whortleberry, which is a low-growing woody plant that is easily damaged, versus camping on grasses, which recover more easily," said Shannon Rochelle, the school's research manager in 2015. "It is something where we got results and it changed practices."

Another innovation that changed practices and gained a quick and welcome toehold was electric mesh bear fences. Developed by John Gookin, the fences were tested beginning in 2002 in cooperation with the US Forest Service, Wyoming Game and Fish Department, the National Park Service, and Grizzly & Wolf Discovery Center. Game cameras monitored wild grizzly bears trying to get at animal carcasses inside of various fence designs, showing what worked, what didn't, and failure mechanisms. With more than 1,000 user nights in the Absarokas and Winds by the spring of 2003, the fences met the testing requirements and were approved by the Interagency Grizzly Bear Committee. The hard-to-pack, heavy bear cans became mostly a thing of the past in many places (although bear cans were still mandated in some branch locations in 2015). In 2013, NOLS published data showing over 50,000 fence nights in bear habitat, with no fence failures using the design NOLS developed.

In 2003, NOLS research shifted from a recreational ecology focus to education, measuring what students were really learning, what program factors correlated with greater learning, and what transferred beyond NOLS. Findings from those studies informed revision of the NOLS educator notebooks, "so NOLS was truly using evidence to develop teaching practices," said Gookin.

In the 2010s, the school began looking at some of the less tangible outcomes of a NOLS education. According to Gookin, the data showed that "NOLS students develop a lot of aptitudes and 'non-cognitive factors' like creativity, motivation, grit, and self-regulation." Those outcomes helped students excel in their studies when they returned to their traditional classrooms. "NOLS is not replacing traditional education, but rather complementing it," he said.

At the same time, research continued into the natural sciences. "The sort of research Chris Monz used to do [was] looking at how our practices affect the natural world, and providing information that land managers could use," said Rochelle. "We're aiming to do some more of that, working with natural scientists more in the citizen science realm where we get courses collecting data that can then be used by biologists, or geologists, or hydrologists to look at something that can actually help with land management questions."

For example, in 2015, NOLS students in Patagonia began collecting snow samples and melting them down,

The NOLS bear fence has been exceptionally effective in keeping bears and human food apart and works much better with large NOLS rations than do bear cans. *Ashley Wise*

filtering them out in the field and then sending the filters to a scientist at the National Center for Atmospheric Research in Boulder, Colorado, who was studying black carbon deposits on glaciers. "He then can see how much black carbon has been deposited," said Rochelle, "and he even has methods he thinks will allow him to identify the source of the black carbon, so land managers can then know if they need to work with a particular industry to reduce black carbon emissions. A similar study with the same researcher was slated in the Winds the following year.

Another task managed in the research department was gleaning data generated by the school's Course Quality Survey (CQS). Started in the 1990s as the Student Satisfaction Survey, the information to be scrutinized shifted over time. In 2015, it included three parts: program quality factors related to positive student outcomes (such as connecting with instructors, quality of feedback from fellow students—indicators of a high-quality course); the elements of NOLS's service (such as getting pre-course information, feeling safe while driving to and from the backcountry, and food quality); and customized questions arranged by each branch or school location.

The NOLS research department also worked with the many people—often graduate or medical students and professors—who applied to do research at NOLS. "I work with those folks to figure out whether what they want to do would actually work with NOLS, and whether the research information would be useful enough to NOLS to be worth the challenges it adds to a course to have them collect data," said Rochelle. In addition, wildlife research was ongoing, with citizen scientists collecting data on such things as bear sightings, sea turtle nesting sites in Mexico, and, in Wyoming, pika sightings over concerns of climate change and resultant habitat loss. In many cases, such research was aided by recording location coordinates using the modern method of GPS.

"Measurement of the changing environment and these many outcomes of NOLS help pave the way for a future where use of public lands, the risks associated with wilderness travel, and the expense of remote learning may all need to be justified," said Gookin. "Research findings help NOLS answer some of these tough questions with the authority of peer-reviewed evidence."

Risk Management Revisited

Systematic incident data collection from the field generated statistics about injuries, illnesses, evacuations, and near misses that were unparalleled in volume and quality. Risk management, though, was never intended to mean risk free. While the majority of incidents were not serious, the ability to carefully review the information proved to be an important element of the school's abundant credibility in the outdoor education profession. It was a way for NOLS to learn from its experiences, hearkening back to Petzoldt's lessons about developing judgment.

Sadly, the school marked its twelfth fatality on September 22, 2011, when Thomas Plotkin, 20, died while on a semester in India. Plotkin's death was the first at the school

Prayer bells are a common sight in the Indian valleys where NOLS semesters travel.
Annemarie Vocca

John Gookin, NOLS curriculum manager from 1989 through 2015, demonstrating the dangers of ground currents from lightning strikes at the NOLS Faculty Summit.
Brad Christensen

in 12 years, since the death of Thomas Nazzaro in 1999.

Like every incident in the school's history, Plotkin's death caused NOLS to take a hard look at its management of critical situations. "These are not static systems," said Leemon. "They're dynamic. We're always evaluating what works and asking, 'how do we make it better?'—whether that's [regarding] a decision someone made, a system itself, or an element of our training. We're always learning."

One subtle but important development in risk management that had evolved in the wake of Katy Brain's and Thomas Nazarro's deaths in the late 1990s was better methods for determining when students were ready for independent student group travel. "Back in the day," said Tod Schimelpfenig, "in the 1980s or so, instructors could send students out for independent travel just because it was Day Six, rather than by examining whether the students were competent to go." Such guesswork had been replaced by scrutiny of the curriculum and development of clearly articulated measures and sequences to assess student readiness for the various tasks of wilderness living.

In addition, new communication technology was a benefit, especially for independent travel by students. Changes in evacuation systems had evolved with technology, going back to the adoption of ground-to-air radios in the wake of David Black's death in 1989. By about 2003, hand-held satellite phones were available, and NOLS courses began carrying them. "That was a game-changer," said Leemon, "because now we had direct two-way communication with instructors in the field."

In 2010, the school started outfitting independent student travel groups with personal locator beacons (PLBs)

—simple devices that, when activated, used a network of satellites and rescue coordination centers to alert NOLS of an emergency and provide the location. When a group of seven students on their student expedition was attacked by a grizzly bear in the western Talkeetna mountains of Alaska in July 2011, four were injured, and they activated their PLB. "It made a big difference in the promptness of response," said Leemon. "Help arrived in hours instead of possibly days, as was more the case before having these devices."

In the case of the bear attack, "the students responded admirably, because their instructors had taught them what to do before they went out on their own," said Leemon. "They were focused on treating the injuries, they quickly activated the PLB, they set up shelter and took refuge from the rain, and worked effectively to keep each other warm."

Between the 2011 Plotkin fatality and the school's 50th anniversary in 2015, some 16,728 expedition students completed 667,163 program days with no more than typical medical problems and injuries, though there were a handful of notable exceptions. That November, two students got stuck in quicksand (one for more than nine hours) in Utah's Dirty Devil River area. A student having a seizure capsized her kayak in Norway the following July, but was rescued by an instructor within seconds. That same month, an instructor hiking in Australia with one other instructor while students

traveled independently was attacked from behind by a feral bull and sustained significant, but not incapacitating, long-term physical injuries. Another instructor, this time in Wyoming's Bighorn Mountains, was pinned under bathtub-sized rockfall, shattering her femur in eight places in July 2015. She activated her PLB and was evacuated by helicopter in 12 hours. "From the point of view of student service, and given the expectations of today's society of 'being connected,'" said Schimelpfenig, "having these devices is prudent and necessary."

Sea kayaking in Scandinavia.
Fredrik Norrsell

Public Recognition . . . or Not?

ASK STUDENTS coming off their NOLS courses to rate the experience on a scale from 1 (being worst) to 10 (being best), and the school consistently averages over 9. Ask a sampling of random people in the wider world whether they know about NOLS, and they more often than not say, "Who?" Many such anecdotal experiences across the decades of the school were supported by a 2005 nationwide survey commissioned by the school called the Bzz Report. It found that only 24 percent of respondents were "slightly, somewhat, or familiar with NOLS."

Pete Colhoun called it the 2-9 model: name recognition of the school was consistently at the level of a 2, yet its product—an outstanding specialized education that changes lives—was a 9. "You're hiding your product under a bushel," he said, pointing to an organizational modesty that, while admirable in some ways, had never served to promote the NOLS name. Struggling to overcome the school's histori-

cal cultural aversion to marketing was an ongoing battle, despite the in-house efforts of the marketing department and the advice of former instructor, board member, and career marketing consultant Ben Toland.

Altering the school's 2-9 record to a 9-9, as Colhoun advocated, remained a challenge as the school reached the half-century mark. It demanded the work of people in departments at the school that, while less immediately student-centric, were nonetheless important partners in developing public recognition, including marketing, publications, and "creative" (as it was dubbed in 2013). Each promoted the school in various ways. The NOLS Bus was a quirky but innovative traveling roadshow for NOLS. Publications rolled out a cornucopia of NOLS-branded books—more than 15 titles by 2015.

And the world of audio-visual media was exploding. An in-house video production team generated the popular

"Mythcrushers" series in 2008 to address many outdoor topics, including safety on the water, blisters, snakebites, and lightning. They also posted newly created footage to market NOLS, and many AV classics (including *Thirty Days to Survival*), on YouTube. In 2015, they organized the NOLS Exploration Film Tour. When social media came along, the school hired a "social network engineer" to manage its presence on Facebook, Twitter, YouTube, and other social media platforms. And in a nod to the most traditional NOLS method of marketing, the marketing department also hired a "NOLS word of mouth coordinator" to organize an array of uncoordinated initiatives into a cohesive program, as well as manage relationships with the school's 250 "preferred retailers," which were outdoor equipment stores that supported the NOLS mission, including international chains in the Netherlands and Germany.

Vision 2020: A New Strategic Plan

As 2014 approached, and the Expedition 2013 strategic plan wrapped up its mandate, NOLS was operating in 15 locations: the Rocky Mountains, Mexico, Alaska, East Africa, the Northeast, Teton Valley, the Southwest, the Pacific Northwest, Patagonia, Yukon, India, the Amazon, Australia, New Zealand, and Scandinavia. The school was large, far-flung,

and still growing. It made sense to lose no time launching the next strategic plan.

John Kanengieter was invited once again to help the school chart its new course, and guide the process of identifying its next priorities and challenges. Social demographics in America were changing rapidly. Wilderness was increasingly devalued. Urbanization and obesity were mushrooming. Thus Vision 2020 was born. Five strategic initiatives for the plan emerged:

- extend NOLS's influence with improved marketing
- exceptional student experiences
- alumni engagement
- planning for the dynamic outdoor classroom
- services and systems optimization

For each of the five areas of strategic concern, context was articulated, the strategic initiative defined, and a precise implementation plan created with measurable goals and benchmarks to strive for. Each area had a leadership team to navigate the details and keep the process on track as it grew and morphed until 2020. "Because, you know, we don't know what 2018 is going to look like for the school, for the global economy, and for what's happening in [the various NOLS locations] at that time," mused Chris Agnew in 2015,

THE NOLS BUS

In August 2004, a new venture for marketing the school rolled out of Lander. The "NOLS Bus," as it was known, was a way to promote NOLS's leadership and alternative energies nationwide. Since the 1990s, Bruce Palmer had been striving to build an outreach and recruiting program, and then in 2003, he got a phone call from the parent of a NOLS grad. His son and 10 friends were traveling cross country in an old bus they'd converted to run on vegetable oil, he said, and Palmer told him he'd be happy to feed the group when they came through Lander—and the idea for the NOLS Bus was hatched.

Actually, Palmer's idea was not original. In his May 17, 1975, report to the board, Petzoldt addressed public relations and marketing when he wrote of an eight-point plan that included the idea to "send out a traveling vehicle to visit schools, clubs, etc., to give slide shows and lectures . . . staffed by NOLS instructor types."

They found a suitable diesel bus in North Carolina, and Steve Matson was dispatched to inspect and drive it back to Lander for conversion into a solar and vegetable oil-powered "biobus." "By the time that vehicle rolled out of here," said Matson, "it was a sophisticated piece of equipment in many aspects. In looking back, it was an incredible learning opportunity."

Palmer, who was charged with making the project self-sufficient, recruited Peter Roy, who was on the NOLS Board at the time and was a founder of Whole Foods, along with Steve Demos, founder of Silk soy milk, to help sponsor the project.

For more than three years, the vagabond bus with a climbing wall on the side and other fun elements took the NOLS message to schools and colleges nationwide. In August 2008, after 48 states and two countries, the NOLS Bus retired with 151,601 miles in 1,503 days on the road. On the way, it had consumed countless gallons of recycled vegetable oil. "It was a fun chapter, and it got a lot of media coverage," said Gans. "It was the right project at the right time."

The Bus was a unique marketing tool for NOLS.
Brad Christensen

then the Pacific Northwest director. "This allows us to be way more adaptive, and I think it also lands NOLS in a better place overall at the end, because we can be more flexible."

The "CL" for the exceptional student experiences pillar was Scott Robertson, director of faculty and studies for the school. Robertson took his IC in 1996 during a sabbatical from his career as a litigator in Maine. As has happened with many, the course changed his life's direction. Robertson worked full-time in the field until 2000, when he began doing field staff coordinating and then operations at the Southwest branch before becoming its director in 2002. As director of faculty and studies beginning in 2006, he oversaw WMI, NOLS Pro, risk management, staffing, human resources, and the newly created department of education.

Robertson's part in the Vision 2020 process, he said, was "articulating [the school's] educational goals and objectives, sharing those with students so they could understand the goals on a course, and then aligning things such as staff recruitment, hiring, training, and evaluation to those desired outcomes." Two tangible outcomes of the committee's work were hiring Liz Tuohy as director of education in 2015 and publication of the NOLS Learning Goals and Objectives the following year.

Cynics might say fussing so endlessly seems like tinker-ing; most would likely applaud the school's insistence on never resting on its laurels. There is a lot of grand language in Vision 2020, such as, "We will equip graduates to have a life-long positive impact on this world," and "We can no longer assume that we know best what our students want and instead must become more quantitatively, research-, and metrics-driven," and "To stay relevant in a changing world, NOLS must remain true to our mission but must be culturally open to trying—and failing at—new things."

As when striving for any high pass, achievement would come one step at a time. "We have a strategic plan, Vision 2020, which takes a look where we want to be between now and 2020," said Deborah Nunnink in 2015. "That for us is our roadmap. We have to continually do map checks, and make sure we are where we want to be, and be flexible enough to rethink if things aren't working the way we thought. . . . It's going to be difficult and challenging, but the school will be in a better place when we get to 2020."

Time would prove the school's ability to maintain its top-notch standards, but Vision 2020 felt to those using it like an apt guidebook. After all, the school was on its own expedition through time, and having a plan was always helpful. Backed up as it was by a half century of hard work, intentional discussion, expedition behavior, tolerance for adversity, leadership, and, above all, judgment, it appeared to have every chance of doing just fine.

Full Circle

September 2015 was not an especially busy month for the school, but it was a case study in how the school had evolved from that June morning in 1965 when the first NOLS students arrived. Between September 1 and 30, seven semesters left the Rocky Mountain branch, including a Wilderness Medicine and Rescue Semester, and one specifically for outdoor educators. Three semesters started in Mexico, one in east Africa, two in the Southwest, two in the Pacific Northwest, one in India, and four in New Zealand, which also hosted an instructor course. NOLS Northeast sent out two two-week backpacking courses for adults, and there was one lightweight backpacking course in the Southwest. WMI started a total of 65 courses, including WFAs, WAFAs, WFRs, WEMTs, and refreshers, at sponsor locations around the world. NOLS Pro organized three courses for the Winterline Global Skills Program, eight for 11th graders from The Archer School for Girls, one for executives from the Northstar Café, a leadership navigation challenge for NASA flight directors, plus a Leave No Trace Master Educator course in Colorado.

Practicing lowering a patient in technical terrain.
Tim Doyle

The alumni office organized two hiking trips in the Dolomites of Italy, one in Tuscany, and a sea kayaking expedition in Croatia. Risk Management Services, which came out from under NOLS Pro in 2015, led a training program in Denver. The staff training office ran a facilitation and debriefing seminar, and an expedition for aspiring

The rare Scandinavian beach cow. *Lena Conlan*

mountaineering instructors in the Pacific Northwest. In all, NOLS counted over 1,800 students that month.

Interestingly, not one was a 30-day wilderness course, although those courses remained the mainstay of the school's expedition offerings; each year roughly 30 Wind River Wilderness courses still left the Rocky Mountain branch. Others explored the North Cascades, the New Zealand Alps, Alaska's Talkeetnas and Wrangells, not to mention other expeditions that sea kayaked in Scandinavia or Patagonia, or rafted and canoed on the rivers of the world.

Instructor and Artist Craig Muderlak's interpretation of the Cirque of the Towers in the Wind River Range.
Craig Muderlak

On September 10, 2015, instructors Gaurav Gangola, Catie Quinn, and Rebecca Yaguda walked among the students of FSR-8 at NOLS Rocky Mountain. This was the first day of their semester, and they were checking student hiking gear. As instructors had for 50 years, Gangola, Yaguda, and Quinn examined each item, rejecting cotton T-shirts, giving advice on socks and boots, and addressing concerns. They shepherded their students to the Gourmet Gulch to bag rations, and to the issue room for backpacks, wind pants, and whatever else the students still needed. The gear looked different than it had that June day in 1965, but putting on a pack still began with hoisting it up on one knee, and it still felt dauntingly heavy to those who had never carried their life on their back before. Later, the students climbed aboard the bus that waited outside, and it took them out to Fiddlers' Lake, on the east side of the Winds, to learn about the wilderness and themselves.

For 50 years, NOLS students have formed community in the wilderness.
Tracy Baynes/STEP

ONWARD

An Epilogue

This . . . is life. This is tasting the pain, the sweat, the raw intense beauty of life. Living as a wild human, in the dirt and the stars. I love it. I hate it. It's wonderful. It's hard. But it's beyond amazing . . . I feel like every moment of my life led up to the beautifully harsh experience of NOLS, and now that it's over, I think about it every day. Every memory reveals some new and significant lessons to carry into today, in the "real world," the "frontcountry," where the lessons of the wild are needed the most. The world would be a very different place if every person on Earth spent three months sleeping on the sand and carrying their food on their back.

—Hazel Underwood, Fall Semester in Baja, 2014

To leave, and then return, is to remember yourself as you once were. Stepping outside from the Lander Community Center's bustle on reunion weekend, October 2015, one could look to the mountains etched against the vivid blue of the sky, breathe in the sharp, clear western air, and remember the feeling of being up there, out there, away from the crowds. A summer-green high meadow bursting with wild onions and spring beauties. A scree slope stretching endlessly. A pass or a peak, hard-earned. One could be transported to the lapping shorelines of Baja or Alaska, or to the steady background roar of whitewater rapids near camp, or to the dun-colored tsavo of Africa. Overhead, one could sense the cosmos still holding NOLS course after NOLS course in the studded dome of starlight, just as it had for half a century. It didn't matter if you graduated from NOLS in 1965 or last week, or if your portal was a traditional course, WMI, or NOLS Pro: Everyone who is part of NOLS shared that weekend, a worthy celebration.

About 700 people from 44 states plus the District of Columbia and eight countries, some of them legendary in the

In honor of the school's 50th anniversary in 2015, a proposal for a life-size (well, larger-than-life, as was the man) bronze statue of Paul Petzoldt to be placed in the courtyard of the NOLS headquarters was made. The $85,000 to pay for the artwork, the statue, and its installation was raised by 151 members of the NOLS community. The committee members were Andy Carson, Nancy Wise Carson, Peter Simer, Cyndy Hicks Simer, Neil Short, Kevin McGowan, Skip Shoutis, and Diane Newbury Shoutis. *Kirk Rasmussen*

lore of the school, came back to Lander for the 50th reunion. There were instructors and board members, some who made their mark decades earlier. Nametags jogged memories, some rendered familiar from reading *The Leader*. Members of the in-town staff, many from the 1960s and '70s who had their start at the old Lumberyard, welcomed those who traveled in, including many from the school's outlying branches. Folks from the hippie era mingled readily with Gen-Xers and Mil-

lennials. Everyone was family: NOLS family.

One who came was a middle-aged man from Omaha who had driven in with his dad. He was shy, and it was difficult to draw out his story. A student from a 1992 Rocky Mountain semester course, he'd never returned to Lander and just wanted to be part of the scene that weekend. NOLS, he said, is still a big thing in his life. Always will be. Perhaps he, best of all, exuded the quiet power of the NOLS experience that has emanated from this modest Western town since 1965.

Another face in the crowd that weekend was Neil Short. An instructor and in-town staffer in the 1970s, he resigned from a board position in 1979 during the second time Paul was let go. Short spoke at the dedication of the life-size bronze sculpture of Petzoldt on the front lawn at NOLS headquarters. A practicing lawyer in Casper, Short put words to what countless others—perhaps including the man from Omaha—were thinking. He said, "I have a couple of degrees, but NOLS is my alma mater. You're all the finest people I've ever met. I think the world of you."

Old friends reunited with joy and whoops of laughter. Stories swirled as memories were recounted of the hungry days of "survival," or dealing with adverse weather (the "fourth instructor"), or improvising a workable splint, or being leader of the day across miles of difficult terrain. Some old wounds were healed, some hard feelings finally let go. It was a time of celebration, a time to look back over the years spent creating the school, blowing gently on the embers of its beginnings, watching the flame almost doused, then rescued to flare more and more brightly as time proved Paul Petzoldt's dream. There were times when much was in doubt, and the cast of characters shouldering the load is a lengthy list.

At the outset of a lunchtime gathering of former members of the NOLS Board of Trustees, executive director John Gans asked everyone to reflect on two questions: first, what was one crucial inflection point in the history of the school; second, what hopes did they have for the future of the school. After the sandwiches and chips were gone, the answers came.

The earliest event that affected the trajectory of the school was, of course, the airing of *Thirty Days to Survival* on the January 1970 *Alcoa Hour*. Enrollment tripled that next summer, to the joy and consternation of those, led by Petzoldt and Hellyer, who miraculously pulled off the daunting logistics. The *Alcoa Hour* helped launch the school.

The next vital moments came in the next several years, when the sheer scope of the project resulted in a wobbly financial situation that culminated in the 1975 transitions of executive director. First was Petzoldt to Jon Hamren. "Credit goes to Jon for being enough of a force to get us through that summer," recalled Bill Scott. By December, Peter Simer was in place. Although somewhat unlikely when appointed (leading Bob Hoffman to say, "The corporal never looks like a sergeant until you give him the stripes"), Simer's ferociousness at the helm is now widely regarded as lifesaving for the school. Remember, someone said, at the time, Hamren was just 24 years old, Peter, just 28.

Another early tipping point was the bank's forbearance of the school's loans in 1976-77. "The school was seriously bankrupt," recalled Hoffman. The bank could have called the note, which would have been the end of NOLS. Instead, it chose to work with the school as it eked its way over several years toward solvency. Much of that hard work was credited to the hands-on dedication of the board of trustees (who, it was noted, have always been volunteers), and how the original members, mostly locals, moved over on the bench

Lisa Johnson teaching on an early winter course.
NOLS Archives

to make room for outside people with more business savvy. The resulting "Homer Luther era" was another shift for the school, strengthened by the decision to institute a term-limit policy for board members. In addition, the mid- to late 1970s innovation of semester courses garnered much-needed revenue, as well as work for instructors during the "shoulder" seasons of spring and fall.

There was only a little financial breathing room by the early 1980s, when the somewhat counterintuitive decision to purchase "the farm" in Palmer, Alaska, was made. Over time, the school's practice of owning, not renting, its properties would pay off handsomely.

By the mid-1990s, the school faced another important inflection point when rising turmoil among staff disgruntled by inadequate compensation and lack of recognition (among other things) brought more changes, and Gans began his tenure. In that decade, the school made several essential cultural shifts: marketing beyond the traditional word-of-mouth method; connecting better with alumni; and more extensive fundraising, which added appreciably to the school's endowment.

Acquiring WMI in 1999 and establishing NOLS Professional Training in 2000 were recognized as important diversification initiatives. The positive impact of encouraging graduates of those programs to regard themselves as NOLS

grads was also noted. Around that time, another debate ended with the decision to stay in Lander and build the headquarters in the school's original hometown. With Lander as the school's home base, the historical link to Wyoming and the Wind Rivers was forever sealed—while at the same time, "home" for many in the extended NOLS family had grown to have broad national and international scope.

The vital turning points often represented very tough, intense decisions, the group agreed, but any time a chance came along to stick to the mission, people did. The former board members often spoke of the courage it required for the NOLS community to face times of adversity and make the best of them. As Homer Luther said, "It was easier when we didn't have options. We were in freefall. We were over the cliff. The choices were stark. But then we began to build." The people of NOLS—instructors, administrators and staff, board members—faced the need for rigorous financial discipline. They weathered fatalities and other unfortunate incidents in the field. They closed the much-loved Kenya branch. They didn't panic in 2008 and jump out of the stock market. They kept the school going.

The NOLS Department of Education

The appointment of Liz Tuohy as the NOLS director of education in the spring of 2015 resolved a long-standing missing link in the school's administrative roster. (Technically, Tuohy wasn't the first person to be so titled; Del Smith briefly held the title of "director of education and special programs" in the spring of 1994.)

Tuohy first came to NOLS in 1989 for a sea kayaking course in Alaska, followed by a Mount Waddington expedition the following year. She took her instructor course after graduating from college in 1994, and began working full-time at NOLS that fall. Within a few years, she became a program supervisor, first in the Southwest, then at the Rocky Mountain branch from 2000 to 2005. She moved into the position of business operations manager for NOLS Pro through 2007, when she became that department's risk management consultant (along with a brief stint in admissions). Tuohy brought to her new position a respected reputation and a broad view of the school.

Even before the decision to hire a director of education was made, an initiative to review, refine, reinvent, and rewrite course objectives was launched under the "exceptional student experiences" pillar of the Vision 2020 strategic plan. Core educational content of each course was examined for how it aligned with that theme. The goal, according to committee member Katie Baum Mettenbrink, was to raise the level of specificity and intentionality underlying the curriculum, to try to articulate the "magic" of a NOLS course.

"The thing is," said Tuohy, "nobody really knows what is happening on all NOLS courses. Part of my job is finding that out. You can't know it totally, but you can do it better than we do it right now.

"What happens now is that talented instructors and program staff in different parts of the world make fantastic program developments. Once in awhile the innovations take off globally, but often they stay localized or get lost when staff moves on. Because we're not a unified group, we don't have the ability to evolve or capitalize on our good ideas as well as we can."

Historically, the need for a director of education had not seemed crucial, with curriculum and research manager John Gookin looking after what was being taught in the field, and Tod Schimelpfenig performing the same role as WMI curriculum director since 2002. But as the school sprawled, the need to coordinate what students learned and what promulgated the most effective ideas grew. Instead of creating new course descriptions or grading rubrics, the focus was to identify the subtle difference between "What am I going to teach?" and "What do I want my students to be able to do?" Such an approach could better facilitate what students might go on to accomplish after their NOLS courses. As Jamie O'Donnell, an instructor and veteran program supervisor at NOLS Rocky Mountain, said, "The awesomeness

Jeffrey Post teaches anchor building. *Brady Robinson*

of being an educator is that everything we do is to serve our students after the experience is over. We don't get to see if they learn, grow, and manifest the things we spend time on." The lessons of NOLS spread far and wide.

Tuohy's charge was to develop centralized program oversight within NOLS and also to influence the broader conversation outside of the school. "To some degree, we would like to influence the rest of the world and what is happening out there. We would like wilderness education to be better accepted and better delivered worldwide, whether we're the ones delivering it or not.

"I think the next major evolution is going to be what our training systems look like," she continued, noting that in 2016 the processes of evaluation, training, and recruitment were slated for review within the context of the Vision 2020 strategic plan. "We have faculty with very high competence levels in a bunch of very individual areas. [For example,] WMI has a really amazing training for the skill of teaching. NOLS Pro expeditions target specific leadership objectives. NOLS Patagonia is improving semester progressions. The system isn't broken; in many ways our training is the envy of the industry. Still, there's some fine-tuning we can do to make everything a little better and to cross-pollinate our strengths."

Over time, mused Tuohy, the attitudes of the instructor team have shifted. "There's a piece where NOLS was built in the 1960s, and like so many organizations in the 1960s and '70s, we had a counterculture spirit which was both freeing and limiting. People defined themselves in reaction to what was already there as much as inventing what the world could be," she said. "I think we're subtly moving out of that because of the way the world is evolving. Independence has always been highly valued by our instructors, in part because they're out there on their own in dynamic environments and they have to make decisions on their feet. [But] I think people over time are becoming more comfortable with [cultural] shifts toward centralization. You see it with the NAFPs or the wilderness medicine curriculum. We just need not to blow it by overdoing things."

At the front line of many of those shifts are the school's program supervisors. They are experienced instructors, and are probably best suited to provide consistency because of their proximity to what actually happens on courses through briefings and debriefings. For example, Tuohy said, "in 2000 there was an expectation that we were teaching the new leadership model in the field. We saw as P-Sups that a lot of people weren't doing it, and if [the school] wanted it, we needed to assume the role of this implementation. We just started simple, by telling people that they needed to use the leadership language. Then we created dialogue between field staff about how it was working out. We were in a posi-

The annual faculty summit and WMI staff meetings provide a venue to share best practices among a community that rarely gets to work in the same place.
Brad Christensen

tion to connect the 250 [Wyoming] instructors who never had a chance to talk to each other. There's an artful blend of providing direction while inspiring people to make their courses better, to be more effective instructors."

Tuohy also noted that creating that consistency on a worldwide basis is also getting easier, through such technologies as video-conferencing. "We might have 30 people from 10 different countries calling in all at once. That's cool," she said.

George Newbury, still teaching after 45 years at NOLS. *Ben Lester*

Moving Forward

IN 2015, NOLS field operations were in 15 locations worldwide, teaching 15 outdoor skill specialties, often in combination. Add in WMI, risk management services, alumni courses, and NOLS Pro, and the number of locations grows into the dozens, in multiple languages. The duration of field courses was still often the traditional 30 days, but ranged from 5 to 135 days. So-called "catalog" course types included Adventure (for ages 14 and 15), Classic (the 30-day version, with separate offerings for 16- and 17-year-olds only), and Prime (for people ages 23 and over), plus the semester and year-long options, including a Wilderness Medicine and Rescue semester. A wide variety of "Career" courses was offered for outdoor educators, including instructor courses. WMI programming included the 16- to 20-hour Wilderness First Aid course, the 40-hour Wilderness Advanced First Aid, 80-hour Wilderness First Responder,

and a 200-hour Wilderness EMT, plus recertifications for all levels. NOLS Pro offered customized options for groups of different sizes, using blended aspects of the NOLS core curriculum elements of leadership, technical skills, risk management, and environmental studies. Pro continued to support five-day LNT Master Educator courses around the country as well. Alumni courses ranged in difficulty and focus, sometimes skills-oriented, sometimes more oriented to cultural experiences.

No wonder explaining NOLS succinctly could be daunting. It had developed well beyond *Thirty Days to Survival*. But to move forward, the school recognized the need to evaluate and prepare for the new world and its place in it. The general social landscape was increasingly populated by diminishing attention spans and rising impatience to wait even a nanosecond for results. People becoming aware of NOLS asked,

Packrafting, here in the Talkeetnas of Alaska, started in 2011. *Roo Riley*

why? Why NOLS? How is it different from a summer camp, or Outward Bound, or other outdoor recreation outlets? How could I possibly afford a week away, much less 30 days? What answers does NOLS have that can't be obtained in a hundred other ways?

From its own point of view, NOLS, too, had questions. In a world of changing demographics, who would be drawn to wilderness education? How could the school be brought to their attention? In addition to finding students, NOLS had also to fret about the school's wilderness classrooms. Would there continue to be a wild outdoors to go to as the world's population placed increasing pressure on wilderness? Was it possible to preserve the wilderness as we knew it? How could future generations value something they might be unable to reach?

The question of preserving the backcountry from becoming overused, mistreated, and ruined was a real concern. Many people were seeking time outdoors, thanks largely to the sheer numbers of a rising population. "In the last year, 42.5 million people went camping, and our national parks saw over 278 million recreational visitors," according to the Leave No Trace Center for Outdoor Ethics in 2015. The work of teaching the principles of Leave No Trace had never been more critical.

One fact that has never changed is that, as Petzoldt said, kids need adventure. If they cannot find it in one place, he was fond of saying, they'll look for it somewhere else, for better or worse. Young people will remain the key focus of the NOLS experience. The biggest challenges will be whether they can be wrestled away from techno-distractions and if marketing can reach youth of all walks of life. As former NOLS instructor Phil Powers said, "The personal growth and confidence, and transition from adolescence to adulthood that we gained from NOLS, are extraordinary. I find myself thinking about that a lot with my children: Where can they find that threshold through which they can go to really grow up? It's not college or your first job. It's something where you really have to own the responsibility, be challenged." Something like the classrooms of NOLS.

The topic of the NOLS students of the future (and the courses that will be available to them) will necessarily be ongoing. "There is much pressure to predict what NOLS will need to be in 20 years to be relevant or interesting," said Rich Brame, although perhaps, he indicated, the conversation should be less about what new programs or products are needed and more a process of discovering what people will want.

"To me," he said, they want "challenging, eye-opening experiences in the wilderness, safe experiences, flexible calendars, quick and smooth customer service, and tangible proof of value, such as college credit. Pursuing those 'knowns' is doable, and well within the context of what NOLS has always done. We can't truly predict the future, but if we stick to the knowns, we'll do all right."

Over time, many will be added to the roster of NOLS alumni. The question of who is a NOLS grad is increasingly moot as the school diversifies. The school could be viewed as "a growing 'ecosystem' that addresses the life-long interests of our constituents," suggested Brame. "Each piece of

Students moving through High Spur Canyon, in Utah.
Aidan Shafland

the ecosystem reinforces the others: publications, catalog courses, NOLS Pro, WMI, alumni networking, research, etc., etc. I find this a helpful vision."

As an institution, NOLS differs from others that seem similar; the difference is the same as when Paul Petzoldt wrote in a 1981 article in *Backpacker* magazine that ". . . many have the idea that teaching skills will also teach judgment, leadership, and conservation. Many universities and outdoor schools are skill oriented . . . without teaching judgment, how to plan and execute trips, how to keep within the ability and limitations of the group and its leaders. We have produced a country full of gung-ho specialized experts, many of whom are outdoor idiots." In expeditions, as with wilderness medicine, it is the emphasis on the core curriculum areas that sets NOLS apart. As for how much of the future of NOLS education lies in the remote wilderness where it started or in frontcountry classrooms, wilderness expeditions remain at the heart of the organization and its mission. Aptly put by WMI director Melissa Gray, "The core doesn't have to be the biggest part of the apple."

Legacy Planning

At the 50th Anniversary in 2015, John Gans handed out 85 Service Awards to employees who had worked for NOLS for 20 years or more (accepting one himself for his 35 years). A parade of NOLS veterans stepped forward to receive their handsome engraved marble bricks, gleaned from the Noble Hotel remodel. Of them, 28 had been with NOLS for at least 30 years, and five for at least 40 years: Tod Schimelpfenig, Don Webber, and Leslie van Barselaar (41 years each); Dave Kallgren (43 years); and George Newbury (45 years). Dozens of others who worked for NOLS for at least 20 years but were not still employed there in 2015 could fill another volume of stories and experiences. Many of them, including Willy Cunningham (39 years) and Doug Dahlquist (28 years), were also in the room.

While impressive, the numbers also portend unavoidable changes for the school as younger generations begin to fill big shoes. As Anne Cannon reflected, "I think it has been fun to see the school grow and branch out and become worldwide. Back when [the executive director] was Jim Ratz, I said to him, 'You know, people are actually going to retire from NOLS.' Who would have ever thought? Although those early days were a lot of fun, a lot of adventure, a lot of willingness to do things that I'm not sure people would be willing to do today, nobody was envisioning 50 years down the road."

Big shifts in staff, especially in the upper levels of the administration, are surely on the near horizon as retirement begins to beckon to many. Even though NOLS as a permanent career stop had yet to evolve when many of these people arrived, they somehow endured the early struggles and made it work. Some benefitted from the credit line Petzoldt maintained at the grocery store so his troops could get food. Gans spent one shoulder season waxing and polishing the floors of the Noble Hotel to earn his keep. Through the worst of the school's dark and worrisome times, that group was steadfast in its belief in NOLS, its lessons emblazoned by their direct experience with multiple rounds of spending 30 days in the field. As former instructor Tim Rawson said, "That whole generation worked together in the field, and there's no better way than that to forge bonds. This has been a remarkable group of individuals that has formed the senior team."

As Steve Matson mused, "Could the school have done it without us? Certainly without me, but the collective 'us'? I don't know." What's coming down the pike for NOLS is not precisely known, but the school is clearly arriving at a junction. For one thing, whoever succeeds Gans as the next executive director of NOLS is likely to be the first without a direct personal relationship with Paul Petzoldt.

The nature of change, while often regarded as fearsome, is not all bad. The upside, when considering organizational personnel shifts, is a broadened opportunity for fresh thinking. Those who have guided NOLS have respected the gravity of their charge. As Bill Murdock said of his time on the NOLS Board, "It was really palpable for me, to understand

Paul Petzoldt and John Gans in the late 1980s.
NOLS Archives

High spirits on a beach in Prince William Sound.
Tracy Baynes/STEP

I found it. That is a huge burden of stewardship. I have never, never been associated with any crowd that has the vigor and the independence and the intelligence and the worldview and the sense of mission that the crowd at NOLS has."

Asked what he regarded as the finest achievements of his 20 years at the helm of NOLS, John Gans said, "My biggest achievement is putting leadership solidly back in our name." Defining leadership in order to teach it as a skill, as opposed to a character trait, has rippled well beyond the confines of NOLS into space, under the ocean, and into uncounted other places and endeavors. Second was building the NOLS Accepted Field Practices (NAFPs) firmly into the culture—no small feat at the time, but by 2015 widely understood and accepted.

Third, Gans was proud that the effort to develop philanthropy had evolved successfully, not for the sake of the money, but for what it allowed the school to do, especially for students from broad backgrounds. After so many hardscrabble years financially, it was also with pride that Gans could report a net worth that had grown from $8 million to close to $80 million in his time, ensuring a brighter future for the school. It will always be mourned by some that NOLS morphed from a hunter-gatherer culture with small society values, and it will be for future leaders to determine the simmering question of how large is big enough; the NOLS of

that this was my time to hold the reins. I needed to make damn sure that when I handed those reins off, that they had been well and carefully managed, that people's livelihoods were on the line and had been preserved on my watch, that the school was stronger and that I was leaving it better than

2015 was a school that educated leaders from a solid business-based foundation that was built to last.

Finally, Gans returned to the field when pondering one final achievement: "Brass-ring programs," he called them: those special courses that shine with such brilliance that they draw out the best and brightest of both students and staff. "When I was an ice and snow instructor in Alaska in the 1980s, people always asked, 'Who's leading Denali?' [That course] was sort of a culminating brass ring for the instructors, and also for the students. I noticed how things like that improved everything at NOLS."

Likewise, bringing in WMI raised wilderness first aid to more professional levels. Delivering the leadership curriculum in a concentrated fashion through NOLS Pro "really solidified this curriculum that we had developed and worked on," Gans said, solidifying the school's emphasis on leadership overall. Working a NASA expedition is a goal for many. What if, he speculated, the concept of brass ring programs was applied to, say, the natural history area of curriculum, or environmental studies? Perhaps it will be up to future leaders to determine the brass ring concepts that could raise up such things.

Hopes for the Future

It's not a regular school where regular things happen in the

Young students plan their independent student expedition route. *Evan Horn*

academic sense, but it is a school nonetheless—one that goes outside, gets dirty, doesn't mind the sweat. By 2015, the school had more than a quarter million alumni—over 100,000 from expeditions, and close to 150,000 who had taken a classroom-based course.

As Gans said when asking his former board members for their hopes for the school's future, "While 50 years is a noteworthy milestone, my overwhelming feeling is a phenomenal sense of optimism and relevance as we look forward to the next 50 years."

As the discussion moved from one person to the next around the lunch table, people were thoughtful. The inevitable and upcoming transition of leadership was on the minds of many, because it would not be just one person; an entire generation would soon pass the torch. As Jon Hamren reflected, "NOLS is emotional. Everyone played a role. . . . We're getting old, and this will come to a head soon, when Gans retires. We have to have the strength to let go of our child and let it go in the direction it needs to go."

That sentiment gave rise to other voices that hoped future leaders would stay true to the mission, keep doing things that can't be measured, and not forget the school's roots. In fact, deepen those roots, said some. That would mean instilling in future generations an appreciation for the past—starting with the founder. To that end, there is powerful symbolism (and a touch of whimsy) that when delivering the annual State of the School address, the board chair should continue to wear the wool hat worn by Petzolt on his 1994 attempt on the Grand Teton, a tradition begun in 2001.

Additional hopes included teaching teamwork alongside leadership. Building diversity, both within the board of trustees as well as through international expansion. Doing

what it takes to stop losing youth to their techno-devices; reminding (and returning) them to the joy of their "hopscotch places." Keeping it simple. Keeping it authentic.

After describing the impact of the *Alcoa Hour* in 1970 as "the first WMI," one person hoped the school would continue to seek out "the next WMI"—meaning being open and agile enough to leap on new opportunities that might further transform and improve the school's ability to carry out its mission. One suggestion was to build the curriculum to include more emphasis on the hard sciences inherent to the wilderness; such an innovation, they said, could help solve both diversity and curriculum issues by attracting people for complementary reasons.

Not surprisingly, there was widespread hope for ongoing stewardship of the environment. Sell "wild." Teach and guide "wild." Find a way to acquaint tomorrow's leaders with the glory of the outdoors.

Finally, those with a financial bent hoped that the school would keep an eye on the ball while not just taking a "follow the dollar" stance. Stay a little desperate, a little hungry; it's a good way to keep making good decisions, they said.

———

A lot of things occurred the year NOLS was born. A loaf of

bread cost 21 cents, the average cost of a new house was $13,600. The St. Louis Gateway Arch was completed. African Americans were guaranteed the right to vote. The epic film *Dr. Zhivago* premiered in New York City. In 1965, NOLS wiggled into infancy and eventually matured until, in 2015, with some silver highlights showing as handsomely as on any dignified 50-year-old, it stood confidently, poised to move forward as the well-conditioned, thoughtful school that it is.

"There's a transcendence of the greater good over personality at NOLS, and I think that that's remarkable," said Bill Murdock. "That's what NOLS is: It is the tribe. It's not the individuals, it's the tribe that counts. And that's a baseline ethic that comes all the way back from Paul Petzoldt. *You* don't get to the summit; *we* get to the summit." Those who came first believed they were building a new world order. While having a lot of fun, they were also dead serious about it, as were those who came later.

"NOLS touches lives in an immensely important way," concluded Jon Hamren. "The trick is to honor history without finger pointing. It's a broad, wonderful tent with room for everybody in it."

Although no one knows exactly what the next 50 years will bring, it's a sure bet that the NOLS community will move toward its future with clear eyes, deliberate planning, and the confidence of a true leader.

Paul taking a break on the trail. *NOLS Archives*

zero!*

* NOLS-speak for "stop" when climbing or mountaineering on a rope team. Also used when you've had too much of something and want it to end.

ACKNOWLEDGMENTS

The joy and honor of writing this book would not have been possible without substantial support, input, and attention from a huge cast of characters. Chief among them are the following:

– Ben Lester, editor and friend. My heartfelt thanks for so very much, not least your impressive editorial talent—and for knowing, too, how to kindly manage me in my moments of uncertainty.

– Linda Lindsey, my childhood friend and NOLS touchstone for umpteen years. You and Monty provided me with a warm home and delicious meals during three trips to Lander to work on this book. And it was you, after all, who urged my participation on the Dolomites alumni trip in 2014, during which I overheard John Gans chatting with a board member at breakfast about needing to find someone to write this book. My application followed . . . and the rest is history.

– Diane Shoutis, for your consistent, cheerful, and speedy help with the archives, contact info, and my endless questions.

– My manuscript readers, whose collective memory of the school is so abundant and rich. John Gans, Drew Leemon, Tod Schimelpfenig, Liz Tuohy, John Gookin, Rich Brame: You kept me honest, sent thoughtful and prompt answers to my many questions, and helped me feel secure that we were on track.

– The designers who made this book such a wonderful feast for the eyes: Eryn Pierce and Brad Christensen at NOLS, and Maggie Peterson at Falcon.

– My stalwart transcribers: Allie Maloney, Annalise Grueter, Rachel Glass, and Michael Froehly.

– My ace copyeditors: Molly Herber at NOLS and Kristen Mellitt at Falcon.

– Katie Benoit and the team from Falcon for guiding this book through all its twists and turns on the way to press.

– The NOLS community at large—always so friendly and welcoming during my lengthy visits while writing the book. Great EB, everyone.

On the home front, my enduring love and appreciation go to: Melody, for being there. Always. You too, Tag. Margaret Idema, as well as Penny and Jamie Ladd for love, support, and many delicious meals. The Smolek family, for the fresh eggs and support. My animal "aunties," Fran Rood and Bev at Hylock Kennels, and Kathy Walters for keeping an eye on the horse herd (Marque, JB, and Jake). Kent County SAR K9 Unit, for helping me continue training Amazing Grace ("Mayzie") while distracted by the demands of writing. My brothers (and sister) at Ada Fire Department. My real brother, Tom. And those who helped keep me physically able for those hours at my desk: Tom Traynor for the strength training, Jon Richardson for massaging that persistent rhomboid knot and "mouse hand," and Eric DeLamielleure, the Healer.

I spoke with legions of people about NOLS. There were more than 110 taped interviews, plus some interviews graciously provided from an earlier start to the book. The following is a list (in no particular order) of those who played a role in this work: Rob and Martha Hellyer, Jack and Alice Nicholas, John Gans, Peter and Cyndy Simer, John Hamren, Homer Luther, Willy and Tina Cunningham, Skip and Diane Shoutis, Kevin and Anne McGowan, Steve Matson, George and Mary Jo Newbury, Jim Halfpenny, Kathy Dunham, Anne Cannon, Don Webber, Randy Cerf, Lucy Smith, Mike Williams, Steve Gipe, Pookie Godvin, Steff Kessler, Q Belk, Paul Calver, Vini Norris, John Kanengieter, KG Kagambi, Doug Dahlquist, Lannie Hamilton, Dave Neary, Joe Austin, Leslie Appling, John Stoddard, Andy and Nancy Carson, Haven Holsapple, LT Chu, Don and Donna Ford, Leslie van Barselaar, Dave Kallgren, Del Bachert, Bill Scott, Claudia Pearson, Jeff Buchanen, Liz Nichol, Bob McConnell, Neil Short, Drew Leemon, Tod Schimelpfenig, Phil Powers, Rachel Price, Linda Lindsey, Sam Talucci, Bruce and Molly Hampton, Steve Goryl, Deborah Nunnink, John Gookin, George and Paula Hunker, Vince Fayad, Duncan Dayton, Herbie Ogden, Tom and Dorothy Warren, Nancy Pallister, Bruce Palmer, Janet Jahn, Nick Storm, Louisa Hunker, Michael Lindsey, Nene Wolfe, Chris Agnew, Raúl Castro, Patty Nicolas Trautman, Rich Brame, Reb Gregg, Molly Doran, Maurice "Rick" Horn, Pip Coe, Rick Rochelle, Molly Absolon, Doug Anisi, Melissa Gray, Bob Shoultz, John Sullivan, Marco Johnson, Scott Robertson, Jim Acee, Morgan Hite, Charley Fiala, Wilford Welch, Blackie Bolton, David Hellyer, Steven Harper, Dave Glenn, Janeen Hutchins, Howard Tomb, Shannon Rochelle, Judd Rogers, Joe Thomas, Nathan Russell, Trina Peterson, Gary and Jani Golding, Geoff Heath, Jim Culver, Katie Baum Mettenbrink, Jaret Slipp, Jon Kempsey, Shana Tarter, Abby Warner, Pete Colhoun, William Foster, Lee Frizzell, Jim Allen, Jamie O'Donnell, Iris Saxer, Nate Ostis, Michael Schmertzler, Tony Jewell, Dave Schimelpfenig, Jake Wallace, Anna Haegel, Adam Crenshaw, Liz Alva Rosa, Carolina González Cortés, Patrick Mettenbrink, Kary Sommers. If your name is missing, the fault is mine alone. You know who you are. Thank you. Thank you all!

BIBLIOGRAPHY / RECOMMENDED READING

American Alpine Journal. "Proceedings of the Club," III:3, 1939, 330-31. (About the 1938 K2 Expedition)

Bachert, Delmar W. "The NOLS Experience: Experiential Education in the Wilderness." Doctoral dissertation under the direction of Dr. Arlene Figaret, 1987.

Birkby, Robert. *Mountain Madness.* NYC: Kensington Publishing, 2008.

Bruce, Jeannette. "Snowplace Like Home." *Sports Illustrated.* February 11, 1974, 38-43.

Burnett, Derek. "Grizzly!" *Reader's Digest.* June 2012, 195-201. (About NOLS students after a bear attack.)

Cline, Andy, ed. "Special Edition: Highlighting Risk Management," in staff *Newsletter*, May 1999.

Cockerill, Tom and Bernard Kelly. "Paul Petzoldt's Outdoor Geewhizery." *Empire Magazine (The Denver Post).* May 23, 1971, 10-14.

Craighead, Charlie, ed. *Glenn Exum: Never a Bad Word or a Twisted Rope.* Moose, WY: Grand Teton Natural History Association, 1998.

Dowling, Claudia Glenn. "Death on the Mountain." *Life Magazine,* August 1996, 32-46. (About the 1994 deaths on Mount Everest.)

Fadiman, Anne. "Under Water," *At Large and At Small: Familiar Essays.* NYC: Farrar, Straus and Giroux, 2007.

(A nonfiction account of a 1972 drowning on a NOLS course.)

Gentile, OA, JA Morris, T Schimelpfenig, SM Bass, and PS Auerbach. "Wilderness injuries and illnesses." Annals of Emergency Medicine, July 1992, 21:853-61.

Greiner, James. *Wager with the Wind: The Don Sheldon Story.* NYC: Rand McNally & Co, 1974.

Grove, Noel. "Winter Challenge in the Wind River Range," in *Wilderness U.S.A.*, Seymour L. Fishbein ed. Washington, D.C.: National Geographic Society, 1973, 162-79.

Hite, Morgan. "30 Days to Oblivion: How to CL Your First Course and Live to Tell the Tale." (1991), at www .hesperus-wild.org.

——. "Briefing for Entry Into A More Harsh Environment." (August 1989), www.hesperus-wild.org.

——. "Coyote Goes to NOLS." (1991), www.hesperus-wild .org.

——. "An Industry in the Wilderness: An inspired outdoor community wrecks on the reef of a corporate model." (1997), www.hesperus-wild.org.

House, William P., "K-2—1938." *The American Alpine Journal* III, 3, 1939, 229-54.

Howard, Jane. "Last Mountain Man? Not If He Can Help It." *Life* magazine, December 19, 1969.

Husband, Evelyn, *High Calling: The Courageous Life and Faith of Space Shuttle Columbia Commander Rick Husband*. Nashville: Thomas Nelson, 2003.

Jenkins, McKay. *The Last Ridge: The Epic Story of the U.S. Army's 10th Mountain Division and the Assault on Hitler's Europe.* NYS: Random House, 2003.

Johnson, William Oscar. "Just Blowin' in the Winds." *Sports Illustrated*. December 14, 1981. 66-86.

Judge, Joseph. "Wind River Range: Many-Treasured Splendor," *National Geographic*, Vol. 145, No. 2, February 1974, 205.

Kanengieter, John and Aparna Rajagopal-Durbin. "Wilderness Leadership—on the Job." *Harvard Business Review*, April 1, 2012.

McDonald, Bernadette. *Brotherhood of the Rope: The Biography of Charles Houston*. Seattle: The Mountaineer Books, 2007.

Petzoldt, Patricia. *On Top of the World*. NYC: Thomas Y. Crowell Company, 1953.

Petzoldt, Paul. "Leadership: The Most Dangerous Game," *Backpacker* 44 (April/May 1981), 21-22.

——. *Teton Tales And Other Petzoldt Anecdotes*. Merrillville, IN: ICS Books, 1995.

——. *The Wilderness Handbook*. NYC: WW Norton, 1974.

——. "Why I Climb Mountains." *Collier's*, June 15, 1949, 24-25.

Price, Raye. "Outdoor Finishing School." *Field and Stream,* March 1968, 68-69.

Ringholz, Raye C. *On Belay: The Life of Legendary Mountaineer Paul Petzoldt*. Seattle: The Mountaineers, 1997. (An in-depth biography of Petzoldt's life.)

Roper, Steve and Allen Steck. *Fifty Classic Climbs of North America*. Sierra Club, 1979. (Climbers featured include instructor Shari Kearney.)

Sampson, Scott. *How To Raise A Wild Child*. NYC: Houghton Mifflin, 2015.

Seghers, Carroll. "Snowplace Like Home." *Sports Illustrated*. February 11, 1974, 38-43.

Smutek, Ray. "An Interview with Paul Petzoldt." *Off Belay*, August 1979, 33-34.

Warner, Abby. "Special Edition: Highlighting Risk Management," in staff *Newsletter*, March 1996.

Wilson, Stephanie F. "Pioneering Women in Outdoor Education: The History of Women at the National Outdoor Leadership School." Master of Science thesis, Mankato State University, Mankato, MN, June 1998.

INDEX

Halfpenny, Jim, 51, 63, 69, 104–5, 106, 115, 119
Hall, Gary, 100, 180
Hampton, Bruce, 113, 115, 155;
    Soft Paths, 185–86, 202
Hampton, Molly, 113, 115, 136, 154–55, 162, 239, 266
Hamren, Jon, 67, 70–71, 91, 148, 353, 369;
    as executive director, 110–11, 113, 115;
    leaves NOLS, 118–19
Harvard Affiliated Emergency Medicine Residency (HAEMR), 314
Hauf, John, 189, 215–16, 237
Heath, Geoff, 58, 69, 143
Hellyer, Martha Newbury, 22, 38–39, 42, 48, 66
Hellyer, Rob, 21, 22, 28–29, 35, 42, 69, 81, 110, 353;
Hess, Rob, 195–97, 198
Hidden Valley Ranch, Wyoming, 3, 29
Highland, Carolyn, 278–79, 301
Hildebrandt, Kevin, 135, 146
Himalayas, 120, 193
Hite, Morgan, 260–61
Hoffman, Bob, 131, 132, 133, 156, 353–54
Holsapple, Haven, 47, 54, 63, 85, 91–92, 119, 143, 153
Houston, Charles, 14, 167–68
Hudecek, Laura, 78, 79, 264
Hunker, George, 98, 100, 109–10, 113, 117, 142
Hunker, Paula, 72, 268, 113
Hutchins, Janeen, 98, 174, 175, 290
Hutchins-Cabibi, Ryan, 175, 290
hypothermia, 9, 169–70

incidents, 41, 95, 98, 100–1, 132, 168–73, 193, 198, 239–40, 338, 340;
    debriefings, 173, 212–13, 273;
    searches, 47, 176
independent student travel, 243–44, 340
industry standards, 179–80
instructor courses (IC), 139, 160–61
Instructor Development Fund (IDF), 161, 192
instructors, 48, 138–39, 167;
    morale, 229–30, 232, 239
instructor's courses (IC), 66–68, 77
international HQ, 287–99
Into Thin Air (Krakauer), 199
IRS Exempt Organizations examination, 104–6

Jahn, Janet, 104, 106, 110, 117, 119, 124
Jewell, Tony, 143–44
Johnson, Jean, 40, 42, 85, 223
Johnson, Marco, 160, 217, 258
judgment, 45, 61, 166, 242–43

K2, 13–14, 167–68, 194, 198
Kagambi, James (KG), 52, 237, 293–94, 303
Kallgren, Dave, 61–62, 147, 182, 237, 239
Kanengeiter, John, 173, 212–13, 236, 256, 275–77, 344
kayaking, 78–79, 97, 258

Lander, Wyoming, 1, 29, 91–94
Landmark Learning, 269, 314
leader of the day, 62, 79, 166

ABOUT THE AUTHOR

Kate (Boyd) Dernocoeur is a many-time NOLS graduate: Wind River Winter Mountaineering (1973), Wind River Horsepacking (1974), Wilderness EMT (2011), plus alumni sea kayaking in Baja (2005) and hiking in the Dolomites (2012). Kate holds a bachelor's degree from Boston University's College of Communication, and an MFA in creative writing from Western Michigan University. She worked as a paramedic for the City & County of Denver from 1979-1986, and is the author of several hundred articles and personal essays, primarily within the emergency medical services field. Her first book, *Streetsense: Communication, Safety and Control* (1985), went to three editions, and she also co-authored *Principles of Emergency Medical Dispatch* with Jeff Clawson, MD (1988). An avid adventure traveler, Kate was expedition medic on the first descent of Ethiopia's Blue Nile in 1999. At age 59, she graduated from fire academy to become an EMT-firefighter with the Ada Fire Department in Michigan. In 2016, she was active both there and with Kent County Search & Rescue's K9 Unit, as well as being an active horseman with a herd of three. She lives a mile up a gravel road in Vergennes Township, Michigan, which shares her heart with her roots in the mountains of Colorado.

The author as a NOLS student, 1974 *Kate Dernocoeur*